NOT LIKE THE REST OF US

An Anthology of Contemporary Indiana Writers

Not Like the Rest of Us: An Anthology of Contemporary Indiana Writers

Editors: Barbara Shoup and Rachel Sahaidachny
Book Design and Layout: Andrea Boucher

ISBN: 978-0-9967438-3-9

Printed in the United States of America

INwords PUBLICATIONS
PRESENTED BY THE INDIANA WRITERS CENTER

Editors' Note

We knew that there were many wonderful Indiana writers when we proposed creating a collection of their work to celebrate the 2016 Bicentennial—but we had no idea how many. One of the greatest pleasures of working on this project has been discovering Indiana writers whose work was new to us. That said, *Not Like the Rest of Us* is by no means a comprehensive collection of wonderful Indiana writers. Aside from residence in Indiana or a strong connection to the state, our primary consideration in selecting writers was the quality of their work and whether they had been published nationally. We also considered geography, diversity, gender, and age. The most experienced writers in the book are in their nineties, the youngest in their twenties. Some are best-selling authors, some widely known in literary circles, some just beginning. Some fine Indiana writers are not included here due to the limitation of space, others we have yet to discover.

To learn more about the writers represented here and others, please visit www. indianawriters.net

Table of Contents

Nonfiction

Poetry

8

Fiction

Introduction

MANY YEARS AGO, on my way home from a week of solitude, I was passed by an open semi filled with carrots. They were piled high in the bed, sticking through the slats on the side: thousands of carrots disappearing into the distance. I was alone. It was a long trip. I couldn't stop thinking about them. How many carrots were in the truck? Where did they come from, where were they going? How did the farmer know how many carrots to plant each spring, how did he know what to do with them when—do carrots get ripe? What do you call a...finished carrot? How does a restaurant or a grocery store know how many carrots to order? How do carrots *work?*

The logistics of carrots pretty quickly overwhelmed me, as logistics often do, and took on the weight of an existential question. If I could understand the logistics of carrots, I wondered, would I, at long last, understand how the world worked?

No surprise. When I shared this idea with my very sensible husband, he looked at me like I was insane. But the idea kept its hold on me. I told the carrot story to a lot of people over the next few weeks and here's what I discovered: those who navigated the real world with ease had no idea what I was talking about; those who found the real world confounding knew exactly what I meant. That latter group was made up almost entirely of fellow writers.

There are numerous reasons people write. Not the least of them is the fact that the act of writing frees us from the real world, which we will never, ever understand, allowing us to live for a little while in a world of our own making, one we can shape and control. Paradoxically, what we write is made of the real world. How could it be otherwise? When we're lucky, the process of wrestling words to the page teaches us something about the world and about ourselves that we desperately needed to know.

The real world is where you are. It's where you've been and who you were in those places. Every real world is extraordinary in its own way. The work in this anthology is made of Madrid, New York City, Nanking, Port au Prince, Chicago, San Francisco, Kathmandu. It's made of small towns and cities, farms and country roads, lakes and rivers in Indiana. It was created by writers who were born and raised in Indiana, some who stayed and some who moved on, and by writers who came to our state by way of jobs or marriage—or choice!

Note the exclamation point after "choice." It's a kind of self-deprecating thing some Hoosier writers do, probably so the reader knows that the writer fully understands that, while we may love our home state, it isn't the first place that comes to mind when thinking about where writers are likely to settle. The title of this anthology comes from Cathy Day's essay, "Not Like the Rest of Us: A Hoosier Named Cole Porter," in which she captures the peculiar nature of Hoosiers' relationship to the arts. Here's how the conversation went when she asked her grandmother, a member of the local historical society, why Peru, Indiana didn't celebrate Cole Porter, its native son.

"[Her grandmother] said, 'Well, because he left.'

"What she meant: *Why should we celebrate him if he thought he was better than us?*

"What I wanted to say: *But he was better than us!*

"Instead, I said, 'He had to leave, Grandma. He wrote Broadway musicals.'

"She said, 'Well, it's also because he was different.'

"What she might have meant by different: homosexual, high falutin', pretentious, East Coasty, snobby, strange, European, hoity-toity.

"What I wanted to say: *I'm different, too. And different isn't a bad thing, Grandma. It's a good thing.*

"But I didn't say that, because I knew she'd say: *Cathy, you're not different. You're a nice girl from Indiana. Don't be getting too big for your britches.*

But writers—all true artists—are different, no matter where they are or where they're from. They all experience moments when suddenly even something as ordinary as a truckload of carrots reveals the inalienable strangeness of the world they live in, so riveting their attention that they find themselves standing outside the circle, observing, wondering, memorizing. Asking, What if? Asking, Why? They remake the world with words or clay or choreography, with musical notes or paint, trying and failing, until it makes some sense to them. The best of them remake the world in ways that make sense to others, too.

Indiana can claim many gifted writers, and the ones represented in this anthology reflect the richness and diversity of our state. Years from now, the stories, poems, and essays here will make the world of Indiana in its Bicentennial year real for those who come after us.

Barbara Shoup
Executive Director
Indiana Writers Center

nonfiction

How to Stop Smoking

A. LYN CAROL

1. Notice smoking around age five, specifically the heavy, cut-glass lighter your grandmother uses and the way the etched glass throws prisms against the wall when it catches the afternoon sun. Be fascinated by the way smoke curls out of her lipsticked mouth when she talks. Mimic this at age twelve with the cigarettes you swipe from her green glass cigarette case, the one that matches her lighter. Resolve to be that elegant when you grow up. Develop a habit.

2. Continue smoking until you've accumulated twenty-odd years of tar in your lungs. This will take some resolve and steadfast denial. To help with the denial, make sure you have maximum amounts of stress and poor coping skills; that way, you can ignore how your lungs ache in the morning and the wet sound of your coughing in the evening and how you're always clearing phlegm from your throat. Also ignore the smell of smoke, which you actually hate. Carry perfume with you wherever you go, along with mints and gum, to cover up the smell.

3. Up the stakes by having a child who grows old enough to learn about cancer. Listen sympathetically as she begs you to stop smoking, remembering

how you did the very same thing with your own mother. Promise her that you will quit, effective immediately. Then start insisting she go play with her neighborhood friends at their house instead of yours so you can sneak a cig. Smoke behind the shed on the mornings she sleeps in, until the day she wakes up from a bad dream and comes out into the yard looking for you. After such a close call, swear to yourself that you will quit once and for all. Go a day or two until someone in your family does another crazy thing or your boss harangues you about being two minutes late to work, and then go ahead and smoke that well-deserved cigarette. Keep this up until the tally of years you've spent inhaling burning leaves into your lungs is equal to two-thirds, or sixty-six percent, of your life.

4. Gradually start resenting the hold the habit has on you, but not enough that you actually quit. Be annoyed at the anxiety that creeps up when you open the last pack of cigarettes you had hidden in the garage. Grow weary of worrying if your daughter catches whiffs of smoke in your hair because no amount of coconut-vanilla body spray will cover it completely. Start the stopping now, because it usually takes at least a couple years.

5. Be hard-headed and slow to learn. Have knee surgery and smoke your first night home from the hospital while still woozy from the narcotic pain medication. Ignore the warnings your husband gives you. Wait until he goes to bed and light up right there on the couch. Immediately regret it as intense dizziness and nausea bowl you over. Vomit down your nightgown because you're trussed up and can't move. Sit in the stench of bile and smoke and swear that was the last time. A few days later try again and find that you don't get sick. Get right back to it, but this time add the clumsiness of maneuvering yourself outside on crutches while holding the plastic grocery bag that carries your scented lotion, mints, water, cigarettes, and lighter. Really, really start hating it. Cut down significantly because it's not worth the hassle.

6. But don't stop just yet because you are going through a rough patch with your husband. Spend many hours in the yard soaking in self-pity. Use

your angst to justify your chain-smoking, just like the old days. Start buying cigarettes by the carton again. Continue to ignore and deny.

7. The following spring, lose a favorite aunt to cancer. The next week, hear about a former coworker who has cancer now. Two days after that, get an email telling you that your sister-in-law found a lump in her breast, and she doesn't even smoke. Go through your own scare when a radiologist says your mammogram is suspicious and requires further diagnostics. Feel the fear make its final click into place when the young man who mows your lawn, the one who's closer to your daughter's age than yours, starts crying in your yard when you ask how he's doing. He just lost his mother to cancer. Hug him underneath the poplar tree he planted six months ago, when his mother was still alive and everyone thought she was coming down with a cold. Become scared—very scared—of cancer. Start accepting your stupidity. Start worrying that it's going to be too late. Recognize that you've finally arrived at the quitting point but wonder how.

8. Decide to become something else.

9. Become a birdwatcher. Do this because you realize that you need a new routine that will replace the cigarettes, because right now being outside equals smoking. Buy some binoculars and a bag of unshelled peanuts for the blue jays. Buy thistle for the finches and safflower seed for the cardinals. Tell yourself that you won't smoke a cigarette until you have seen a red-bellied woodpecker. Wait. And wait. Learn patience. Learn to delay gratification. Learn to be more excited about seeing a woodpecker than you are about flicking the lighter and taking that first drag. Learn to sit and wait and sit and wait until you've waited a day to smoke, a week, a month ... until you're at four years and counting.

10. Keep watching birds.

That's What You Remember
[An Essay in Third Person]

JILL CHRISTMAN

S HE WAS IN THE GROCERY store sulking past forbidden sugar cereals when
she stopped, looked around, and realized she could put a box of Froot
Loops in her cart if she wanted. Could she? She was thirty-four years old. She
did. Nobody stopped her—who would stop her?—but she kept checking her
back until she made it out to the parking lot and got all the bags into the car.

At home, the milk turned a putrid gray, and even dry, the bright sugar rings
weren't as good as she remembered them. She sat at the wooden table in the
kitchen with the baby, sliding the red ones into place for the top arc of a cereal
rainbow and remembering the Atari her brother had won back in the mid-sev-
enties with his drawing of Toucan Sam in the Kellogg's "Stick up for Breakfast" contest. The only game was Pong, a drifting dot and two straight-line
paddles locked in a perpetual bling-boing-bling. How would she ever communicate to her new-millenium daughter the excitement, the thrill, of the day
that Atari arrived in its plain brown box? For months, her brother—celebrated
artist, creator of the winning Sam-in-the-jungle scene—reigned as king of the
neighborhood.

She was down to the greens in her ROY G. BIV rainbow when she realized
something, something big: They could catch a plane. They could buy tickets,

fly out of dreary, frozen Indiana and celebrate the rest of Christmas vacation
somewhere sunny—and alone. This was revelatory. A full year into her daughter's life and Jill suddenly understood that she was the mother.

SHE chose a family-run hotel in Madeira Beach near St. Petersburg. Their
room had a little kitchen with one of those undersized stoves and a too-bright
fluorescent light, but the double glass doors looked out over the bay where the
proprietor seemed always to be busy on his sailboat, Island Woman. That's
the thing about men and their boats, she thought—they can never get enough.
There's always something to fiddle with, a reason to pull her out of the water,
sink her back in, sand her down, shine her up. A man with a boat never lacks
for something to do.

Her own husband, boatless, was still sleeping in the king-sized bed under
the giant straw fan, and Jill sat cross-legged next to the baby tossing Cheerios
onto the tray of her booster chair. They faced the water and the man. Boat TV.
A pelican—the baby's first!—sailed in and landed hard on a piling. "Look,
Ella! Look! A pelican!" She could have called that bird anything—a sea gull,
a loon or an osprey, an ostrich for heavensakes—and the baby would have believed her. But she didn't. She called it a pelican.

That afternoon, they set up the booster chair on a picnic table and drank
margaritas and ate blackened grouper sandwiches on the dock. The baby
munched fries and smeared ketchup in her hair. Men in tight suits buzzed
by in weird parachute machines that reminded her of the jet pack police in
Farenheit 451. A gull dove down to steal a fry and her husband covered his
head with his hands, threatened to scream like a little girl. That night was New
Year's Eve and she fell asleep on the couch in front of the glass doors despite the
blasts of color exploding over the water. Her husband woke her up with a midnight kiss just as Regis talked the ball down in Times Square (Regis? Where's
Dick Clark?) and they went together into the bedroom to kiss their sleeping
angel on her fat cheeks. She felt a kind of surreal happiness and thought, This
is probably as good as it gets.

THE next afternoon, while the other two napped, Jill took her book down to the dock to show her Indiana-white legs to the Florida sun, breathe in some air the wind had cleaned on the salty water. She was never alone these days. She found a spot on a bench and another sea plane pelican, all pouch and hold, skimmed low across the water, eyes trained down, looking to scoop up some morsels, swallow them whole and squirming. From a distance, the pelican had seemed so exotic. Up close, she could see the pelican was filthy, mangy. A dirty bird.

Her book wasn't even cracked before a little girl came skipping down the planks of the dock on her bare feet and cast a towel in a flap of rainbow colors down on the warm wood.

"Mmm," the girl said. "I think I'll set up here for awhile!" She was six, she reported, her name was Cameron, and she was here in Florida with her mom and dad for a whole week. After this they'd go to see her sister's baby who had just learned to walk. Cameron wanted to know if Jill had any sisters or babies and she told her, feeling lucky, that she had both. Two sisters and one baby, my own little girl, also one, who's sleeping up in the room. Cameron took that in, told her that Ella was a good name, and then mentioned the brother she never sees. He was in some kind of trouble, she's wasn't sure. She'd like to see all of them more—the sister with the baby, the baby, the brother—but she was careful to let Jill know they don't all live together. They can't. They live all over the country. All over the country. Jill noticed Cameron's flare for emphasis, one word in every sentence, often where she'd least expect it.

As Cameron talked, lying on her belly, her bare feet stirred the air in rapid circles and her palms patted the colors of her towel. Every paragraph or two, she required a bit of information. "Do you have any brothers?"

"Yes," Jill reported, "and he has a little girl exactly your age." Jill's eyes flicked up to the mother lying by the kidney-shaped pool, a pool only big enough for children to really get going in, but beautiful in a tropical way, palm trees and shine. The mother looked to be about forty, so she would have been about her age when she had Cameron. Not a young mother. The other mother's sunglasses pointed down towards her book. An older man sat two lounge chairs away, talking business on a cell phone—probably almost sixty, and that explained the sister with the baby, the brother too far away to see, maybe in some kind of trouble. . .

Cameron popped up from her towel, all long brown legs and round eyes. She couldn't stay down for long. She was made of springs and tendons. "Well," she said, "I guess I'd better throw these shells back in the water so they can become sand!" She produced a handful of shells out of nowhere, scuttled to the edge of the dock, still chattering about the fish she saw earlier, bigger than these little fish, much bigger, but look at all those fish now. Do you see them? And she cast the shells, a handful of tiny white shells, like beads or confetti, across the calm surface of the water and they sprayed down, a lovely sprinkle of sound. Together they watched them sink down through interested fish and onto the sandy bottom. "Watch," Cameron instructed, "now watch." And the sand on the bottom shifted and danced—was it moving all that time? before the shells?—and Cameron's luminescent shells absorbed into the tawny grains. "See? See? Now they will become sand."

Although she'd be loathe to confess, Jill wasn't always one to enjoy the company of other people's children, but she liked this Cameron. She sparkled, but the way she talked to her was terrifying. Jill found herself wishing she wouldn't tell her so much. There's too much not to trust in this world, and strange ladies sitting on docks are probably one of them. Also, there was something behind her eyes, something old. Something that reminded her of herself.

HER husband walked down to the dock carrying the baby. Ella squinted into the bright light to marvel at the lively creature standing on the dock next to her mother, so much better than a pelican. "This is my baby," she told Cameron. "This is Ella." Cameron reached out for Ella's cheeks and pinched them just as an old woman might do. Ella hated to be pinched, but she didn't cry. Cameron's eyes were too round. Too much like her own eyes.

With a bigger audience, Cameron turned business-like, played the experienced tourist. After all, they'd been there for a week. She gave her review of the Dali museum. At first, they heard "dolly" because she was six, but their misimpression didn't last long. "You have to touch the fur when you first go in. It's red. You have to touch it." Cameron was full of instructions. "Then you look into this box and it's like a frame. Inside it's a face, but it's not a face. There are two pictures on the wall and they're the eyes. Then there's a fire. That's the nose. And a couch is the mouth."

FOR the rest of the afternoon, Cameron trailed Jill and the baby wherever they went on the hotel grounds. She followed them when they took the bag with the dirty diapers to the dumpster, and then she skipped behind her until her nose pressed against their glass door. She must have known she wasn't supposed to come in, and she hadn't been invited, but she came terribly close. "We're in four," Cameron announced. "Right there." Pointing. "Okay, I guess. I'll see you later." When she backed away, her eyes were funny again, that same look, darting around to see if anybody was watching.

Shouldn't somebody be watching?

Jill remembered a time when she was a graduate teaching assistant at the University of Alabama, hanging out with boys, the kind of boys a good feminist wouldn't hang out with on a normal day—body-ogling, PBR-swigging boys who were fun to play pool with because they were smart and funny and could quote poetry even when they were many, many sheets to the wind. These boys were graduate teaching assistants just like her, and one day, an out-of-a-magazine co-ed from her English 101 class came into her office weeping about her life, pledging that she would do anything to make a C in the class. She was wearing a tank top over another tank top, both lycra, no bra, and she put her breasts on the desk. Put them there. The act seemed unconscious— why would it be otherwise? force of habit?—but there they were, placed there, like a bottle of Coke or a literature anthology. On the desk. And she couldn't help but look at them, sitting there. She explained about the final paper and the revision process, but she was thinking: Shit. My God. What if I wasn't me? What if I was one of those boys?

LATER, entering the red mouth of the Dali museum in St. Petersburg, Jill stopped to peer into the hole, and with one hand on the baby's stroller and the other on Dali's box, she could see that Cameron remembered everything exactly: the frame eyes, the fire nose, the couch mouth. "Don't you think that's pretty impressive, Mark?" she asked her husband. "She's only six."

"Not really," her husband said. "That's what you remember. You remember what's at the beginning and what's at the end."

She put her own eyes back up to the box and forced her mind to turn: a face, a living room, a face, a living room. The baby tossed her Dali finger puppet onto the floor and Jill took this as a signal to keep moving.

WHEN they pulled into the hotel parking lot, she waved when she saw Cameron in the back seat of a white rental car. Cameron looked down without waving back. Jill couldn't see the other mother's eyes beneath her dark sunglasses, but she could tell she was looking right at her. The other mother's mouth was a straight line, a couch—no cushions. More of a bench, really.

IN the morning, Cameron was not by the pool. The family had checked out.

Jill was disappointed. She had wanted to thank Cameron for recommending the museum. She wanted to tell her they'd touched the red fur, and everything in the box was just as Cameron had said it would be, she'd remembered exactly: a face, a living room, a face. . . and still, she had imagined saying to Cameron, there's no place to relax, is there? No place to sit, not without messing up the face. What's that blot on the mouth? A bad tooth? A canker? Oh. No. It's Dad, sitting on the couch. Jill had thought maybe this would make Cameron laugh. Such a serious little girl—she had wanted to make her laugh.

Outside the glass doors, the man worked on his boat, sanding down the bowsprit. He whistled while he worked. The day was so perfect, the sun on the water, it made her eyes hurt. Under the rippling surface, Jill imagined Cameron's shells, everything becoming sand.

She wiped the applesauce from the baby's face with a wet cloth and walked to the open door of the bedroom. She could see her husband lying spread eagle on the floral bedspread. The straw fan on the wall was a kind of sombrero, the open fingers on each of his hands a fringe of flirty lashes, eyeball palms, head and torso nose, legs forming those lines that trace from our noses to the edges of our lips—what are those lines called?. . . but no mouth. She imagined curling herself onto the bottom of the bed to finish the picture. She could reach up and around her husband's feet, touch her fingers and toes to bold hibiscus cheeks on the horrible bedspread, and become a grinning mouth. Maybe she could grab the baby from her chair and plunk her, round and perfect, on the bottom corner. She could be a mole. A beauty mark!

Yes, she thought, scooping up the baby. That's what you remember. You remember what's at the beginning and what's at the end. Even if nobody was there to see her, she would be the smile.

Not Like the Rest of Us:
A Hoosier Named Cole Porter

CATHY DAY

How I Discovered Cole Porter

When I was twenty-one years old, I broke one of Indiana's commandments: *Thou shall not leave.* And I broke it by going to the one place Hoosiers fear most: New York City. It was 1990, and one day, I walked into a Tower Records store. I came across a CD called *Red, Hot + Blue,* a tribute to someone named Cole Porter to benefit AIDS research, and it contained songs by some of my favorite artists at that time (Sinead O'Connor, U2, Annie Lennox). So I bought it. I opened up the jewel case to read the liner notes, and right there, "Cole Porter was born in Peru, Indiana..." I was dumbfounded, because, you see, I'm also from Peru, Indiana, and at that time, I had no idea who Cole Porter was, nor that he was a fellow Peruvian.

I bought the CD, of course, and as soon as I played it, I recognized the songs. "Night and Day" and "Begin the Beguine." I'd heard them all my life in movies and television shows, in commercials, on the radio in the doctor's office. Even if you don't know who exactly Cole Porter is, you know those songs.

Six Reasons Why I Didn't Discover Him Sooner

1. I come from a non-musical, working-class family that listened to Kenny Rogers, not Cole Porter.

2. It was 1990. There was no Internet yet. I couldn't Google anything.

3. I didn't know what NPR was.

4. Cole wasn't on the "Welcome to Peru" sign.

5. Back then, we celebrated our town's *circus* history (of which I've written, in *The Circus in Winter*) with museum exhibits and a festival, but we didn't do the same with our Cole Porter history.

6. I often rode my bike past the Cole family plot at Mount Hope Cemetery, but there was no marker, no sign to let you know: Here Lies Someone Famous.

A Conversation with My Grandma

When I got back from New York, I went to see my maternal grandmother, a member of the local historical society. I asked: "Why don't we celebrate Cole Porter more?"

She said, "Well, because he left."

What she meant: *Why should we celebrate him if he thought he was better than us?*

What I wanted to say: *But he was better than us!*

Instead, I said, "He had to leave, Grandma. He wrote Broadway musicals."

She said, "Well, it's also because he was different."

What she might have meant by different: homosexual, high falutin', pretentious, East Coasty, snobby, strange, European, hoity toity.

What I wanted to say: *I'm different, too. And different isn't a bad thing, Grandma. It's a good thing.*

But I didn't say that, because I knew she'd say: *Cathy, you're not different. You're a nice girl from Indiana. Don't be getting too big for your britches.*

What Is a Hoosier?

Back in 1900, Hoosier writer Booth Tarkington published *The Gentleman from Indiana*. The protagonist John Harkless says of Hoosiers: "I always had a dim sort of feeling that the people out in these parts knew more—had more sense and were less artificial, I mean—and were kinder and tried less to be somebody else, than almost any other people anywhere."

Well, is this statement true? I left Indiana in 1990, and for the next twenty years, I lived all over the country—New York, Alabama, Minnesota, Pennsylvania, New Jersey. And then in 2010, I moved back home again to Indiana, where (supposedly) people are kind and sincere and have good sense. I still can't tell you whether that's true, but I can tell you that the people of Indiana *believe* that it's true.

Disclaimer So That Everyone in Peru Won't Hate Me

Not long after I had that conversation with my grandma, Peru started celebrating its Cole Porter history. You see, June 9, 1991 was the 100th anniversary of his birth, and his fans from all over the world wanted to make a pilgrimage to the place where he was born and where he is buried. They called the city and asked what we had planned to celebrate our native son. So: we planned something. This is how the first Cole Porter Festival came to be, and since then, there's been a much bigger Cole Porter presence in Peru. His name is on the welcome sign. There's a sizeable Cole Porter exhibit at the local museum, including one of his Cadillacs. There's a sign at Mount Hope Cemetery to help you find his grave, in case you want to leave some flowers. You can spend the night in the room where he was born (although it really could use a new coat of paint). And do you know why you can do all that? Because they found a meth lab in his neglected childhood home, and a bunch of nice townspeople spent a year restoring it into a bed and breakfast. The mayor said the house went "from meth to magic." I can tell you thousands of things that suck about Indiana, but for every bad thing, I can also tell you something good.

Things I've Heard Hoosiers Say about Cole Porter

"His music has nothing to do with Indiana. It's like he's ashamed of us."

"He never came back because he thought he was too good for this place."

"He wasn't like the rest of us."

"I know he visited his mom a lot, and he had a standing order at Arnold's Candies, and yeah, he's buried here, but he's not really from here, you know what I mean?"

"I guess Cole Porter's B-day was today. Does anyone still listen to him?"

The Problem of Celebrating Cole Porter in Indiana

So: what happens at the Cole Porter Festival in Peru, Indiana? Performances of his music, of course, and a bus tour of all the places that inspired his songs or where he might have slept. Historians usually give lectures on "The [insert subject] of Cole Porter." The local cinema shows one of the two movies about his life: *Night and Day* (1946) or *De-Lovely* (2004). But don't go to Peru expecting you'll somehow "channel" the mythic Cole Porter. You're not going to drink a martini in a 1920's nightclub, like in *Midnight in Paris,* eat a fancy French meal, nor attend a hedonistic pool party with a bevy of attractive young men. No sir. But you can go to the local theater group's annual revue— Cole's music incorporated into wildly different themes. Prehistoric Cole. Cole in Space. Country Fried Cole.

No, I'm not making this up.

Another main attraction is the antique car show. One of my prized possessions is a T-shirt that reads "2003 Cole Porter Days Car and Bike Show" in orange neon, and features a chopper and a 1950 Mercury hot rod painted with flames.

No, I'm not making this up.

And you need to know this: I love this shirt, and I love the revue. I love the question that these things raise: How do you celebrate one of the 20th century's most sophisticated artists in a place where his brand of sophistication and artistry is not generally valued?

Hoosiers According to the Office of Tourism

In 2014, the Indiana Office of Tourism Development unveiled its new marketing slogan: "Honest to Goodness Indiana."

This is who we want to be, but is it who we are?

We weren't honest to goodness on August 7, 1930 in Marion, Indiana when two young African-American men, Thomas Shipp and Abram Smith, were lynched in the town center while the town looked on. A photograph of their bodies hanging from a tree sold thousands of copies and has become iconic with lynching in America. And it didn't happen in the South. It happened here.

We weren't honest to goodness when we tolerated "sundown towns," when lots of communities in Indiana posted signs at their city limits that said, "Nigger, don't let the sun go down on you in [name of town]."

We weren't honest to goodness in March and April of 2015 when Governor Mike Pence signed the Religious Freedom Restoration Act, which allows a business to discriminate against LGBTQ individuals if such a business believes that homosexuality is a sin.

As a friend of mine who is writing her dissertation on branding says: If you want the world to see you as loving, be loving.

The Problem of the ExMid

For twenty years, I lived as an expatriate Midwesterner. I was what writer Calvin Trillin calls an "ExMid," a term he uses to denote "someone who lives on either coast or abroad but still prefers to think of himself at least partly as a Midwesterner." The ExMid harbors a particular fear: "The fear that his mother or aunt or cousin will be cornered by some neighbor at his hometown supermarket and informed that he has become too big for his britches." Cole Porter was not an ExMid, but I am. Big time. In fact, I am petrified that someone from my hometown will read this and corner my aunt at Harvey Hinklemeyers and say it's really a shame I couldn't find something nice to say about my hometown. (See disclaimer!)

But these questions haunt me. How do you become the person you need to become when there's so much pressure to be "normal"? How are you supposed to stay down to earth and shoot for the stars? How do you live an intellectual life in a state that values folksy wisdom and bristles at big words and big ideas? How do you become extraordinary and stay ordinary?

Things I Have Heard Hoosiers Say about Why They Won't Try

"I just can't see myself doing that."

"What would people say?"

"I don't know how to get there."

"I'm scared to drive on highways/fly in a plane/get on a bus."

"My family needs me."

"I have everything I need right here."

"I don't want everyone looking at me."

"It's too hard."

"God is not calling me to do that."

"Only stuck up people/gay people/weird people do that."

"Everyone will say I'm getting above my raising."

"If I try and fail, everyone will say I told you so."

"If I try and do not fail, everyone will say I'm an asshole."

Hoosiers According to Meredith Nicholson

In 1918, Hoosier writer Meredith Nicholson tried to articulate our character in his book *The Valley of Democracy*. In the first chapter, titled "The Folks and their Folksiness," he said that we are "the real bread and butter people." In spite of every facility of communication, we are disposed to be scornful of the world's experience because we believe it doesn't relate to us. We believe you can learn just as much in your hometown as in China, and he said we're prepared to prove it.

How's that for a new marketing slogan? Hoosiers: The Real Bread and Butter People.

How Do You Pronounce Peru?

I get this question a lot. I say Puh-roo, but others say Pee-roo or Pay-roo.

People also ask me why Indiana has so many towns named for foreign places, but that are mispronounced: Brazz-ill instead of Bruh-zil; Monti-sello instead of -cello, Ver-sails instead of Ver-sigh, Lebbin-in instead of Lebbin-on. For a long time, I said we just didn't know how to pronounce them correctly, but now I think that we *did* know, but that we mispronounced them on purpose because if we said *Ver-sigh,* people might think we were putting on airs.

Folks and Their Folksiness

I don't think Indiana is honest to goodness. Sometimes, I think it's the angriest place I've ever lived—and I've lived in a lot of places.

Indiana can be a real bully, and we all know that bullies hurt because they themselves hurt. They're unhappy, so they want you to be unhappy, too. And why is Indiana unhappy? Because deep down, we believe that—by virtue of having never left or having ended up here or having returned—we have somehow failed. I worry about that a lot, actually. And even if you don't believe that you've failed, you still worry that's how you look in the eyes of others—like someone who couldn't do better.

What keeps me from feeling like I failed is the fact that I left. That I chose to come back. It's the people who never left who tell themselves they are the real bread and butter people. And then they meet someone who makes them uncomfortable, someone who makes them aware of how much they've sacrificed to folks and their goddamn folksiness. That's where all the trouble begins.

Hoosiers According to Theodore Dreiser

In *An Indiana Boyhood,* Dreiser wrote: "The very soil smacked of American idealism and faith, a fixedness in sentimental and purely imaginative American tradition in which I alas could not share. This profound faith in God, in goodness, in virtue and duty that I saw here in no way squared with the craft, the cruelty, the brutality, and the envy that I saw everywhere else. These parents were gracious and God fearing but to me they seemed asleep. They did not know life—could not. These boys and girls, as I soon found, respected love and marriage and duty and other things which the idealistic American still clings to. Outside was all this other life that I had seen of which apparently these people knew nothing. They were as if suspended in dreams."

How's that for a marketing slogan? Indiana: Join Us in Our Bubble.

A Story about Bullying

These days, I'm working on a new novel about Cole Porter and his wife Linda. A few years ago, I got a fellowship from the Houghton Library at Harvard University to study Linda Porter's personal scrapbooks. I was at a tea party for the visiting fellows, talking with a reference librarian when another fellow, a woman from California, came up and introduced herself. I told her that I taught at Ball State in Muncie, Indiana. And then I waited for it, and sure enough, she obliged. She cocked her head and said, "Indiana. Tell me, why do people live there?"

This is what bullies do, of course. They're at a party, feeling insecure, so they make you feel insecure, too.

Sure, okay, but I was also battling rube-a-phobia, a profound fear that I'd say or do something stupid in the company of these eminent scholars that would demonstrate that I had no business being in that room and they'd take away my coveted Harvard library card.

So I took a deep breath and said, "People live there because they work there or they're born there or they come back there. Cole Porter was born in Indiana."

"He was?" she said, surprised.

"Yeah, in my hometown. Peru."

The reference librarian standing next to me said, "You're from Peru? I was born in Marion." Turned out he majored in English at Purdue, and we continued talking and eventually the lady from California drifted away.

Another Story about Bullying

But the worst part wasn't what that lady said to me in Cambridge, MA, but what someone else said when I returned home to Indiana.

I was scheduled to speak at an event, and one of the hosts, an Indiana native, kept introducing me to others like this: *Cathy Day, who just got back from Hah-vahd, who probably thinks we're small potatoes compared to Hah-vahd, and I'll bet the coffee is so much better at Hah-vahd, isn't it Cathy? Ha ha! You know I'm teasing, right?*

All day, this person shamed me like this. And so, even though I was at that event to talk about researching my book, I never mentioned Harvard. Not once.

The Most Hoosier Song Cole Porter Wrote

If by "Hoosier," you mean honest to goodness, sentimental and nostalgic, then by all means, it's "Old Fashioned Garden" or "Don't Fence Me In," but if you mean something else, then I say it's the little-known ditty "Experiment," written in 1933 for the musical *Nymph Errant*. A professor gives some final advice to his graduating students about what to do in the face of "philistine defiance."

Experiment.
Be curious,
Though interfering friends may frown.
Get furious
At each attempt to hold you down.
If this advice you always employ
The future can offer you infinite joy
And merriment
Experiment
And you'll see.

Playwright Ben Hecht said, "Old songs are more than tunes. They are little houses in which our hearts once lived." Cole Porter built more than twelve hundred of those little houses, but "Experiment" is the one he built for me. And for any person—from anywhere—trying to come to terms with being different in a place where folks ask, *Why can't you just be like everybody else?*

The Hoosier Identity

PHILIP GULLEY

I WAS IN THE FOURTH grade, in Mrs. Betty Conley's class, when I first remember hearing the word Hoosier. I'm certain I heard it before then, but
that was the first time the word stuck. We learned about the state bird, car-
dinal, the state tree, *Liriodendron tulipifera,* and the state stone, limestone.
In the fifth grade, we moved on to U.S. history, but for one glorious year we
dwelled on all things Indiana.

Mrs. Conley was an evangelist for the small town, believing its citizens
possessed a degree of nobility lacking in city dwellers. When anything bad
happened in our town, she blamed it on people from the city. So for the first
twenty-nine years of my life, I avoided Indianapolis like the plague, then was
wooed there by its siren song. Unlike the Greek tragedies, my time there ended
well. I only moved back to my hometown because I fell in love with a house
that had a woodstove in the kitchen, which was, and remains, my idea of high
living.

I've lived in Indiana for fifty-five of her two hundred years, have traveled
in every one of her ninety-two counties, speaking in libraries and churches,
and can report, with a high degree of confidence, that there is no such thing
as the Hoosier identity, if by identity we mean a common trait shared by all.

Hoosiers are no more all the same than are Californians, Iowans, or Texans. This isn't to say most of us don't aspire to a collective goal, in this case Hoosier hospitality. Just as a cowboy lurks in most Texans, so does the wish to be friendly dwell in most Hoosier hearts. In our 199th year, our legislature voted in a law perceived to be unkind to gays and lesbians and such an outcry was raised by Hoosiers the politicians had to run for cover. We Hoosiers can be contrary, slow to change, and impossible to lead, but once we get it in our minds to welcome someone there's no stopping us.

I've been fired twice in my life, once by a man from Oregon who tossed me overboard to the sharks, and the other time by a Quaker meeting in Indiana whose elders held my hand and wept as they eased me out the door. I returned the next month for a pitch-in dinner and they ushered me to the front of the line and slipped me an extra piece of pie. I'd like to think it was because they were Quakers, but now I believe it was the Indiana in them, that part of us that can't bear to be the cause of someone else's distress, however slim our fault. I once wrote a letter to a man newly arrived to our state, apologizing for its lack of an ocean.

In Indiana, guilt runs a close second to hospitality. We feel guilty about everything. I majored in theology at Marian University in Indianapolis, which was actually a four year course of study in things I should feel bad about. William Henry Harrison, a governor of the Indiana territory-turned-President, died on his 32nd day in office, throwing the nation into a tizzy about presidential succession. Mrs. Conley told us his last words were, "I wish to apologize for causing you all this trouble." I think she made that up, because no one knows what he said, though it sounds like something a dying Hoosier would do, apologize for something he couldn't help.

Or maybe he could have helped it, had he not violated another maxim dear to Hoosiers, wash your hands. That's the third thing every Hoosier learns. First, be nice; second, be ready to apologize; third, always wash after shaking hands. But William Henry Harrison forgot, caught a cold, which led to pneumonia, which led to his death, which led to John Tyler being sworn in as President. That led to the annexation of Texas and its eventual inclusion as a state, for which we Hoosiers would like to apologize.

I'll be the first to admit that my love affair with Indiana has had its ups and downs. Whenever our legislature meets, I think of leaving Indiana, but I stay put, mostly because of the woodstove in my kitchen and because my hero, Eugene Debs, was a Hoosier, born in Terre Haute on November 5, 1855. It was Eugene Debs who said to the judge after being convicted of violating the Sedition Act in 1918, "I am opposing a social order in which it is possible for one man who does absolutely nothing that is useful to amass a fortune of hundreds of millions of dollars, while millions of men and women who work all the days of their lives secure barely enough for a wretched existence."

The judge was unimpressed and sentenced Debs to ten years in prison, where he ran for President in 1920 and received nearly a million write-in votes. But, and here's the bright spot, Hoosiers had the good sense to elect Eugene Debs to the Indiana General Assembly in 1884. Any state that would elect Eugene Debs to public office has something noble, something virtuous, in its DNA. That nobility might well be a recessive gene, only popping up every now and then, but I intend to stick around to see if it emerges again.

When I was in the fourth grade, Mrs. Conley, that lover of all things Indiana, recited from memory Eugene Debs' 1918 speech before the federal court. Even now, I recall that wintry day, his glorious words warming our room and stirring our hearts, thinking that if Indiana never gave the world another gift, at least we had given it Eugene Debs.

Faith

JEAN HARPER

IN THE GREENHOUSE, WHERE I cut roses for a living for only four short months of my life, but long enough to be changed forever, I learned about the men and women in my crew during our breaks from the day's work. We broke three times a day: in the morning and in the afternoon for fifteen minutes; at noon for thirty. Each break of the day we sat together as a crew on makeshift seats of overturned ten-gallon white plastic buckets. On hot days, we sat on the loading dock, out of the heat of the greenhouse, in the wake of whatever paltry breeze we could find. On cool days, we retreated inside the greenhouse, sitting along the walkway between two houses. Most breaks, every one of us ate; every break, most of us smoked. In my crew, of the seven of us, three of the four women were Christians, two of them born-again. At our breaks in the morning, at lunch, and again in the afternoon, the women talked, and they often talked about Jesus.

Lil, fifty, short and doughy, had a personal relationship with Jesus Christ. "I was brought up in a Christian home," she would remind us, often. Joy, seventeen, wore shiny red lipstick, and came to work every day carrying a tiny blue purse that swung at her hip, a purse that she retrieved at breaks and rummaged in, meditatively. She had been saved at a revival two months before she had started at the greenhouse. "I accepted Jesus as my Lord and Savior," she would say. Sammie Jo, seventeen too, translucent as a Barbie doll, was raised a Christian and had been a true believer since birth. Of these three women, Sammie Jo was the only one who smoked.

"If He wanted me to quit, He would show me the way," she would say.

Lil and Joy would nod; the rest of the crew, the men and I, would listen in silence. It sometimes seemed to me that the men, with their noncommittal quiet, believed that religion, God, Jesus—all of that—was women's work. For my part, I kept quiet for other reasons: I knew if I spoke up and asked questions that arose out of my transplanted, East Coast naiveté about all things Midwest—whether I asked about Jesus or Christianity or God or what it really meant to be "saved" or "born again"—Lil would pounce on my questions, taking my idle interest as dawning faith. So I too ate and listened in silence every day while the three women talked.

It was talk about Jesus that was curiously intimate. Lil and Joy and Sammie Jo talked about Jesus as if they knew Him personally, as if He were a distant, beloved uncle living some kind of important life in a big city—Manhattan, Chicago, L.A. Somehow, wherever He was, their Jesus always kept tabs on everyone. Jesus, according to Lil and Joy and Sammie Jo, was intimately aware of the lives and troubles of everyone, no matter who or where they were.

Did you wake up with a headache? Jesus felt it.

Last night, did you have a fight with your husband? Jesus heard it.

Was your rent overdue? Your son in trouble with the cops? Your ulcer flaring again? He knew these things, felt what you felt. And He cared. He cared about all of us, kept track of all us, all of the time.

"He is by your side," Lil would say.

And Joy and Sammie Jo would nod. But even though Jesus knew us intimately, and seemingly kept elaborate ledgers of our constant troubles and intermittent triumphs, it was clear, the three women said, that we couldn't always count on His intercession.

When and how and who He helped was up to Him. Your headache, your husband, that looming rent, that restless son, your burning ulcer—sometimes He would answer your prayers for intercession and relief. Sometimes He would not. You never knew.

Lil and Joy and Sammie Jo not only talked about Jesus, but they protected Jesus and they worked for Jesus, doing the things they knew He liked, avoiding the things they suspected He did not. At the greenhouse, they carried out His work in many small ways, in all of their tasks.

There was one task that tested the particulars of their faith. Every six weeks, we worked in our crews pinching back the roses to encourage new and predictable growth. To pinch back meant that we cut off vegetative shoots on the roses down to a good five-leaf; every shoot pinched off would be the site of a new rose within another six weeks.

Pinching back was both science and faith. It was based on the knowledge that the rose would respond to the pruning by producing a shoot which, if properly watered and fed and sprayed and kept in a temperate environment, would flower on schedule. That was the science. The faith was in the timing. Roses are animate beings, growing and flowering by way of complex systems of cellular response. Along the way to their full flowering, roses have preferences and irritants. They like good steady light, enough water but not too much, the right brew of food; they don't like mildews and fungi, aphids and spiders, persistent cloud cover, dampness and chill.

In the greenhouse, we interceded as we saw fit. We sprayed, watered, fed, turned on heaters, pulled back overhead curtains. We cut, we pruned, we pinched back. We made judgments about which plants would bloom, and when. When I cut off a vegetative shoot to a good five-leaf I would hear the clip of the cutters on the shoot, that quick juicy snap of blade on stem. I would toss down the slender shoot of the plants on the path between the benches of roses and step over it, feeling it ever so softly crush beneath the sole of my boot as I walked forward, reaching for the next shoot and the next.

As part of our work of pinching back, we kept count of the shoots on our mechanical counters. We tallied our counts; from them, we would project out six weeks and estimate production. In a single day, pinching back more than a thousand shoots was nothing unusual. In a week of pinching back, we tallied up numbers in four and five digits.

One morning in September, during a break, we sat on our overturned buckets on the loading dock and compared our counts. That day, I remember we read out our precise numbers to each other. The exact numbers are gone, but I remember how we measured up to one another. Hank had the highest count, something near nine hundred. Bo was next, then Lil at about eight hundred, then me, followed by Joy, Sammie Jo, and finally, dead last at only three hundred, Eddie.

It was Lil's count that was different, not for the number, but for the way she had arrived at it. She had added two counts: first six hundred and sixty-five and then another couple hundred.

I had to ask. Why two counts?

Lil smiled patiently at me, a What Would Jesus Do kind of smile, and then she explained. When she got to six hundred and sixty-five on her counter, she said, she would stop, turn the counter back to zero, and start again. I remember her nodding sensibly and Joy and Sammie Jo nodding too, and the men, who were smoking and listening and watching the toes of their boots, even they were nodding. Everyone seemed to know something I didn't. I remember asking again, even as I suspected I was treading onto hallowed ground:

"How come you go back to zero? Is your counter broken?"

Lil smiled at me again, with even greater patience. "No, honey. It ain't that," she said. "It's that next number. That's the Devil's number. I don't want no Devil's number on my hands. So I don't go no further than six hundred and sixty-five."

It was Sammie Jo who explained further. "You gotta just get by that number," she said. Her approach was to go over it fast. "It," I slowly gathered, was more than simply a number; it was the mark of the Beast, the signature of the Devil, that Biblical warning: 666. When Sammie Jo got to six hundred and sixty-five, she clicked twice and got to six hundred and sixty-seven, seemingly before the Devil had time to register that the verboten 666 had appeared on her counter. She shrugged as if to say: not perfect, but better than nothing.

I gazed at my counter. I rolled the numbers back to zero again; four o's winked up at me. I looked at Lil. Our fifteen-minute break was almost up.

"What would happen if you stopped at six hundred and sixty-six?" I asked.

There was a moment of silence. Sammie Jo pulled out a second cigarette. Eddie flipped his cigarette butt off the loading dock; Bo lowered his ball cap and exhaled a long stream of cigar smoke.

Lil turned to me. "I just don't go that far," she said. "I just don't tempt no Devil."

I imagined I saw Him nodding sagely, wherever He was—Chicago, a five hour drive to the north; New York, nine hundred miles to the east, L.A., almost two thousand to the west. I clicked my counter carelessly, ticking through digits one after another. I thought about clicking the counter six hundred and sixty-six times and letting it sit, there in my hand, like some kind of tiny time bomb for Jesus. Would anything happen?

Would anything change? Would the world as I had always known it end in fire—or ice? Would the rapture commence in a resounding flash and only the blessed and saved be transported upward through the searing heavens to dwell forever by Jesus's side kindled by the warmth of His lambent skin? Would the rest of the trammeled masses—those of us resolutely unsaved, obstinately unrepentant, dim and unschooled in the ways of Jesus—would we now howl in mortal agony, our feet rooted to the ruined earth, our flesh torn and scorched by the flames of the ascending Lucifer, our haunches burned with his irremovable brand: 666.

I did not know about these things. Yet—I was alone in my ignorance. I clicked forward through the numbers on my counter—578, 579, 580, 581. The white digits paraded inexorably onward across its silver face. 623, 624, 625. Then, at last, the greenhouse whistle blew, a long, mournful, nearly human wail I have never forgotten, not even now a decade away, that cry summoning the end of our morning break. Lil and Joy and Sammie Jo got up; the men slowly rose in turn; everyone began to gather their gear.

I crumpled the paper sack that had held my lunch and stood up. We all went back to work. What else, what else, would there have been to do.

Fort Wayne Is Still Seventh on Hitler's List

B.J. HOLLARS

IN THE 1940S, CITIZENS WOULD tell you that Fort Wayne, Indiana was so wrapped in magnetic wire, superchargers, sonar systems, bombshells, pistons, amplidynes, and dynamotors, that for a brief moment, the people there became important enough to fear obliteration. Employees at General Electric, Rea Magnet Wire Company, and International Harvester clocked in seven days a week to support the war effort, churning out all the necessary parts.

Without Fort Wayne, perhaps there would be no B-24 bomber.

Without Fort Wayne, perhaps there would be no atomic bomb.

When *Little Boy* was dropped over Hiroshima, a small piece of Fort Wayne was lodged inside. On Taylor Street, Joslyn Steel Manufacturing shaped uranium to ingots, contributing to the killing of 160,000 people 6700 miles away.

Days later, when *Fat Man* was dropped over Nagasaki, once more, Fort Wayne was to blame. Twenty-one-year old assistant flight engineer Corporal Robert J. Stock of 415 Downing Street—just five miles from where I grew up—peered down from his instrument panel at the mushroom cloud ballooning 30,000 feet below.

His mission: measure destruction.

Which he did, admirably, making him better prepared than most to know the effects of the bomb had Hitler dropped his own upon the steeples of the churches of Fort Wayne.

A questionnaire from a May 18th, 1942 citywide meeting clarified Fort Wayne citizens' questions on how to respond if Hitler bombed the city.

Q. Aside from ordinary fires due to combustion or any other natural source, do you feel there is any danger from fire that we might expect?

A. Yes, there is another danger we must face now that we are at war. That danger is from enemy airplanes dropping incendiary bombs.

Q. What is an incendiary bomb?

A. It is a small bomb weighing about two pounds.

They burned at 4500 degrees Fahrenheit.

IN a coffee shop on Broadway, old men still talk about the planes humming over their city.

"Probably twenty or thirty of them," a retired mailman shrugs, sipping his coffee. "We had to look up and try to figure out if they were our planes or theirs. We were always waiting for the day when we saw a swastika on the back wing."

That day never came.

With their heads tilted skyward, they spied only skywriters or C-47s droning high above.

The only strike they ever knew was lightning.

In October of 1941, in the months prior to Pearl Harbor, Charles Lindbergh spoke to a crowd of ten thousand at the Gospel Temple on Rudisill Boulevard. His noninterventionist group, America First Committee, was opposed to the American invasion of Europe and Lindbergh looked forward to sharing his feelings with Fort Wayne. The city was proud to host him, onlookers sprawling along the streets and sidewalks to catch a glimpse. But in the early afternoon on December 7th, 1941, as Fort Wayne citizens stepped from their churches and received word of the attack on Pearl Harbor, Lindbergh and his isolationist policy was quickly forgotten. The American First Committee disbanded within days while the men of Fort Wayne rushed to recruiting stations. Six hundred and twelve men who were raised on Wayne Street and Sherman Street and Clay Street would die in places they never knew existed.

MY father gets his oil changed at a service station on Covington Road.

"Eighteen bucks for the full service," he says. "You can't beat it."

Once, many years back, I attended Lindley Elementary with the owner's son. His name was Ryan, and for a time, our desks sat in the same row. During free-reading period, Ryan and I often hunkered into beanbags that swallowed us whole, taking turns holding *The Illustrated Guide to Fossils,* pointing out which fossils we would most like to find on our way home from school. We had never heard of Hitler, nor had we ever been told that Fort Wayne—our beloved home—was important enough to make it to the top of any list.

"I want to find a trilobite," Ryan once told me, so I said, "Okay. I want to find one, too."

Nearly twenty years later, Ryan died. Small arms fire from insurgents in Balad, Iraq. He was a corporal. He was a paratrooper. He was no longer in the beanbag chair beside me.

Once, during an oil change, my father asked his father how many tours his son had served. Ryan's father didn't speak, just held up grease-stained fingers.

IN the coffee shop on Broadway, just a few blocks from General Electric, old men still talk about the German prisoners of war.

"Probably thousands," the retired mailman continues. "I was just a little boy then, but we used to sit on my grandmother's porch and wave to them as they jogged by for their daily exercise."

Reports show that by 1945, six hundred German prisoners had infiltrated our city.

Camp Scott was originally constructed for the 130th Railroad Battalion, but by 1944, it had transformed to a prison camp. Guard towers were erected, barbed wire rolled out.

The camp was situated just beyond McMillan Park, between Wayne Trace and the Pennsylvania Railroad. The Germans were captured from Rommel's Africa Korps before flying into Fort Wayne.

The men at the coffee shop recall Sunday afternoons spent driving past the camp, the prisoners peeking out from the fences. Once the prisoners arrived, some parents no longer allowed their children outside after dark. But some parents did. There are stories of German POWs playing soccer in the park, of children accepting nickels to buy the prisoners sodas from nearby drugstores. The prisoners had access to radios and received more generous beer and cigarette rations than American soldiers overseas. They enjoyed Ping-Pong. They found girlfriends. They stuck around.

You ask them, they'll tell you—Fort Wayne is a good place to live.

THE night after three hundred and fifty-three Japanese aircraft attacked Pearl Harbor, the General Electric factory on Broadway turned off its glowing sign for the first time since 1928. The GE symbol had become a stalwart of the Fort Wayne skyline, though the red encircled letters remained dark until war's end. Nine hundred and twenty-five bulbs quieted their hum, and six months later, GE produced its last civilian motor before focusing entirely on war production. Security fences were constructed around the factory, and employees were given high-level identification badges. Armed guards were stationed in guardhouses. The war had reached our backyard.

Nearby, at the Wolf and Dessauer department store on Calhoun Street, the forty thousand lights depicting a glowing Santa and sleigh flickered into darkness as well.

The citizens of Fort Wayne knew one thing for certain:

They did not want Santa Claus in the German crosshairs as the bombs began falling from the sky.

CLOISTERED in the backroom of Fort Wayne's History Center sits a gray box filled with various manila folders, one of which reads simply "Bombs." Inside, a list of the most likely threats Fort Wayne may have endured, as well as information related to how citizens were to respond if Hitler bombed the city.

One pamphlet reminds Fort Wayne citizens that should they find themselves in a blackout, they are to remain calm, obey all traffic signals, and assist the infirm, the frightened, and the lost.

And remember, the pamphlet chides, "a blackout or air raid warning is a warning and not a promise of one."

Q. WHAT usually happens when an incendiary bomb strikes a home?

A. It will penetrate the roof of any ordinary constructed home. The force of the contact will ignite it and the chemicals within the bomb itself will start working. It will generate heat at about 4700 degrees Fahrenheit. At that heat almost anything will burn.

Q. A lot of questions have arisen on air raids. What would you suggest as a first step in protecting yourself from an air raid?

A. Every person should select in his home a place that would be suitable for occupancy during an air raid. It has been suggested that a basement room is preferable for this purpose.

THE questionnaire also recommends that a radio, table, chairs, books and magazines be kept in the basement, as there is no telling for how long the bombing might continue. Newspapers described basements filled with water and non-perishable food, of men preparing to darken the city at a moment's notice, air wardens stationed at the top of the Lincoln Tower, scanning the skies. Posters plastered to telephone poles and trolley cars reminding citizens, "Loose lips sink ships."

If the blackouts were done properly, even the posters would disappear.

MOST blackouts were announced in advance, but not always.

One flyer reads:

Black Out
Sunday Night
May 24, 1942

From 10 p.m. to 10:15 p.m.
Please Follow This One Rule:
Turn Off All Lights During This Period!

Yet in late May, the flyers were replaced with a confidential memo, one in which Carter Bowser of Fort Wayne's Command Control Center informed the FWPD of a surprise blackout scheduled for June 4th, 1942 from 9:30 p.m. until 9:45 p.m. Bowser hoped the unannounced blackout might better simulate the conditions of a true bombing, might strike fear into Fort Wayne's citizenry by keeping them on full alert.

On June 4th, a siren rang and light bulb filaments throughout the city rattled and died away. The trolleys stopped in the streets, their lights dimmed, while cars killed their engines. When Colonel Robert Harsh of the Office of Civilian Defense came to inspect Fort Wayne's preparedness, he left quite impressed by the city's ability to turn itself invisible, returning the land to fallow fields, the city to grids on a map.

A month later, an instructional film entitled "Bombs Over Fort Wayne" premiered at the Murat Temple Theatre on New Jersey Street in Indianapolis. Though the sixteen-millimeter film is lost, the original script remains.

Narrator: "It's a warm spring night in the city where three rivers meet. Late theatre-goers and workers have long since departed for their homes. A lone policeman patrols his beat. Far off—an automobile horn shatters the stillness of the night."

Then—silence, the city settling in for a night of rest.

Moments later, the calm of the Fort Wayne night is disrupted by the German air strike.

Controller: "High explosive bombs at Calhoun and Pontiac! Casualties approximately ten. Fire in three buildings. Electric wire down."

Police: "Enemy aircraft crashed through high tension wires at Delaware and Alabama. Some persons still in plane, some thrown out. Approximately six persons injured."

Incendiary bombs explode at the corner of Berry and Union as messenger boys are sent sprinting through streets.

"Several enemy escaped from the plane and seen going east!" actors cry. "Several unexploded bombs scatter in vicinity. Some smell of gas!"

Bomb squads and decontamination teams enter into the scene. Officers in riot gear chase after the six downed Germans as they scatter past the Embassy Theater, their swastikas reflecting on their aviation suits.

By movie's end, it's made clear that Fort Wayne's quick thinking and preparedness has saved the city.

As the house lights come up the narrator notes: "You've observed the drama of self-defense."

Fort Wayne citizens deemed the film a success, and Commander Bowser encouraged representatives from the Office of Civil Defense in Washington D.C. to buy the rights to the film and screen their production elsewhere.

James Landis, the director of Civil Defense, congratulated Bowser on a "very excellent job" before informing him that they would not be purchasing the film but wished Fort Wayne and its movie the best of luck.

Q. WHAT precautions can a person take and what can be used to combat an incendiary bomb?

A. Sand is the most efficient material which can be used to smother such a bomb. Water can be sprayed, but not poured in a steady stream on the bomb first to avoid the possibility of the fire spreading. Then the sand should be poured over the bomb until it is entirely covered. It can then be picked up in a shovel and placed in a partially filled bucket. A bucket with about six inches of sand in it will be satisfactory. The bucket can be carried out by using the handle of the shovel thrust through the handle of the bucket.

IF I had been alive during the blackouts, I would have lived in District 5. My warden would have been Donald H. Jones of 3424 N. Washington Road. He would have called me the day prior to a blackout to remind me to close my blinds, extinguish all light, do my part to obliterate ourselves from the aerial eyes of the Luftwaffe. He would have informed me not to strike a single match, and that if I needed to smoke—if I needed to calm my nerves—then I should have the courtesy to strike my light in a hallway far from the planes.

People still speak of the Civil Defense demonstration held in Hamilton Park years before. How the Civil Defense representative struck a single match from the outfield of the baseball diamond and how the citizens' faces erupted in firelight. How you could read the street sign: *Poinsette.*

Today, just a few hundred feet from that baseball diamond, a plaque reads, "In honor of all who served in the armed forces of the Second World War from the Third Civilian Defense District."

I would have been in the Fifth District. I have yet to find our plaque.

Q. TO sum up the situation, what would you say would be most essential then for the protection of a home?

A. A hose of approximately fifty feet in length. A bucket, a long handled shovel and a supply of sand are the most essential requirements.

AS other cities and manufacturers became aware of Fort Wayne's bombing problem, Fort Wayne Mayor Harry Baals began receiving literature on the latest anti-bomb technology in order to safeguard the city from foreign attacks.

For just $2.50, one could purchase a Bomb-Quench.

"Bomb-quench may be used with complete ease by anyone in home or factory," claims the brochure. "Simply remove top from the tube carton, sprinkle free flowing Bomb-Quench over the burning bomb or magnesium fire."

Or if Fort Wayne citizens preferred, they could invest in the Bomb-Snatcher, an orange metal scoop that stifled unexploded bombs.

"With the Bomb-Snatcher, Removal of Burning Bombs is Speedy and Safe," the pamphlet promises.

However, the people of Fort Wayne were far more interested in simply buying bombs themselves. A dozen practice incendiary bombs could be purchased for just over seven dollars.

"Our Bomb is low in cost and its action similar to a real one," the pamphlet assures. "Dispel the fear which nearly all persons have of an Incendiary Bomb by giving them an opportunity to see these PRACTICE INDENDIARY BOMBS demonstrated and actually allowing them to practice with one."

Intrigued, Commander Carter Bowser wrote the Baltimore Fire Works Company.

"Will you please advice [sic] us if you have available for demonstration purposes any small incendiary bombs. Also, quote us prices, quantities and delivery date."

There is no evidence Fort Wayne ever purchased a bomb, nor is there evidence we ever endured one.

A few years back, while driving along Jefferson Boulevard, I momentarily lost sight of the city's one and only skyscraper. Thankfully, it remained intact—just hidden in the fog.

Q. DO you feel that because of our inland location, the possibility of an air raid is very remote and that all these preparations are in vain?

A. I certainly do not want to say such a raid is impossible here, nor do I want to say that it is sure to come. I do however know that if we are raided these precautions and this training program will be invaluable. You don't carry fire insurance on your home because you are sure you will have a fire. You carry it for protection when it might be needed.

IF you look hard enough in Lindenwood Cemetery, eventually you'll stumble across the gravestone of Victor F. Rea, the man responsible for creating Rea Magnet Wire Company and bringing Hitler's name to every citizen's lips. If you look harder still, you'll find Ryan Woodward's grave as well, a slab of perfectly polished black marble, photos of him and his family laser-etched into the stone. Fourteen flags surround the monument, and even though the burial took place in 2007, at last glance, there were still fresh roses resting their petaled heads against his name.

I wonder what room we were in at Lindley Elementary when Ryan and I first learned of Hitler, learned what a bomb was, what small arms were, wondering if we would ever die by them and if so, who would remember our names.

THE day Truman announced the end of the war—August 14, 1945—the Fort Wayne newspapers were on strike. Airplanes buzzed over the city, though they did not drop bombs.

They dropped leaflets.

Japan Surrenders! Tune Into WGL For News.

According to newspapers, Fort Wayne's children crouched over the fallen materials and struggled to make out the words. When they finally did—sounding out every last syllable—the children ran up and down Bowser Avenue banging pots and pans, no longer even fearing fear itself.

On Calhoun Street, cars honked as bells rang from the spared church steeples, while not far away, the GE symbol re-lit the sky. No longer a target, Santa Claus followed soon after.

For the first time in a long time, Fort Wayne filled a newspaper with good news.

Q. IF we were to be subjected to a bombing attack, what type bombs would probably be used against us?

A. We would first, in all probability, be bombed by Incendiary Bombs.

But we were not.

We were just prepared for it.

You, too, have observed the drama of self-defense.

Walking in Outer Space

MICHAEL McCOLLY

Wherever I walk no traces are left,
And my senses are not fettered by rules of conduct.
—*Hsiang-yen Chi-hsien*

WHEN THE LAST IRON DOOR clanked behind me, my legs began to lighten. Exchanging my badge for my ID, I tried not to rush the guards, but once I got that first glimpse of the outside, my mind was already in my car, racing down the Indiana Toll Way back to Chicago. I sped through the decaying town of Michigan City, passing the shuttered stores and factories, the concrete cooling towers of the power plants, and then hit the expressway, grateful to be swallowed by the chaos of traffic. In a little over an hour I was back on the North Side of Chicago, lying spread-eagled on my bed, whiskey in hand, wondering why I'd ever thought it would be good for me to volunteer to sit with a Zen *sangha* of inmates in a maximum security prison.

Though I'd had a long history as a pilgrim on the proverbial spiritual path—trying just about everything this side of Transcendental Meditation, I was not a bona fide Buddhist. But there I was, sitting cross-legged on the concrete floor of an old chapel, surrounded by a dozen inmates, a guard with a loaded shotgun on his lap, looking down at us from a chair on the altar.

I did little more than show up and go through the rituals as we followed an ailing professor of Eastern philosophy, who had begun the *sangha* a decade ago. Mostly though, it was the men who guided me on the proper forms of practice. If I lost my place during our chants of the sutras, down came a tattooed knuckle to direct my eye to the right line of transliterated Korean. More than once, too, an inmate had to catch me from falling flat on my face, after getting up too fast from our meditations. "Whoa there, man, have to wait a few seconds 'fore you can walk. Got to let the blood get down to your feet."

We held our sessions on Fridays in an unheated, dimly lit chapel painted entirely in industrial grey—wooden pews, concrete floor, brick walls. The only colors came from the humiliating Kelly green sock caps the men were forced to wear, the American flag, and the golden Buddha. But for the inmates, worship of whatever faith was a welcome break from cramped cells and regimented lives. By the time the professor and the rest of the volunteers got there, the prisoners had pulled out a ceramic Buddha and set it on its cardboard storage box, arranged cushions for meditation and, with ceremonial pride, donned their robes. We prostrated one hundred and eight times before the Buddha, chanted the sutras, meditated, and then passed around a book of teachings of a Zen master, from which the inmates read word by word. Then we made tepid black tea from the bathroom tap, and awkwardly made small talk until the guards came to take them back to their cells.

Not surprisingly, the first couple of times I volunteered, the intensity of the experience and the Zen rituals immediately altered my mood and state of mind, which, honestly, was what I desperately needed. Once you walk through seven locked gates and feel the reality of where you are, a place of such visceral tension and ghastly history, your little psychodramas shrink to their proper proportion. My journalistic eye scanned every corner and face, fascinated and appalled all at once.

I was moved by the men and how the hours of practice altered them—the brightened faces, the lifted chins, the belting chants of the *Prajnaparamita*. I was changed, too; sitting with these damaged souls and walking behind them about the chapel often left me for brief moments freed from the need to measure and critique. The man beside me, the walls, the shotgun, the physical world, my body—all became a formless fabric turning itself inside out before my mind. I didn't feel so much contentment as simply relief.

But as is the case for the subtle practices of the spirit, no matter of what sacred tribe or method, there is a common pattern: a rise and a fall, a hallelujah and the despairing dark night that follows. And sure enough, after those first few times, the spell of Zen's charms and my professional curiosity about life behind bars gave way to the bitter anger I couldn't help but feel as I observed the business of housing the damned and dark-complicated. No quietist round of chants and meditative walks could quell the echoing bark of the guards or sweeten the stench of a century and half of humiliated souls. Perhaps, it was where I had been and what I'd seen in my past, perhaps it was my own sense of feeling close to death because of my own illnesses, but I found myself at times not wondering at the smart psychologist that was the Buddha but at the bodies of the men themselves and the desperate cries for power and meaning etched in ink on the only thing not taken from them—the canvas of their own skin.

Zen Buddhism, they say, is the practice of the middle path, in which the adherent learns to keep the mind aware of its tendencies toward emotional extremes of either attachments or aversions. By meditating, one practices holding onto the middle, literally, by carefully observing and feeling the effects of the mind's habits as it spins thought into memory and emotion in response to a steady stream of agitation from the physical world.

My problem was that when I opened my eyes, the practiced observer wouldn't quite turn off, and what it saw—with the keen eye of the meditator—was a world more clearly visible, more starkly drawn, a world of extremes, both surrounding me as well as within my own mind. I would like to say that the practice of meditation made me a better person, more conscious, more compassionate, more at ease, but at that time in my life, it had the opposite effect: it made the anger inside me toward much of humanity just that much more real.

ONE winter Friday, our teacher had arranged for a special meal for the *sangha*. I can't remember now why we were celebrating. It might have been a Buddhist holy day or an inmate's taking his vows. But at the end of our practice, a few of the other volunteers went into town and brought back big platters from a Chinese take-out, and after the men set up some tables, we sat and did something we rarely did, socialize.

I mostly listened to their conversations, a bit self-conscious and nervous. But I liked listening to the men, because sometimes out of their stories of home and families, came the name of a town, a highway, a place name I knew from the map of my youth growing up in Indiana—*Kokomo, State Road 13, Clifty Falls.*

But when one of the inmates, Larry, began to talk about camping to the guy next to him on a river where I'd fished and camped myself, I broke my silence.

"It was on the Mississinewa, that campground, wasn't it?"

Larry leaned over his food to put his face as close to mine as he could. "The Mississinewa? You know that river?"

"I grew up on that river."

"You been to that campground over there by I-69?"

"There was an old trestle bridge, wasn't there?"

"Yeah.

"You took a gravel road."

"That's it."

"There was a bend in the river, nettles on the bank, cottonwood."

"You catch catfish?"

"Yeah, we did. My dad baited up trot lines, and we set them out."

"You use chicken livers?"

"Nope, a ball of night-crawlers on a hook."

I hadn't thought of these landscapes of rural Indiana, not with the pleasure he'd made me feel for it, in a long time. I'd camped in the remote wilderness of Montana, hiked through the savannahs of West Africa, climbed into the Andes and walked along the great rivers of Europe. The farm lands and factory towns of my family had long ago lost their power to evoke wonder and natural beauty. But there it was in the air as we sat eating Chinese food in that old drafty Methodist Chapel: the trestle and the catfish, the nettles and hooks.

Then one snowy afternoon, after another long day of sitting and walking with the men, I found myself in my car, staring out at a line of oaks and cottonwoods behind the prison, as I tried to warm up my numb body and my poor car before starting back to Chicago. My vision seemed altered in some way, the intensity of the light had changed, objects and sounds appeared exaggerated in texture, as if the air was clearer, the sun brighter. For some reason, I had no desire to leave. I looked at the prison and it seemed to become a monument of rock, a castle, sinking into the sandy earth, its heavy brownstone walls, gates and turrets like a surreal dream dropped back to earth from 16th century Scotland. The forest behind the prison fixed my gaze, a wall of naked black trees, impenetrable and dense, protecting the tangle of forest and old sand dunes beyond from this factory of human misery.

Behind that stand of hardwoods, I could see just a hint of the oaks atop Mt. Baldy, the last of the great dunes left along Indiana's shore, saved from the bulldozers of industrial growth and sand mining of decades ago. Rising next to it like a giant child's top was the concrete cooling tower of what was once to have been a nuclear power station but had been reengineered for the coal burning furnaces of Northern Indiana's energy monopoly, NIPSCO. For the first time, it seemed, I let myself try to simply feel where I was: the prison, the city, the heavy weight of human grief, the winds off the lake blowing through the trees.

I'd seen all of this before. But this worn and weary landscape of power plants and prison camps and the grim disappearing neighborhood around it appeared now newly minted, its colorless qualities sharpened in the snow and afternoon light. Something felt familiar and necessary in what was there for me to see and study.

Slowly, I drove through the town I was always so eager to leave, past its lakefront casino, by its outlet mall, crossing and re-crossing railroad lines, some abandoned, some still alive with commuters and cars of coal for the power plants. The buildings and houses were of another time, another generation— my generation—unchanged it seemed from the early seventies, when the steel industry and everything around it collapsed, and the locally-owned shops and stores, the schools and the churches, emptied one by one. On a street by the prison, only a few old wooden houses now stood where there were once blocks of them, cheek by jowl.

I recognized these old, wood-frame two-stories, the tar-shingles, the lattice work on the porch cornices, the garages leaning off their concrete foundations. These were the houses of my hometown, my neighborhood of forty years ago. These were the houses of my schoolmates whose parents worked at the glass factory, at General Tire, GM, and RCA. These were the houses of my grandparents and aunts and uncles—houses with tall ceilings and stone porch steps, bedrooms where I first tasted sex, kitchens where my parents argued late into the night, family rooms where we watched man land on the moon.

I headed southwest out of Michigan City on State Road 12, rolling through the dunes and marshes, past the empty roadside motels and old sand quarries. A sliver is all that is left of what was once one of the most unusual landscapes in North America, some of the largest fresh water dunes in the world, miles of them along the southern shore of the lake, created by the northerly winds that swept across the long water, sculpting great mounds of sand and moving them, literally, inland, year by year.

I'd forgotten how the snow could recast the dunal landscape, diminishing the distant machines of man, the cold air sterilizing and defying the heat and clamor of commerce. I headed off into the snowdrifts making my own trail. I tramped upward, falling into hidden drifts unable to read the land, walking to walk, to move, which, as I walked, I realized was exactly what I needed to do.

I walked among the bones of black oaks long ago buried by the winds and sands, solemn sculptures, trunks and limbs sticking out of the snow, a graveyard of wooden remains. There were pines, too, clusters on the dune ridges, some strongly rooted, others warped by the winds. In the sheltered swales and blowouts, a single cedar stood and under its protection chokecherry and other grasses grew, specific to these miniature valleys walled off from the winds of the lake. Even in winter and under the cover of snow, the unusual ecology of the dunes struck the eye. Next to the boreal pines and burberry down closer to the beach were the rugged dune grasses, and over the dunes, on the leeward side, were the hardwoods, where woodland ephemerals would pop up in spring, and across the road, the wetlands held tamaracks and ancient plants of the Ice Age. If I kicked about under the snow, I could find the poor prickly pear far from its southwestern home.

I traversed up into the wooded ridges along the lake, awaiting that first sight of it to appear through the trees, a sight that even if you live for years by the lake somehow still startles the eye. And there it was, the vast void of slate blue, churning with chunks of ice. From here, I could see all around the lake, my eye following what was once the trail of the Indians and, before that, creatures of the Ice Age—the lion-faced bear, the wolves, the sloths and saber-tooth tigers that I drew as a boy over and over again on the margins of my school papers, fantasizing a past that had long ago been buried by the needs of man.

To the north, rising out of the pines, was the great Mount Baldy, and from there, if I were standing on top and looking inland, I could see the prison not a mile to the east, with its old stone walls built by its first prisoners, Confederate soldiers captured and shipped north. And inside, there would be the rec yard and the infirmary, the graveyard and the chapel. All of this, I thought as my eyes scanned the scope of land and lake before me, the forests and marshes, the dunes and the vast waters of the lake, which can be clearly visible in space, and yet unseen by my *sangha* mates behind those old stone walls.

I'd initially dismissed the meditative potential of our walking meditation at the prison, as it seemed more like desperately needed exercise for the men than official Zazen. In fact, it often reminded me of following a gym teacher in my grammar school days in a game of follow-the- leader, as the professor led the men around the chapel, cutting down an aisle between pews, then whipping us back down the next, hardly the formal meditation practice I'd learned in Thailand. But over time, by doing nothing more than watching the tottering gait of the khaki trousers and white-stocking feet of the man before me, I would fall into our collective rhythm and for a while feel as if I were upon some path, a pilgrim on his long journey.

I walked on down the beach, content for once, for now, to watch my feet and listen to their weight as they made their mark in the snow.

AFTER my winter walk into the dunes that day, I made a point to take my time on trips back to Chicago. I explored more of the dunes, places I'd seen on maps but assumed were too close to industrial wastelands. I took the highway rather than the expressway and discovered patches of wilderness and other odd wonders of the landscape that once had symbolized my anger and disgust. I looked now for the contrast, the foreground of nature and human survival against the backdrop of dross and industrial baroque. The coal cars covered in graffiti rolling through the dunes, the beauty of oxidized iron girding among the grasses and goldenrod, the woman dragging her tank of oxygen down the beach as she searched for bits of colored glass.

It wasn't that I didn't feel the toxic ugliness and its effects on those who were surrounded by it, I did. But what was important now was to hold onto the suspended way of seeing that had begun back at the prison among my *sangha,* among men whose very sanity depended on seeing beyond the sorrow. The point was not to speed by but to practice simply seeing what was there.

And so it was through the fallen cities of East Chicago, too, a silence pervaded the scene as I drove around the refinery towers, the tanks and pipelines coming up and over the road, the gargantuan mills next to the casinos next to the power plants along the lake, the empty spaces, trains crossing under the highways, crossing over the city streets, the tire fix-it shops, the *taquerias.* I crossed the Calumet River and entered Chicago, drove along the super fund site left by US Steel's famed South Shore Works, and then the highway zig-zagged and turned into a south shore neighborhood of proud old brick black churches, crumbling two flats, and weeded lots, the lake peeking through as I wound my way back onto Lake Shore Drive. Here, among the foreclosed and forlorn, I felt the same heavy silence I'd felt in Gary, the same solemn weight of history, as the steel and glass empire of the city rose out of the evening spring light. I drove on feeling the silence in me, as tangible and as real as my thoughts, making me have to acknowledge that what we see and what we feel are who we are. The layers upon layers of life, fallen and fallen again, and rising up through the dead, was this city; was, for better or worse, who I was as well.

IN the spring, my schedule changed and my trips to the prison became more difficult, and by the end of summer, my participation in the *sangha* came to an end. I'm ashamed to say I never told the men goodbye, never properly bowed before them as one does before the Buddha upon entering a room where it rests. I'd meant to. I'd meant to tell them many things that I knew only they would understand, things about myself only they could help me feel.

But on the day I knew would be my last, I got a call from my friend who'd invited me into the *sangha* in the beginning, a woman I'd learned to listen to for how she navigated through her own lot in life. I was glad she'd called because I wanted to tell her of my plans. But before I could tell her she told me there had been trouble at the prison, a fight had broken out between rival gangs, and a man had been brutally stabbed to death, a young man, a member of our *sangha*.

In my mind, as she told me that the prison was under lockdown and we would not be meeting, I saw the young inmate, who'd joined the *sangha* as I had over the course of the last year; I could see him leaning against one of the pews, telling me of his love for science fiction, his eyes lifting to the grey wooden ceiling of the chapel, fantasizing himself into the wilderness of outer space.

Neighbors

SCOTT RUSSELL SANDERS

ONE NIGHT, DEEP IN WINTER, deep in the Ohio countryside, midway through the 1950s when I was a boy of ten or so, there came a knocking at our farmhouse door. Glad of an excuse to escape from the scary movie that was playing on our brand-new TV, with its round screen and murky black-and-white picture, I ran to answer the knock.

Opening the door, I found our neighbor from down the road, Mrs. Thompson, with a baby in her arms and her other four children huddled behind her, shivering. The look on Mrs. Thompson's face was even scarier than the movie. "I need to ask your parents a favor," she said.

Before I could fetch them, my father and mother came to the door, having heard the urgency in Mrs. Thompson's voice even above the spooky music on TV. To my relief, the one-eyed monster, as my father called it, was now silent.

My mother hustled them all inside, laying a hand on the head of the baby and on each of the kids in turn as they scurried by like a troop of ducklings. They were wearing pajamas under their raggedy coats, and worn-out sneakers caked with snow. No boots, no gloves, no hats. No wonder they were shivering. I knew they were poor, because the two kids who were old enough for school climbed on the bus wearing the same clothes every day. My parents often sent my sister or me down the road to their place with vegetables from our garden or Mason jars from our canning shelves. "To share the wealth," my mother would say.

The favor that Mrs. Thompson shyly asked was if she and her children could spend the night until they found some other place to live, because their house had burned down. Only then did I notice the smell of smoke.

"Burned down?" my father repeated. He flung open the door and stared out, but there was nothing to see except the snowy fields and starry sky, because the Thompsons' place was half a mile away, beyond a bend in the road. "Where's Jimmy?" my father asked, about the man whom I knew to call Mr. Thompson and knew to avoid because of his foul temper.

"Took off in his truck," Mrs. Thompson said. "It was him as started the fire. He fell asleep smoking."

My mother and big sister quickly made up pallets for the kids; put the baby, who had slept through the whole ruckus, in a bassinette that my own little brother had recently left for a crib; and put fresh sheets on my bed for Mrs. Thompson.

I slept on the couch that night, and off and on for weeks afterward, until my father and a dozen or so of our neighbors finished building a new house on the foundations of the tarpaper shack that had burned. The materials were donated or purchased with money gathered in local stores and churches, and, of course, the men, mostly farmers or carpenters or factory workers, volunteered their labor. Women delivered casseroles and cakes and soup and a feast of other foods to our door almost every day while the Thompsons stayed with us.

Soon after Mrs. Thompson and her children moved into the new house, Mr. Thompson returned from wherever he had been wandering. But he stayed only a few days, and then he left for good.

Why he left for good I did not learn until years later, when I asked my father if he knew the reason. My father explained that Jimmy Thompson used to beat Mrs. Thompson and the kids, who often showed up at school or the hospital covered in bruises. When my father learned of this, he talked to the sheriff, who talked with Mrs. Thompson and then secured a restraining order. When the beatings continued, despite the court order, my father paid a visit to the house and had what he called a heart to heart talk with Jimmy, who saw the benefits of moving elsewhere and leaving the family in peace.

Knowing that my father had been a Golden Gloves boxer in his early days, I asked, "Did you threaten him?"

"I told him if he hit anybody in his household one more time, and I learned of it, he would have to hit me next, or try to, and he could find out how it felt."

I recall this story as an especially vivid example of the mutual care I witnessed in the rural Ohio community where I grew up. My parents and all the other grownups had lived through the Great Depression and World War II; they knew they needed one another. When someone fell sick, lost a job or a child, neighbors would nurse them, feed them, console them. Neighbors would loan tools, offer rides to town, share garden bounty, listen to happy news or sorrows, visit shut-ins, and swap work. The people in that community recognized one another's dogs and horses and cows, and made sure any stray animal was returned to its own pasture or house. They kept an eye out for one another's children. We kids roamed freely over everybody's land, knowing we could knock on any door for help. Once, when I fell through river ice while checking muskrat traps, I staggered to the nearest farmhouse, where the elderly couple thawed me out by their woodstove and thanked me for livening up their morning.

I do not mean to romanticize that rural community. Jimmy Thompson was not the only scoundrel. There were grumps and gossips among us, but no saints. Nor were there any African Americans or Asian Americans. I believe that my parents would not have distinguished among neighbors on the basis of race or ethnicity, a belief supported by what I observed in their later years when they lived in cities in Louisiana, Oklahoma, and Ontario. How many others on those Ohio back roads would have been equally tolerant, I cannot say, but I recognize that the all-white homogeneity of our community eased the way to a culture of mutual care. It also helped that there were no rich people, so nobody suffered from the delusion that money could buy all the necessary help or comfort. People knew that sooner or later they would need a hand or a hug, a recipe or advice; they would need a neighbor, not a hireling, to rescue them from loneliness or loss. Knowing their own vulnerability, they had a livelier sense of what others needed or suffered.

The neighborly culture I observed in the 1950s was shaped by other circumstances that are less common in America today. Because a greater stigma was attached to divorce and to pregnancy outside of wedlock, and because women had few options for supporting themselves without a husband, nearly every family had two parents. Many women, by choice or necessity, were fulltime homemakers. In addition, households often contained grandparents or other kinfolk. So there were grownups at home during the day, available to look in on an ailing neighbor or help can tomatoes or hold a fretful baby. People often worked outdoors, repairing their houses and cranky machines, weeding gardens or mending fences. There were no electronic attractions indoors aside from primitive televisions, so children commonly played outdoors, requiring no equipment aside from a ball and bat and mitt, perhaps, or a bow and arrows and a bale of hay, and requiring no guidance except from their imagination. Chores also kept children in the open air, filling water troughs in the barn lot or gathering eggs from the chicken coop. In hot weather, families sat on porches in the evening, listening to the radio, reading books aloud, playing cards or board games and telling stories, all within sight of passersby who would stop to chat.

It's clear most Americans would not choose to go back to such a world even if we could. In our millions, we have chosen air-conditioning, jumbo TVs, video games, and sundry other electronic devices, food from grocery stores or fast food joints, and a life spent almost entirely indoors. Without leaving our desks or easy chairs, we can tap into news and knowledge and products from around the world. Who could regret this enlargement of our awareness and reach? Who could regret that our society has become more appreciative of racial and ethnic and sexual diversity, however halting and imperfect the changes in attitude may be? Who could regret that women now enjoy wider opportunities for learning and living and working than they did in the 1950s?

These gains have come at a cost, however. Our mechanical conveniences, proliferating gadgets, and industrially-grown foods have placed an ever-in-

creasing strain on Earth. Since 1950, for example, per capita consumption of
electricity in the United States has nearly doubled, contributing to a tripling of
our greenhouse gas emissions. During that same period, the rate of obesity in
America has also tripled, affecting nearly a fifth of children and fully a third
of adults, and this trend has placed an increasing strain on our healthcare system. Living indoors has cut us off from neighbors as well as nature. Thanks
to electronic technology, we may learn about the needs of people in distant
nations, may donate money to global causes, and that is all to the good, but
we may not know the person who lives next door. Ignorant of our neighbors,
we may be reluctant to walk in the streets, visit parks or allow our children to
play outdoors. The increase in opportunities for women in paid employment,
surely a change for the better, has led to a decrease in the care that women as
full-time homemakers once provided to their children, kinfolk and communities. Insofar as that care is still provided, much of it is paid for, either directly
out of pocket or indirectly through taxes.

The shift from a culture of care based on familiarity and affection to one
based primarily on money has freed us from many burdens. It has also exposed us to risks. Junk food may ruin our children's health; junk media may
dull their minds. Hiring strangers to repair our houses may lead to shoddy
work or scams. The more we count on private wages, savings and loans to meet
our needs, the more we may neglect the public wealth that our ancestors created—schools, libraries, parks, museums, civic organizations—as well as the
natural wealth of healthy soil and water and air. Those who cannot pay for
necessities, such as medicines, may have to do without, unless they can secure
help from government programs or charities. Those who can easily afford not
only necessities but luxuries often resent paying taxes to benefit people whom
they regard as lazy or alien or otherwise unworthy. When that resentment is
turned into public policy, the rich get richer, the poor get poorer, and the majority live in dread of job loss, accident, illness, divorce or other contingencies
that might plunge them into poverty.

LOVING one's neighbors, or at least caring for them without expecting to be
paid, is in keeping with instructions from many of the world's scriptures, in-

cluding the Bible, a respected authority in the community where I grew up. In that community, in that era, people looked after one another, trusting that they would be looked after in turn. They shared their abundance—of sweet corn, say, or plumbing skills—trusting that they would benefit from the abundance of others. Compassion might reinforce this mutual care, as when my mother hustled the shivering Thompson children into our house and fondly patted their heads, but the essential motive was practical. Being able to rely on neighbors made everyone more secure.

Anthropologists call this non-monetary exchange of goods and aid "reciprocity," and they find it in every long-lasting culture. As a boy, I learned to call it neighborliness. Hearing that word today, one might be tempted to sigh or shudder—sigh, if one imagines people have become too selfish, too plugged-in, too mercenary to care for others; shudder, if one fears that neighbors will pry into one's business or add to one's responsibilities.

Isn't life easier if we mind our own business and let others mind theirs? Isn't the American way to be self-reliant, pull yourself up by your bootstraps and let others fend for themselves? Besides, who counts as a neighbor? Is it simply the person next door, whose house might burn down? Is it anyone who lives on my block or my stretch of road? Should I consider as neighbors everyone in my town or city? All the members of my tribe, ethnic group or social class? All those who salute the same flag or worship the same god? Anybody anywhere who needs help? Who is my neighbor?

According to the Gospel of Luke, a wily lawyer asked that question of Jesus, who answered by telling a story: A man traveling from Jerusalem to Jericho was set upon by thieves, stripped of his clothes, severely beaten and left in a ditch to die. First one and then another religious official, seeing the man, a fellow Jew, passed by on the far side of the road. A third traveler came along, a Samaritan, a person who by the customs of that time and place should have shunned the injured man. Instead, he bound up the man's wounds, delivered him to an inn and cared for him through the night. Next morning, he paid the innkeeper the equivalent of two days' wages to look after the man until he, the Samaritan, could return and pay whatever additional charges there might be. On finishing his story, Jesus asked the lawyer, "Which of these three, do you think, was a neighbor to the man who fell into the hands of the robbers?"

"The one who showed him mercy," the lawyer replied. Then Jesus said to him, "Go and do likewise."

That was a tall order when Jesus delivered it two thousand years ago, and it is an even taller order today. On a planet with more than seven billion people, there are more robbers than ever, not only burglars and muggers but also identity thieves, online scammers and financiers who bundle bad mortgages and rig markets; there also are far more injured people abandoned in prisons or camps or slums. The media bring us news of ethnic and religious hostilities that make the ancient rift between Jews and Samaritans seem mild by comparison; they bring us news of wars, coups, droughts, floods, famines and epidemics. Worldwide at the end of 2014 there were sixty million refugees displaced by such turmoil, the largest number ever recorded by the United Nations, and more than half of them were children. Agencies ranging from Oxfam to the Pentagon have predicted that all of these threats will intensify under the combined impact of climate disruption and population growth, placing more and more people in jeopardy. Whose mercy can stretch to embrace so much need?

PSYCHOLOGISTS first diagnosed "compassion fatigue" among nurses, mental health workers and others who care for trauma victims; in recent years they have observed the same condition among people who learn of trauma only through the media. Our screens blaze with images of disaster; our mailboxes and inboxes overflow with appeals for desperate causes. Dismayed by the scale of suffering, caregivers may burn out, viewers may tune out and all of us may retreat into numbness.

Yet neighborliness persists. In barrios, ghettoes, villages and leafy cul-de-sacs, along country roads and disputed borders, inside high-rises and apartment buildings, in churches and synagogues and mosques, the practice of mutual care still goes on. What form it takes will vary from place to place, from person to person, depending on resources and circumstances. For an elder in a slum, it might be telling stories to children, and for those children it might be carrying jugs of water from the public tap to shut-ins who can no longer carry their own. For refugees fleeing war or famine, it might be taking turns carrying those who are too weak to walk. For a teenage girl in a suburb, it might be staying overnight with a woman down the street whose husband of fifty years recently died, and for that widow it might be teaching the girl how to bake bread. For a high school boy it might be sending a portion of his lawn-mowing earnings to UNICEF or CARE.

Even in a wired, crowded, money-driven world, neighborliness will survive. For we are a social species, with an inherited disposition for cooperation and sharing. We also have an instinct for selfishness, of course, a fact exploited by many advertisers and politicians and pundits. We are urged to think of ourselves as consumers rather than citizens. We are told that the pursuit of private greed will produce the greatest good. Despite these appeals to selfishness, however, all but the most affluent or arrogant of us realize that we need one another; we are responsible to one another for practical as well as moral reasons.

Anyone fortunate enough to live under a roof and eat regular meals might volunteer in a homeless shelter or community kitchen; anyone skilled in music or computers or languages might offer free lessons; anyone adept at reading and writing might tutor adult learners or kids who are struggling in school. Sharing money can certainly be an expression of neighborliness. After all, the Samaritan paid the innkeeper to provide lodging for the man set upon by thieves. However much or little we have to spare, we can donate money to support causes in our own communities, such as free medical clinics or after-school programs, and we can support international service organizations such as Doctors without Borders, Habitat for Humanity or the Heifer Project. Even if we have no money to spare, we still have gifts to share—knowledge, perhaps, or laughter, a knack for listening or a kindly touch.

Before binding up the wounds of the man set upon by thieves, so the story goes, the Samaritan salved those wounds with oil. There was courage as well as kindness in that touch, for the injured man was not merely a stranger but a presumed enemy. Courage may or may not be required when we reach out to help others, but kindness always is. The Samaritan was moved by more than an expectation of reciprocity, for he could not hope to receive help in return. He was moved by compassion. To be a neighbor, the story teaches, is to show mercy.

The same lesson is taught in Judaism, Hinduism, Buddhism, Islam and most other spiritual traditions: We should treat with compassion those whom we encounter who are in need. We may encounter them in our travels, as the Samaritan did, or learn about them on television, or meet them in the street, or find them knocking at our door. They may be wounded, hungry or sick; they may carry the smell of smoke in their clothes and need a house to replace the one that burned down; they may need only a shoulder to cry on or a consoling hug. That we cannot meet every need even in our own communities, let alone in the world, is no excuse for despair. If we feel overwhelmed by the barrage of bad news, then let us disengage from the media for a spell, look around, and see what good we might do.

The Artist's Torah

SANDY SASSO

FROM THE EARLIEST VERSES IN the book of Genesis we learn of the power of language to create, not just narrative or poetry, but a world. God speaks: "Let there be…" and there is. It takes naught but sparse language to bring into being not only light but earth and sky, plant and animal, man and woman.

It should come as no surprise then, that we find wisdom in the words of Scripture, not only about a sacred covenant, the fashioning of a people, its beliefs and values, but about the very art of creating itself.

And so we begin—"In the beginning". What appears as a simple phrase is not simple at all. The first word of Genesis in Hebrew, *b'reshit,* yields two different, even contradictory understandings. Does the text mean to say: "In the beginning, God created the heaven and the earth…" suggesting that before God's initial act, there was nothing? Or should we to translate: "When God began to create heaven and earth, the earth being unformed and void…," suggesting that the earth already existed but was unformed? In other words, is creation a crafting out of nothing or is it an ordering out of chaos?

What is the creative process that yields prose and poetry, dance, art and music? Is it an act of breathing in what is, the chaotic swirl of feeling and thought, the jumble of smells and tastes, sounds and sights and breathing out of form? Or is it a calling up from the emptiness, the void of nothingness, of absence, something new and altogether original? Might it be that the very first words of the Bible offer us the possibility that creation is both?

From the first words, we turn to the first story. What appears to be a simple account of the world's birthing is not simple at all. The author of the first chapter of Genesis seeks to capture the wonder of creation in majestic poetry. Yet no sooner than we have completed the poem, taken a breath of rest, then we begin again.

This time, in Genesis' second chapter, the world is formed anew in the rich mythic narrative of Eden, a Garden of Delights. It seems that no literary form can hold the grand process completely; each is a partial glimpse of the mystery of creation.

So it is that in the Bible everything begins as an art project. God is the Master Artist, potter and gardener, painter and musician creating with words and breath. We learn not only of God as Master Architect but of the human being created "in the image of God". As God celebrates creation and argues with it, builds and uproots, affirms and regrets so we construct and tear down, assert and repent, quarrel with the world and rejoice in it. Perhaps the Bible wishes to teach us that our share in divinity is not merely as creatures formed by God, but as divine co-creators in an ever-changing universe.

Fishing in Middle America

GREG SCHWIPPS

IN YOUR DREAM, SOMETHING IS touching, dragging across your face. You lie on your back on a riverbank, mouth gaping to the clouds, in your sleeping bag in the weeds. A heavy dew covers you. You are damp all over and your back feels like it has been pummeled with a steel pipe. You are cold. Something is touching your face again! What is it?

The smell of wood smoke floats to you, along with the sharp stink of your own wet clothes. You open your eyes and try to regain some sense of the world. Something hangs now in your field of vision. It's so close to your eyes it's blurry, but what is it?

Why, it's a little face—a little bluegill's face! It's the severed head of a fish! Part of its guts hang out in loose strands from the cut behind the gills. The guts plop on your face, cold and hard and slimy, and then the fish head rises inches above you, dancing. It bobs on a string.

The first sound in your ears on this new day is laughter. *Now* things come together. You know your older brother's laugh, the small laugh of someone who does not talk much. Your eyes follow the fish head up its string to the tip of a fishing pole. Then back to the person standing there who owns the laugh. He lowers the rod tip again and the bloody fishface plops on your cheek.

"Mr. Fishhead says it's time to get up, sucker," he says.

There are two laughs now.

You sit up—what else can you do?—and look around with a mind cloudy from forty-five minutes of sleep. You focus on the source of the other laugh. Ah yes—it comes from your younger brother. Of course. And he has something he would like to say this morning.

"Hey, just think," he says. "Just think if he'd pushed the cutbait away with his hand. It would've hooked him. Jerkface would've woken up with a hook through his hand!"

Both laughs echo through your sinus pressure. Even without getting hooked, this is a rough way to wake up. But you are a little sad, too—morning light means it is almost over.

so you pull on your boots and take a leak in the weeds up the beach. Your body pulses with the low-grade electrical current of too-little sleep. You look around. Good campsite. Here, where the river curves around, a beach rises from the inside bend. The beach consists of sand and gravel that has been pushed along this current for thousands of years. The fire smolders. Its smoke mixes with the mist rising off the river. No tent has been pitched, because last night you fished with only your brothers, and without the wives along who needs the accoutrements of a tent? You see the sleeping bags, still spread out on the ground around the chunks of still-smoking burnt wood. They're wet and dirty, like the bedding of a homeless person in a big city somewhere. You don't care, because you have a home. Your home is this sand that has been pushed along the river for centuries.

You zip up and walk down the beach to where the boat rests. You feel a flash of love for the boat—aluminum and green and beat all to heck with the name carefully spray-painted on the bow—*ORCA II*. The boat in *Jaws* that the big shark sank.

You lift a rod from the boat, and this too is a thing of beauty, a four hundred dollar fish pole, the reel oiled and machined and made in Sweden. You've spent more money on catfishing gear than on furniture and this makes you a misguided dingdong. No, you're kidding. Of course it was a wise investment. Don't even joke about that, you admonish yourself.

You reach into the livewell, which is now a deadwell, because it's filled with dead baitfish. You lift a bluegill as big as your palm from the deadwell and cut its head off with bone scissors. Blood smears the serrated jaws and you rinse them in the river. Channel cats like cut fish. This is the way God made them. So you stab the head through its eyes onto a large hook. You've done this for many years, and you'll do it until you die, but you may never get comfortable with all of this death. But you'll always use live bait at night, because flathead catfish like that, and cut fish for the channel cats. This may or may not be the way God made you, but you have absolved yourself for any sins you commit on this riverbank this morning.

You cast out where the current sweeps along the far bank and place the rod in the holder before snugging the line against the sinker. Your brothers are fishing on either side of you. You realize you haven't spoken to them.

"You zeros catch anything yet?" you ask. "Or were you too busy dropping cutbait on my face?"

They laugh like little kids, although they are both fathers. The older one has two little girls and the younger one has a son on the way. Or, as he put it when he called with the news, his wife "Has a turkey in the oven."

"I had a bite," the older one says.

"He means he hooked a piece of the current," the younger one says. "We ain't catching crap."

You all sit in folding chairs and watch the current. Now you can relearn the world in the truth of daylight. The logjams you fished around suddenly seem less massive. The river seems narrower. The whole world seems smaller in the light of day.

"You know," the younger brother says, "I hope ol Bop's eyes are all right."

You all nod. Bop is your cousin. He is the fourth brother. His real name is Ben but he has been named Bop for reasons no one can remember. This is a trip he would've been on, but last week his retinas detached and he faces extensive surgeries. The doctors will slice open his eyeballs and drain them before trying to reattach his retinas. They're pretty sure they can save his sight, but his eyes will betray him for the rest of his life. Perhaps he will see this river only ten more times? Twenty? Perhaps he's seen it for the last time.

This news of this problem—it's not something you could foresee—alarms all of you. Detached retinas! What's next, your first heart attack? You're all still kids! It makes you want to take more of these river trips, as hard as they are on your aging bodies and growing families. Your back still aches from the ground even now.

Of course, you deal with Bop's situation with the tenderness it deserves. Daily, you call and email support and encouragement. You write in an email, "Hey loser. Hope the surgery goes well. Since one eye is worse than the other, we'll start calling you Cybop." You do not write that you'll give him one of your eyes, if it comes to that. You don't need to.

"Yes," you say as your line jumps against the current, "I hope ol Cybop can join us next time."

"He's annoying as crap, but I kinda miss the hoser," the younger brother says.

"Dummy," the older brother says, like he is saying amen to a wise and meaningful prayer.

You fish until the sun rises over the trees. The fishing, which has been slow all night, slows even more. You're all thinking the same thing: time to head back to the wives, kids, dogs, jobs.

"What time we going today?" the older one asks. "I want to go squirrel hunting this afternoon."

"You better get some sleep first, or you'll shoot your own hand," you remind him.

"I would shoot your dogs, if they were at Mom and Pop's," he says.

Both of your brothers live close to your parents, near the farm you all grew up on. When you drive down there, you take the dogs and run through the woods of your youth.

"If you shot my dogs," you tell him, "I would take your little rifle and shove it up your butt and blow a hole in your colon."

With that you all stand and pack the gear into the boat. The rods stay out to give the fish one last chance to bite. They are the last things loaded into the *Orca II. Great name!* you think again.

AT the ramp, you fasten the boat to the trailer and check a hundred things to ensure there'll be no accidents on the highway. It's bad enough that you've gotten less than an hour of sleep. The brothers have not slept at all, and they have to drive almost two hours home.

"You all need to stop and buy some pills off a trucker," you tell them.

"Man, this kind of fishing is harder than work," a brother says.

You all laugh. The older brother chokes on the Rooster long-cut tobacco he is shoveling into his bottom lip for the ride.

"Well, you donkeys stay awake. I'll be in touch," you tell them. It's understood you'll talk to them on the phone about four times this week. Every time you'll talk almost exclusively about fishing.

"Well, it was a good time," the younger brother says as he climbs into the truck with the older brother. "They just weren't bitin."

"Yeah, the fish more or less got together and told us to stick it," you say. "It happens that way sometimes.

"See you all later," you add as you start your truck.

"See ya later," both brothers say.

"Let me know when your wife drops that calf," you yell out.

The younger brother stands on the truck floorboard and looks over the cab. "She ain't due for three weeks," he says.

You have driven almost halfway home before you look in the rearview mirror. Your hair's so greasy it stands under its own power. Your eyes are bloodshot. Your skin looks so thin you can almost see the arteries and veins moving their cargo through your face. Dried blood from the fish head smears both cheeks.

You cannot go into Burger King like this! You'll have to hit the drive-through.

You're exhausted, but you need to go home and clean up the boat and equipment. Everything must be washed and dried in the sun. There are papers to grade, the yard should be mowed. Cybop needs to be called. He'll want to know how the trip went, what he missed out on. You'll not be able to put all of it into words. How do you tell someone you laughed a lot?

The highway looks like a grainy videotape of a roadtrip from the past spread out in front of you. You swoop around cars and barely realize you've passed them. These cars grow smaller in the mirrors and then disappear. You'll never see those cars again. You drive for miles and can recall no details from those miles. You are exhausted. Still, you can't help but start calculating. When, exactly, will you be able to fish the river with your brothers again?

Working a Jigsaw

BARBARA SHOUP

T HE SKY IS ICY BLUE. The line of trees across the meadow seem engraved on it, their charcoal trunks dark against the snow, their branches hazy, as if the artist has not yet brushed away the dust made by his burin. I look at this peaceful scene from inside the cabin, where I have come to work. The wood stove burns brightly. A whole week stretches before me, nothing to do in it but write, read, think. I packed everything I could imagine I might need: books, notebooks, computer, printer, paper, pens, letters to answer. As an afterthought, I brought along a puzzle.

Unpacking it, I remember driving the "Black and White Trail" of Tudor villages to Hay-on-Wye, just over the border of Wales. There, my friend and I spent the better part of a morning wandering in and out of musty-smelling shops, each with long, narrow aisles of books shelved floor to ceiling. We browsed rickety shelves of battered paperbacks that ran the length of a winding lane, with a collection box at each end beneath a sign that read: "Honesty Book Shop, All Books 50 Pence, Money Into Letterbox Opposite Please". It was an enjoyable morning, but a little disappointing. The village was full of tourists, much more commercial than we'd thought it would be. We laughed when we came upon the toy and puzzle shop; it seemed so obviously placed there in the hope that parents who had dragged their bored-to-tears children from bookshop to bookshop might spring for an expensive new toy to appease them. There were wonderful teddy bears, trains, dolls, blocks, balls, and bright modern picture books inside. And puzzles. Hundreds of them. The ones toward the front of the store were children's puzzles; but the entire back room was lined with art puzzles. The effect was rather like a cluttered, scaled-down museum. Renoir, Monet, Turner, Rembrandt, Rubens. Vermeer: "A Lady at the Virginals with a Gentleman."

Owned by Queen Elizabeth and rarely exhibited, this was a Vermeer painting that I'd never seen in the original; but I'd looked at prints of it many times and always found it deeply pleasing. Even a picture on the top of a puzzle box reveals that it is one of the artist's most beautiful works. In it, a woman wearing a vivid red skirt stands at a harpsichord, her back to the viewer, a honey-colored cello abandoned at her feet. To the right, between the harpsichord and a framed portrait that is cut off by the canvas's edge, a man dressed in black—perhaps Vermeer himself, watches her, his elegant hand resting on a cane. Just behind her, the ubiquitous blue chair with the lion's head finials is placed at a slant, facing outward. In the foreground, there is a square table covered by a rich Persian rug, a white porcelain jug set on a silver tray upon it. Light pours in from the mullioned window on the left. The placement of table, chair, and cello creates a kind of barrier, protecting the man and woman in this private moment; but the framed mirror above the harpsichord reveals the woman's interest in her companion. This intimate detail and the glimpse of an easel at the top right complicate Vermeer's almost too careful composition, turns the world of the painting inside out.

"Remember me," he seems to be saying. "I made this."

I hadn't worked a puzzle since I was a child, and I hadn't much liked doing it then. It seemed like an absurd activity for an adult. I bought the Vermeer puzzle simply because I couldn't quit looking at the beautiful picture on the box. When I got home from the trip, I put it on a shelf in my office and forgot about it. Every now and then, I'd look at the picture and think again how lovely it was, and how strange the way looking at the top of a puzzle box could make me feel so still inside. I happened upon it again, gathering things for this week of solitude. Why not take it along, I thought? Maybe I'll work on it when I need to take a break.

But when I open the cellophane package of puzzle pieces and spill them out on the kitchen table, I cannot imagine that I will have the patience to put them together. There are so many of them, and each one so small. Then I notice a gold piece with scrolling on it, recognize it as part of the instrument Vermeer's woman plays. I see another piece of it, and another. I'm surprised at the chord of satisfaction that resonates inside me when these pieces interlock. I can't resist searching out another, then another to fill the gap between that one and the three that made the virginals start to emerge. And, oh!, there's a buttery yellow piece, with faint orange markings: one of the letters on the raised lid of the instrument. When I look up from the table, all the letters finally in place, an hour has passed. More time passes as I browse through a book about Vermeer's work to learn what, translated, the letters spell. "Music is the companion of joy, the medicine for grief."

In the next days, I cannot go past the table without stopping to examine the puzzle there. I am mesmerized by the task of fitting the pieces together. I look at each piece carefully. I look at its shape, its markings. Is there any clue in it to the whole? A dash of orange, a thin green line, a silver curve? An eye, a fret, a finger? Usually, there is not. Usually, each piece seems much like any number of other pieces I pick up—and at the same time maddeningly unique. Hours and hours I meant to spend writing pass as I stand staring at the picture of the painting, then at some section of the puzzle I am trying to complete.

I imagine Vermeer staring at the scene, fine-tuning it. He places the table, the cello, the pitcher, the mirror, the rug, the harpsichord, the chair just so. He directs the man closer, then farther from the instrument. He turns the woman's face this way, then that with the palm of his hand. At last, every little thing seems to him in harmony with the immutable angles and patterns in the floor, the roof beams, the walls, the windows, and he steps out of the picture and begins to paint.

Color against color: I once read that that was how he accomplished his magical effect. Vermeer saw with the pure eye of a child. He did not see objects, rather he saw the way the myriad of colors that any one object was made of lay, one against another, on a plane. In a sense, he built a painting with color: a process not so different than putting together a jigsaw puzzle, I think—until I look at the palette of puzzle pieces for the luminous colors I see in the painting before me. There are a few yellow pieces, a few solidly red ones. But the majority of pieces are some dull, unlikely mix of colors or, worse, no apparent color at all. Three bright dots on one piece look like upholstery tacks and tell me that it probably makes up part of the blue chair. But how? The puzzle piece they're on does not seem at all blue to me, rather a kind of steel gray. Yet when I fit it against another piece with similar dots, blue emerges as surely and suddenly as if a chemical reaction had occurred. Another series of what seem to be gray pieces make a long, dark red fold in the woman's skirt.

The complications of the exercise grow deeper. Sometimes, fingering the pieces in the box, staring at the pieces I've organized on the table by color tone or some other identifying element, I think, surely, there must be some pieces missing. There don't seem to be enough of the blue-gray pieces to make the chair, for instance. I'm certain of a shortage when I notice a second blue chair in the background, against the wall. But, remembering my earlier lesson, I concentrate on each piece and how it fits against its mates. I find the gold dots, the upholstery tacks, on a few dark pieces and I put them together, waiting for the moment they will transform before my eyes. This time, however, the magic effect does not occur. No matter how I look at it, this chair is not blue. But I *saw* blue when I noticed it; I see blue now when I step away. Is this because I recognize the chair as the same blue chair Vermeer painted again and again; or would I have registered blue if I had looked at the chair never having heard of Vermeer or seen his work before this moment? Did the artist somehow suggest blue? Is that possible?

There is something in the way I have to look from the puzzle to the painting and back to the puzzle again that is teaching me about the way Vermeer carried information from his eye to the brush. As I must look at the pieces one at a time to complete the puzzle, so he painted the scene before him by looking at it spot by spot. Looking at the painting the way the puzzle demands of me, I see that, in isolation, no color is as it appears in the whole. The pieces that make the shadowy gray wall beneath the window are green. Some of the black tile pieces are green, too. Some are charcoal. The white tiles aren't white at all, but gray swirled with gray. The pieces that make the silver plate beneath the white jug are black and white, with an effect rather like magnified newsprint.

And the light. If I am confounded by how Vermeer made these vivid objects out of what seems like no true color at all, how can I ever hope to understand how he painted the golden light seeping in through the window? If I hold two puzzle pieces in my hand—one from the most luminous section of the wall, and another from the section near the mirror, where the light has begun to fade—I can see that they are completely different colors, different shades of beige. Yet looking at the place between these two sections, and at each of the pieces that make that place, I can't see where the light begins to change.

I look harder, but the essence of light simply will not reveal itself to me. I have an odd thought then. What if it never revealed itself to Vermeer either? What if it felt like failure to him to accept that seeing the way light lay against not-light was as close as he would ever come to defining it, that luminousness was some trick of the earth itself, from which both the painter and the paints were made?

My poor, strained eyes go bleary, looking. I stare at the black and white tiles in the painting and see the black and white Tudor villages we passed through to get to the village in Wales where I bought the puzzle that I am working, here in this quiet place. I see us driving away from Hay-on-Wye that afternoon, up, up into the Welsh hills. The narrow lane winds through dense forest, then fields of waist-high ferns, suddenly giving way to a flat, bald, expanse of green so vast, so foreign in its effect that we cannot comprehend what we see. Light spills from the sky. Sheep rest stubbornly in the middle of the road. White horses graze. One comes so close to our parked car that my friend reaches out and touches its face, and at that moment I cannot imagine wanting to be in any other place or time. I feel exactly as I once felt in the Mauritshaus Museum, standing before Vermeer's *View of Delft*. I must remember this, I think, and I scribble words into my notebook: black ink on a white page.

Just as, now, I am typing these black words onto the white screen. Am I working? I am not doing the work I planned to do. I am working a puzzle, looking hard at a painting in order to put each piece in its place, and, from

time to time, I am writing down facts and memories and odd insights that
float up, pieces of another, bigger puzzle. This puzzle has no picture on its
box to help me, though. Just pieces. And with fuzzy, undefined edges, at that.
A green hilltop in Wales. Sixteenth century Delft. A still-unwritten character
in my head who is as real, as vivid as the photograph of the little girls that my
daughters once were, sitting on my desk.

I look up, look beyond the words and the puzzle to the winter scene outside
my window, and the whole world fractures. The window frame dissolves to a
kind of bargello, brown on brown. The braided cord of the Venetian blind is
no more than a simple red line, hatched with bright, whitened-red, and outlined in a thread of pure white. The push pin holding the cord in place is a
dot of white, a half-moon of lemon-yellow, a slice of duller yellow mixed with
black. Outside, the snow falling is a swirling tapestry of silver, white, and gray.

Valéry said, "Seeing is forgetting the name of the thing one sees." A jotting
from my notebook finds its place. I am seeing as Vermeer saw. If I could look
long enough, if my hand were steady enough, if only I understood the proper-
ties of paint, I could make a world as he did. My world. Sky, snow, trees. Window, chair, desk. Words on a screen. They are all there, in pieces before me. I
would only have to be patient enough to put them together.

But it would take so long. Even this puzzle picture builds so slowly beneath
my fingers: Vermeer's beautiful image made of hundreds of moments of paint.
Sometimes I look at a piece for what seems like forever, trying it in every single empty space left in the puzzle, and ultimately have to set it aside because
I cannot make it fit in any of them. Occasionally, I pick up a piece and see
immediately where it should go. Sometimes, placing one piece, it becomes obvious where a number of others will fit around it. The hardest part of all is the
Persian rug on the table. The pieces are so impossibly similar that I can only
work when the late afternoon light falls across the table a certain way, illumi-
nating them. Even so, more than once, a piece only seems to fit, and when I
realize this, many pieces later, I must take the whole section out and do it over.
It comforts me in my discouragement to remember the X-rays of the painting
that show how Vermeer himself reworked the position of the man, the girl's
head, the lid of the harpsichord, the neck of the pitcher.

The exercise seems so pointless and impossible at times, a bad investment of more hours than I care to count. This is ridiculous, addictive behavior, I tell myself. Stop, cut your losses, do what you came here to do. Then a piece falls into its right place and I see, suddenly, the corner where the line of roof timbers meets the window casing, or the man's face, or the crisscross pattern on the back of the woman's gown, and I feel some small measure of what I am certain Vermeer felt the moment when, after a long patience, the small slice of the world he was looking at yielded to his brush.

And I go on.

Finished on the last day of my solitude, the puzzle seems a work of art in its own right. The colors are luminous, the pattern of pieces effects a kind of craquelature on the surface, and, at that moment, I am as pleased as the Queen herself must be to own something so beautiful. The puzzle becomes a piece of my life. An object. A week in time. The ghost of an unwritten story. And this snippet of understanding: every beautiful thing is made of many pieces, each one complete in its own way, utterly, maddeningly, gloriously itself.

The Labors of Our Fathers

KELSEY TIMMERMAN

HARPER, MY THREE-YEAR-OLD DAUGHTER, HOLDS the metal square, and with all the seriousness of a seasoned carpenter, she seems to be considering what's right and what's outta whack.

She makes a few scribbles on the 4x4 lying in our driveway before looking up to me. I hold the dummy end of the tape. I look up to Dad putting marks where marks need putting. I'm not good at angles and inches. I work in the less finite world of words and stories.

Dad has turned wood into barns and homes, careers and educations. At nineteen he started his own construction company. When I was a boy I told people, "Daddy doesn't live with us." That's how much he worked. He was gone before I got up for school and often not back before I went to bed.

When I came into the world, it was just Mom and me at the hospital. Dad was at home recovering from surgery. He had fallen off the roof of a building and ruptured his spleen. The surgeon had to remove it, but Dad had a second spleen. Leave it to Dad to bring an extra organ.

I lift the 4x4 and put it on the sawhorses. The saw screams to life and Dad's mark disappears. He grabs the router. The sharp corners of the board are made round—a little safer for running, laughing, falling grandchildren.

He returns the router to the bed of his red pickup. It's the last of a long line of red company trucks. Dad bought this particular one twice: once from the dealer and once from the bank at the auction where everything Mom and Dad had worked for was sold to the highest bidder in an afternoon.

Mom and Dad had grown their business, then switched from construction into wood truss manufacturing in the 1980s. Less than half of businesses in the United States last five years. Mom and Dad's lasted thirty-six. A few years back they came to a crossroads: Expand or retire comfortably?

They chose wrong.

We chose wrong.

I was in on the meetings, and I can't help but think their decision to expand was made, in part, to build a business for me to run. I had no interest in running the business, but I loved it because I loved Mom and Dad. I cared about the sixty employees, some of whom I had started working with when I was fourteen. The business was infused with Dad's work ethic, and by working there, I had it instilled in me, too. Up at 5:30, splinters and stitches a nuisance for a moment, and then back to work. I swept floors, inhaled hot plumes of sawdust, and drove forklifts into below-freezing temperatures. I learned the dignity of work.

The most valuable thing a man has to give is his time to another.

Dad runs the electric sander across the 4x4. We can't have anyone getting more splinters. Harper already had one in her thumb. Dad watched as I pulled it out with my fingers. There was a little blood, but she didn't cry. I was so proud of her.

"Now I'm a schmuck." Dad says all too regularly, after years of not being able to find a good job. "Who wants to hire a sixty-year-old failure?"

ON the first leg of the many flights that would take me from Dayton, Ohio, to Dhaka, Bangladesh, I flew right over the thirty-acre property and half-built steel structure that became the business's undoing. I traveled to Bangladesh, Cambodia, China, and Honduras to meet the people who made my clothes.

The experience led to my first book and launched my career as a writer, speaker, and author.

I had a few assignments but no book deal then—nothing that covered the travel expenses. The trip wasn't the kind of thing you'd think a practical guy like Dad would support, but he did. He supported it all the way.

In Bangladesh I met young women and single moms who were struggling to support their families. I encountered organizations such as the Grameen Bank and CARE that have programs mainly focused on women. Economists and development experts believe that the best way to lift families out of poverty is to educate and employ women. NIKE even sponsored a viral video called "The Girl Effect" that highlights an alarming statistic: When you give a man a wage he spends 30-40% of his income on his family, and when you give a woman a wage she spends 90%.

One question kept going through my mind: Where are all the fathers?

The very first garment worker I met was a guy in Honduras named Amilcar. I met him for 10 minutes and didn't learn anything about his life other than he was 25, lived with his parents, and liked to play soccer. I continued my travels and eventually ended up back home. Not knowing what Amilcar's life was like ate at me for seven years. So I went back to Honduras to try to find him. I called the number I had for him and an old woman answered.

"Oh, Amilcar. He's in California."

I spent the next week meeting Amilcar's family. His mom was sick and on medication bought with the money that Amilcar sends from California. His brother runs a business out of a car paid for by Amilcar. I traveled back to Amilcar's home village where I met the mother of his children and his three daughters living in a home and receiving educations courtesy of his work at the counter factory in the U.S., shouldering heavy slabs of granite for wealthy Americans to eat off of.

He had considered his life as a garment worker in Honduras, and it wasn't enough. He wanted to provide lives for his family that couldn't be supported on his wage. So he took a bus through Guatemala, crossed illegally into Mexico, and rode thousands of miles on top of trains to the U.S. border. He was robbed and chased by bandits. He nearly froze to death crossing the mountains into Mexico City. Eventually he made it, and his labors have changed life for his family in Honduras.

"Are you a good dad?" I asked Amilcar at a mall in Indio, California, where we were talking about his journey.

"I don't think I am, because I'm not there to help the girls. I'm there mentally, but not physically... When I go back, I'll tell them I'm failing them."

DAD makes the impossible happen.

We've finished building both A-frames and only have to connect the horizontal 4x6 from one to the other. The only problem? This isn't your average swing set; it weighs hundreds of pounds. We bear the burden together.

I'm having one of those "someone is going to get hurt" moments that I've become so familiar with after years of working with Dad. I felt that way when we moved a piano into a basement, cut down dangerously angled trees in his woods, moved a multi-ton generator the way ancient Egyptians would have done it. Dad always gets the job done.

Before Mom and Dad lost everything, my brother and I stood to inherit a lot of money. In fact, one of Mom and Dad's financial advisors recommended that my brother and I have our fiancés sign prenuptial agreements.

Now there's no money, but we've inherited so much more.

My phone vibrates in my pocket. It's a text from the little brother I have through Big Brothers and Big Sisters. He's asking whether I can take him back to juvenile detention tonight. That's where he lives during the week, and now, after months of good behavior, he's allowed a twenty-four-hour home-visit on weekends.

He has never met his dad.

According to National Fatherhood Initiative, one in three American children grow up without their fathers.

I'M insulted when Dad says that he is a failure. That he worked for all of those years and has nothing to show for it. He taught me to throw a bounce pass and how to drive a stick shift. How to curse and how to have backbone. Doesn't he realize that we were his life's work?

He regrets expanding the business, but I don't think that's his biggest regret.

"You guys were never this cute," Dad says, when he holds Harper or my baby boy, Griffin.

"Yes they were!" Mom corrects him.

He reads to my kids; he didn't read to me. He changes my kids' diapers; he didn't change mine.

We don't just learn from our fathers' strengths. We also learn from their flaws and regrets. We learn from their labors.

Harper has been waiting patiently for us to finish. She wants to swing so badly that she's quivering. I set her in the swing and give her a push and she squeals with delight.

The swing set is imperfect but solid. Mom says my grandkids will swing in it and she's probably right.

The swing will last forever.

Basketball Crazy

DAN WAKEFIELD

WHEN I WAS A SOPHOMORE at Shortridge I went to a High School Journalism Conference in French Lick, Indiana, and shared a room with my classmate and fellow sports columnist on *The Daily Echo,* Dick Lugar. When we turned out the lights at night we spoke of our hopes and dreams, and Lugar asked me, "What would you be, if you could be anything at all in high school?" I answered without hesitation: "High point man on the basketball team."

"Oh, Dan," Lugar said. "You're so frivolous!"

Lugar's high school dreams were more appropriate for a future United States Senator: President of the class, valedictorian, student body president. Neither of us achieved our high school dreams, but Lugar came a lot closer than I did. I didn't even make the basketball team, much less become the player who scored the most points. In defense of my dream, though, I would argue that I wasn't being "frivolous"—I was just "basketball crazy," an Indiana affliction.

I pleaded with my parents for a backboard and basket in our backyard when I was ten years old, and my father hired the Broad Ripple Lumberyard people to do the job (the basket was always supplied with a real net so you could hear the satisfying swish of a score.) This not only sated my lust for the game but also insured my popularity with every kid in the neighborhood.

We played in fall and winter, summer and spring, on ice and in snow, in heat and rain, sleet and slush, in the earliest mornings till the shadows of winter drew us home for supper with the passing of the Monon train to Chicago at the very back of our yard, beyond the Victory Garden, at five-fifteen every evening. Playing in all seasons, I became a good shot, but my flat feet denied me the ability to run at even a normal pace. (I bought a stopwatch to time myself and learned that I couldn't break the seven-minute mile—roughly a minute slower than the average kid my age.)

My only basketball glory was reflected in two of the graduates of my backyard basketball court—Gene Neudigate and Dicky Richardson, the legendary "Itchy," a slender, slithering master of the court and nonstop shooter from any angle. Itchy and Gene were both backyard regulars, and both went on to star for Broad Ripple. Though I'm a true blue Shortridge Blue Devil, my earlier loyalty to School #80 and my backyard backboard allowed me to root for both those guys even though they were Rockets. Not only were they great players they were also a lot of fun. We sometimes tried to spook whoever was about to take a shot by shouting incantation-like curses the moment the ball was about to leave his fingertips: "Oogum-Sloogum!" "Puget Sound!" (Don't ask me to explain why these sappy syllables sent us doubling over with happy hysterics that caused noses to run and stomachs to ache. You had to be there, in my backyard, in 1944.)

Gene Neudigate now sports a neatly-trimmed white beard; he's a retired, respectable businessman, but he still lights up like a kid when he tells me how he averaged fifteen points a game and was seventh in the city in scoring his senior year.

"We beat Tech in the Sectionals when I was a Junior," he says. "They were the favorites, but then we got beat ourselves the next day."

Those were the days when the tournament was played in the "any team can win" era that was dramatized in the movie "Hoosiers," before the schools were divided up according to enrollment numbers into "athletically correct" divisions so more kids could be called "winners," but the sacred *spirit* was lost.

Butler Fieldhouse was filled to the rafters for every game from Sectionals to Finals, rocking in a frenzy of unforgettable March madness that will never be matched. Those were the days when fourteen thousand people came to The Fieldhouse to see Crispus Attucks play in a regular season game when Oscar Robertson was there; everyone waited for "The Crazy Song" that meant The Tigers had the game sewed up, and you clapped in rhythm no matter what school you were from as they sang: *You can beat everybody—but you can't beat us.*

Gene and I were so basketball crazy we not only went across the Monon tracks at night to the Broad Ripple gym to see the high school games and the grade school "curtain raiser" that came before the freshman game that came before the varsity game; we even went to games of "old guys" who played for company teams after work.

"We used to laugh at those 'old men' who were probably in their twenties and thirties," Gene reminds me. "We even made up a cheer for the team of guys who worked for 7 Up. We knew the head man of the company was Tom Joyce, so our cheer was '7 Up's our choice/ Rah Rah Tom Joyce!'"

Gene said sometimes he even went by himself just to watch the Broad Ripple team practice. (I can hear the often-quoted words of the NBA star Alan Iverson complaining that he was rumored to be traded because of missing a practice:

"We talkin' about *practice*—not a game, not a game—we talkin' about practice. We talkin' about practice, man. We talkin' about practice...")

Gene Neudigate is talkin' about walking over the Monon tracks after school to go watch the Broad Ripple high school team practice—not even to see them play in a *game,* man, but just to watch them *practice.* His devotion—addiction—is more understandable when you know he was watching the Broad Ripple team that went to the state finals in 1946 (and was beat by Bosse of Evansville 35-33.)

"Do you remember that the guys from that Broad Ripple team used to stop by sometimes after school at Gene Purcell's Pure Oil station and get peanuts out of the penny machine?" I ask Gene.

"That team was my inspiration," Gene says, and we both, in unison recite the starting lineup: "Allen and Chafee at guards, Chapman at center, Baker and Steinhart at forward. . ."

The coach was Frank Baird. So just imagine how Gene felt one day when he was shooting around by himself at the outdoor basket by School #80, and a car stopped and the driver sat there a while and watched Gene shoot the ball. After a while, the man in the car asked Gene "Are you going to go to high school at Broad Ripple?" Gene said he was, and the man said "Well, I hope you do, and I hope you play for me."

The man was Frank Baird.

That was the neighborhood equivalent of Knute Rockne watching a boy named George Gipp kicking a football and asking him if he'd like to play for Notre Dame.

"Frank Baird was a real gentleman," Gene said. "He never once used a cuss word. But he could make you feel small. Once when we were losing a game and playing badly he told us at halftime "I'm going to deflate this ball and you can use it for a sewing kit—you might as well use it for something, since you don't know how to use it to play the game out there."

Even the low points of basketball memory are high points now.

"Remember who made the shot that beat Ripple in the Finals?"

"Brock Jerrell!"

How could we ever forget?

I remember playing for The Coagulators, an intramural team at Shortridge that won at least half their games (as I remember). I remember being in the starting lineup with Jerry Burton, Don "Moto" Morris, Bailey Hughes, and Johnny "Big Red" Peterson, backed up by the all-star bench of Pete Estabrook and Dick "Ferdie" Falendar. I remember joining Ted Steeg of Shortridge and Jere Jones of Broad Ripple in a pick-up game at an outdoor court in Greenwich Village against three high school guys from Harlem in 1957. I remember being so beat and exhausted after the game that my team-mates and I couldn't speak until we flopped down on the grass in Washington Square Park and Jere Jones summed up our experience: "The Parable of the Three Fools," he called it. We were basketball crazy.

How I Spent My Summer Vacation

LILI WRIGHT

WHILE MOST AMERICANS FRITTERED AWAY their summer with idle sport and leisure, my family spent six weeks on an island in Maine throwing away my grandfather's stuff. Grampy, as we call him, is a retired biochemistry professor, a kindly man with reddish hair and freckles, who in the nineteen intervening years since my grandmother died, managed to fill not one, but two, houses with junk. He cluttered up his house in New Haven, Connecticut, and then he cluttered up the family summer house in Maine. After ninety-one years, a man has ample time to acquire, and my grandfather never saw a dry eraser board he didn't like. Or a magnifying glass or surge suppressor. Somewhere he developed a fetish for jar openers, particularly the floppy rubber kind that look like handcuffs for lovers on a budget. For most of his life, he's lived by two credos: "Never throw anything away," and "If you like something, buy two."

Last summer, Grampy fell down the stairs in Maine and had to be life-flighted to the hospital and later rehab. Though he suffered only a bruised hip, he finally had to give up his car keys and his home. When his perky physical therapist asked if he was excited about moving into an upscale assisted-living complex, Grampy lowered his two-pound dumbbell and closed his eyes, as if the indignity of it all were too much to bear.

"I guess I'm a loner," he said. "I don't like people much."

This summer, for the first time in years, Grampy didn't come to Maine and though we missed his company, his bottles of cod liver oil lined up in the fridge, we gleefully set about to do what we'd longed to do for decades: clean house. We threw away biochemistry syllabi dated 1969. We threw away bouquets of fake yellow flowers, a plastic watch that zaps mosquitoes, a magazine article describing how to cure psoriasis with beets. We threw away paperbacks with titles like *The Vitamin Bible* and *What Your Body Language Says About You* and a lab manual called *The Basic Biology of the Fetal Pig.* We threw out dozens of empty peanut jars labeled with a single word printed adamantly in black ink: SAVE.

When it became overwhelming, we hired professionals. A hazmat team with gas masks arrived on island to throw away my grandfather's chemistry set, which had been molting in the basement for thirty years. Many of the labels had fallen off the bottles, but a few still retained Grampy's hand-scrawled poison labels with grinning pirate skulls.

Of the myriad toxins stored next to Nana's rusty chaise lounges—on which, back in the day, she would bask in the sun with a Scotch and a fly swatter—were several containers of picric acid. When dry—and ours was very, very dry—picric acid is highly explosive, a sister, the hazmat man with the dreamy blue eyes explained, to its more stable sibling, TNT. If the jar had fallen off the shelf, we could have blown up a good portion of our summer house, which, I later realized, would have saved both time and money.

My burgeoning crush for hazmat man number three quickly faded when we learned he was too cowardly to remove a small yellow bottle whose contents were radioactive. No amount of eye-batting would sway him. Or my brother or my father, so we're offering a free vacation in Maine to whoever will stash the three-ounce vial in their trunk and dump it somewhere in New Jersey. The total cost of removing my grandfather's chemicals was $12,000. When asked why he'd put our lives and bank accounts in such danger, Grampy replied with a giggle: "I was a bad boy."

Still, cleaning up Maine was a picnic compared to the mess in New Haven. For years, my dad begged Grampy to purge his sprawling house in Connecticut, but every year he amassed more. One day, fed up with my dad's carping, Grampy stood at the doorstep and refused to let my dad in. After that, they went out for lunch when my dad visited, burying bad feelings in piles of pastrami, and no one knew just how dire the situation had become until it was time to rescue Grampy's valuables—the first step to selling his house.

Grampy gave me careful instructions over the phone. "The German pistol is under my armchair. The gold bullion is in the vitamin closet."

Needless to say, we were surprised to learn that Grampy had removed his valuables from the bank. Then again, we hadn't heard about Bank of America's dastardly plot to seize customers' safe deposit boxes and pawn the contents to line their secret slush funds in Monaco. Luckily, right-wing conspiracy newspapers like *The Spotlight* kept Grampy in the know, and he snuck the family heirlooms home, hiding them in the debris.

When we reached New Haven, we opened the back door, recoiling at the filthy kitchen and its stench. Grit covered the counters. A pile of egg shells balanced on hundreds of bottles of magnesium, melatonin, and B-complex. The bathroom sink had no plumbing, the water simply fell onto the basement floor. In places, the ceiling had crumbled. Half of the rooms were impassable: boxes on boxes on piles on stuff.

Worse than the mess was the smell, a rancid combination of dirt and moth balls and body odor that stuck to your hair, your clothes, the back of your throat. We could only stand 15-minute stretches before staggering onto the lawn in search of fresh air. (Later, the demo crew we hired wore gloves and masks, but that didn't stop one viral fellow with tattoos from barfing in the bushes. In the end, they filled two and half commercial dumpsters.) Giddily, we climbed over boxes and furniture, looking for monogrammed silver trays, Venetian glasses, all the treasures my grandmother had traveled the globe to collect. Peter found Nana's sapphire pin hidden behind olive leaf extract. My father walked out a bedroom wielding the P-38 my great uncle brought back from Normandy. It was loaded.

At first, the treasure hunt was funny. Like a game show or reality TV. Then, I felt guilty, then inconsolably sad, then sick. How could we have let my grandfather live like this? The answer was simple: This is what he wanted.

Even after he'd settled into Eisenberg, he complained that he'd arrived five years too early. "I was keeping up with things," he wrote me in a wistful e-mail. Walking past the shrouded windows, the molded Steinway, I wondered: Is it more humane to let people live as they wish or force them to live as they should? I don't know the answer. I only know that we love my grandfather and we let him live in a house that was killing him.

After the New Haven debacle, our summer cleanup in Maine should have been easy, yet all summer I teetered on despair. I'd like to think I know the difference between a person and his belongings, between the beautiful and the mundane, but I am capable of getting sentimental over a grocery list. When faced with chucking Nana's fifth casserole dish, I hemmed and hawed, examining the vessel, remarking on its merits. Does anyone even make casseroles anymore? I should make casseroles! I should bring back the casserole and when I do, this noble dish will have its renaissance.

My husband does not suffer this disease, and we locked horns one day in early August over a pair of rusty grass clippers. They were lying in the chuck pile on the lawn.

"Are we throwing these away?" I asked. "Don't they work?"

"They work," Peter said. "But we have a weed whacker now so I don't use them. Besides, we already have a pair." He pointed to the garage where a similar pair already hung from a nail.

That he was right made no difference. I dug in my heels: We were not throwing away the clippers. We'd thrown away enough.

Sensing a fight, Peter repeated himself, slowly this time, his eyes turning steely. "I will never use these."

Divorce seemed possible. Marriages have ended over less. You never know when the proverbial last straw will be, but by God I plan to have the grass clippers to cut it.

A half hour later, I wept in the kitchen, as Peter looked on with amazement. It felt like we were throwing out my grandfather, I explained, jettisoning him jar by jar. The clippers were more than clippers. They were memories. When I was a girl, we did not—as our eight-year-old daughter did—spend the summer doing community theatre. We did yard work. My father mowed and my brother and I snipped around trees, daydreaming, listening to the Red Sox lose, itching mosquito bites, sneezing. I am convinced this combination boredom and hay fever is what made me a writer. Chekhov clipped around trees as a boy, I've been told. So did Thoreau. To throw away the clippers was a little death. Of my childhood. Of me as a girl. Of my family and the peculiar way we operate.

My mother has been dead two years now. She is fading in my memory as her things disappear in boxes to Goodwill. We have saved her most beautiful possessions, but even ordinary things are hard to part with. Her swimming sneakers. Her last shell collection. People we love die. Their things outlive them. It is up to us—the living—to throw away their things, even those things that remind us of who they were and what we loved. To cheer ourselves up, we buy new things. Retail therapy. And one day our children will lug all these things to the dump, no matter how darkly or emphatically we write the word "Save."

You might call this recycling. Or the circle of life. *There is a season. Turn. Turn.* But I am digressing. I am singing old folk songs. And people with this much crap to throw away have no business digressing or singing folk songs because the dump is about to close and it's already August.

Lest anyone worry about my grandfather, don't. At ninety-one, Grampy has fallen in love. At Eisenberg, the ratio of mobile women to mobile men is ten to one. "I have been chosen," Grampy announced one day with pride. Her name is Lillie and she is a lovely woman, an Italian American with jet black hair and skin as white as paper. After six months of dating, the two of them have a better social life than I do: They see jazz, eat Chinese, and there is even, Grampy confided, "kissy wissy." That Lillie is suffering from the beginning stages of Alzheimer's makes little difference because she thinks the world of Grampy and he likes caring for her and she recently won Eisenberg's best-dressed award and Grampy is—like most men in my family—a sucker for a beautiful woman. After a complete medical workup, a new wardrobe, testosterone supplements, and, yes, eye-lid surgery, Grampy looks like a million bucks.

As he should. Because despite years of pleading poverty, it turns out our favorite Swamp Yankee is rich, which means if he doesn't live to be one hundred and twenty—his goal—or buy too many flashlights, we may have enough money to get the radioactive goo out of the basement.

So we have our happy ending. In a single year, my grandfather has gone from misanthrope to millionaire, from loner to lover. Meanwhile, next summer, my husband and I will head up to Maine to sweep mouse poop and whack weeds, tending our own private Superfund site.

And so it should be. The old fall in love again. The children do curtain calls to wild applause. And those of us in the middle carry on.

But some day, some summer, we will run out of things to throw away. And on that fine day, you will find me on an island in Maine, reclining on a chaise lounge with a Scotch and a fly swatter, savoring the summer I have waited for my whole life. I will be happy then, happy with a casserole in the oven.

poetry

Being in This World Makes Me Feel Like a Time Traveler

KAVEH AKBAR

visiting a past self. Being anywhere makes me thirsty.
When I wake, I ask God to slide into my head quickly before I do.
As a boy, I spit a peach pit onto my father's prayer rug and immediately

it turned into a locust. Its charge: devour the vast fields of my ignorance.
The prophet Muhammad described a full stomach as containing
one-third food, one-third liquid, and one-third air.

For years, I kept a two-fists-long beard and opened my mouth only to push
    air out.
One day I stopped in a lobby for cocktails and *hors d'oeuvres*
and ever since, the life of this world has seemed still. Every night,

the moon unpeels itself without affectation. It's exhausting, remaining
humble amidst the vicissitudes of fortune. It's difficult
to be anything at all with the whole world right here for the having.

Memo to the 21st Century

PHILIP APPLEMAN

It was like this once: sprinklers mixed
our marigolds with someone else's phlox,
and the sidewalks under maple trees
were lacy with August shade,
and whistles called at eight and fathers walked
to work, and when they blew again,
men in tired blue shirts followed
their shadows home to grass.
That is how it was in Indiana.

Towns fingered out to country once,
where brown-eyed daisies waved a fringe on orchards
and cattle munched at clover, and
fishermen sat in rowboats and were silent,
and on gravel roads, boys and girls
stopped their cars and felt the moon and touched,
and the quiet moments ringed and focused
lakes moon flowers.
That is how it was
in Indiana.

But we are moving out now,
scraping the world smooth where apples blossomed,
paving it over for cars. In the spring
before the clover goes purple,
we mean to scrape the hayfield, and
next year the hickory woods:
we are pushing on, our giant diesels snarling,
and I think of you, the billions of you, wrapped
in your twenty-first century concrete,
and I want to call to you, to let you know
that if you dig down,
down past wires and pipes
and sewers and subways, you will find
a crumbly stuff called earth. Listen:
in Indiana once, things grew in it.

Postcard

FRANCISCO ARAGÓN

Blue sky the Bay
Bridge from afar
arcing like a bow

into Treasure Island,
city skyline
scoring this view

tourists could buy
at Fisherman's Wharf
but for the smudge

clouding the tip
of the Pyramid—panels
deflecting the sun

glint through, as if a beacon
shrouded in fog
were blinking a code

to this green slope: a park
named after a mission:
Dolores   Dolores

—it simmers on my tongue, is
Pains in Spanish, is
her name. And beyond the grass

a dark-haired woman
crouching in the sand
saying to a boy

¡Sácate los dedos
de la boca!
Take your fingers

out of your mouth!

Big Little

MARIANNE BORUCH

Brain leans toward the heart: *I can't hear you!*
It's not a given. Every day
is different as clouds. One's a rabbit
in half-leap
over some interesting clover.
A second cloud's small
as a bee glommed to that sweetening before its
radar's knocked off by a teenager's
cell phone over at WalMart. *Oh hive,*
where art thou? Here, says the brain, right here.

So the brain is
a serious racket, buzzed as rain in a drought
or rain in the middle of rain or three
whole Tuesdays of rain.
The heart too
is complex. Its emphatic narrows to fuse up
the worst possible
chick movie. Or some action film, its thud thud
in the hero weighed down dumb
to really dumb by armor, his faux glory so long ago

it was yesterday. Maybe he can
learn something from grief.

Heart and brain: which one of them
wants more? All is realm, a theory of realm
vs. realm. But it's fun, thinks
a thought, give me a try!

The brain, what a liar. Not desire, all's
freefall to the most common denominator, only
keep beating the brain wires down to
the obsessive, cheerless heart.
I'll figure you out, I promise, the brain keeps
stage-whispering south toward

that thicket. *Promise.* Such a big
little word, the heart
lost and clutch and release.

Love Is Blue

NANCY BOTKIN

I find myself gulping for air which has no melody.
    At best, it's cymbals crashing. Blue ocean
as far as I can see, and my body in love with water. My body
    in love with undercurrents. These are difficult
matters. During revolutions people destroy their own artifacts,
    create a million cacophonies. All that fire. All that roaring.
You'd think lighting a match would be clean and simple.
    Long ago in high school a girl crumpled her math test
before bending over a small mirror to apply mascara
    in a sweeping motion while the rest of us were solving for x.
The enraged teacher stood next to her desk. She paused and held
    the raised wand like an orchestra conductor. Without taking her eyes
off the teacher, she brought it down slowly so that everyone
    in the room would continue believing in music.

Tomato Soup

MARY ANN CAIN

1.
Usually on snowy days
with grilled cheese wedged against bowls,
Mom always pushing the dairy.
I rejected her milk when I learned
for myself how to cut the can, let the tiny blade
pierce the seam until a jagged circle
dropped, edged with thickened
Campbell's, only Campbell's.
Sweet and acidic, that soup
played on my favorite tastes, not Mom's
milk meant to enrich my young bones. I craved
my own bite. I learned to twist and listen
for clicks that signaled the gas
flame. I bent for the copper-
bottomed pot I always scoured,
to smooth pale red globs
as the water, just water, one can, heated.
Later, I leapt to frying—the actual
act, never really grilled—
Wonder bread, Fleischman's, and Kraft

singles, what the household held,
but I found my own ways
to make the meld.

2.
In the infusion room, I expected comfort
in Campbell's, wheeled in on trays and plastic
cloches. I had never looked a free meal
in the face of not being free. Now,
a year's gone by. I still recoil,
remembering the chill, that soup,
the queasy steam. I ate to calm
the chemo laying waste to my gut.
This old comfort even now recalls only sickness.

3.
Today, this snowy day, a storm outside
burdens the power lines, threatens to cut
off all heat and light. As the fire
hydrant out front disappears
under a drift I call back
Campbell's both ways, Mom's
and my own. I reclaim the calm
of hot red hearts, the first meals
after tummy troubles, the slow cold
of hope, that steal me back
to when I learned to taste and ache
and feed myself
on my own.

Returning to Rilke

DAN CARPENTER

who was all about loneliness—
seeking it, that elusive core
whose perfection was denied the artist
by human noise . . .

Returning once again
to the exalting struggle
to comprehend him
is an exquisite loneliness in itself.

Who, to steal the poet's language,
is there
in all of family or friends
to even begin to care
about this quest
to rise to that plunge?

Who comes off the golf course
out of the nightclub
mall or boudoir
to stand alongside the poor reader

even to watch him watch him
wrestle with the angel?

The Measuring

JARED CARTER

You're sickly pale—a crooked root.
But one last remedy remains:
before the dawn we'll go on foot
through grass sleeked down by heavy rains
to the sexton's house. Already he
takes down his spade, and goes
to walk among the whitened rows.
His wife awaits with lengths of string
necessary for measuring.

She has no fire alight, nor words
to spare, but bolts the wooden door
and helps you out of clothes that fall
soundlessly to the floor. Naked,
you mount the table and recline;
she comes, her eight stiff fingers
trailing bright bits of twine. First,
crown to nose, then mouth to chin,
pressing against each crevice, in
and down the length of your cold frame—
whispering unintelligible names.

The feet are last to stretch: from heel
to toe each one must be times seven
the other piece. She nods, and knots
the two together, breathes her spell,
then turns to go. I leave a pair
of silver dollars there, and take
the string to tie where it will rot
the winter long, on hinge of gate,
wheelbarrow shaft, or eaves-trough's fall.

Behind us, where the darkness drains,
a blackbird settles on the roof
and calls back to another that rain
is coming like an awful proof.
The two denounce the scratching sound
the sexton's spade makes on the ground—
measuring off the careful square
of someone else expected there.

My Buddhist Lessons

KYLE D. CRAIG

Five months old, my daughter teaches me how to be Buddhist. Her sleep sack is a simple robe. Her bottle, a begging bowl. A semi-bald head and verbal silence serve as outward signs of her inner refuge. Place a crayon in her hand and she marks the page in Sanskrit. Sit her on a mandala patterned play mat and she mumbles mantras to a sangha of Taggie toys. When she wants to teach me about desire, she lunges for a stuffed tiger. To instruct how desire leads to grasping, she takes the tiger and clutches him to her chest. To teach how grasping leads to suffering, she shakes him and begins to cry. To impart the lesson that liberation comes through non-attachment, she throws him to the floor and squeals in joy. Her compassionate nature even allows me to accumulate merit. *Change me. Hold me. Feed me.* And at night her screams ring out like tiny bells, to remind me that the purpose of my life is to awaken.

sunrise
a tiny thumb rubs
mala beads

When Your Mother Corrects the IN Poet Laureate You Feel Like Yelling

CURTIS CRISLER

When your mother corrects the Indiana Poet Laureate you feel like yelling, "No Miss Sofia!" as if you are Laurence Fishburne and she is Oprah Winfrey caught up in the past. Shame on your brown face like rouge. But a minute later, when he comes back to her acknowledging she is correct, you realize

she's always been correct, and although you never thought where you came from would matter much, a splash resides, and it all crests back to Lake Michigan washing up on your life, and how you would

one day butterfly into a man with legs, matriculate into another day to flap your wings. To never know you'd meet a man who would become your bookmark. A man who would become your eye-loop. A man who would become another man in front of you—a voice you recognize in the wolf's howl. Some

say you should have never been here, but you have always leaned on stargazing and letting the moon burn its lips on yours. Somehow you saw the moment your mother would meet the Indiana Poet Laureate,

and somehow you were always here, and he would be all these men packaged like lunchmeat into some moment of time where you have swallowed life like bites of tart green apple in the backyard of your suburban mess. The yard, your mother built a garage on. The world's a small place full of eyeballs for

huge moments. You wish more brain matter, but your head hits the meso-sphere driving out of the county of lakes—everything behind you is closer than it seems. You still go forward, into the darkness, where a

white line pulls you back to where you'll start propulsion, again. Although the world is not a circle, it is an O-shaped mouth yawning in the hurt of morning sun on its walk of shame. Most times you end up somewhere you have faded out, but begin where there's no footprints—torn edge of rotating beginnings.

✝

MITCHELL L.H. DOUGLAS

After days of murder, more bodies
than nights in a week, you would think
we'd say *Enough*. Instead,
more blood. Don't think
it's just the dealers, that side
of law not in your nature.
It's expectant fathers on morning walks,
it's businessmen minding their business,
selling denim on Sunday afternoons.
Yesterday, my poetry student
who doesn't believe in gun control,
said he wanted to write a poem
about parenting & the right to bear arms,
how slipping on one side affects the other
(you guess
          which way that goes).
& though you won't find me w/steel
in the small of my back (@ least
not by my hand), I know the peace
a poem can bring. So I say, *Yes,
write.* & he goes back to his seat

nodding his head, the room filled
w/the voices his classmates
comparing Dove, Simic & Wright,
the push of my chair
back from my desk to stand & speak
like fingernails
on a chalk board, like a scream
when a gun   fires.

Celebration

MARI EVANS

I will bring you a whole person
and you will bring me a whole person
and we will have us twice as much
of love and everything

I be bringing a whole heart
and while it do have nicks and
dents and scars,
that only make me lay it down
more careful-like
An' you be bringing a whole heart
a little chipped and rusty an'
sometime skip a beat but
still an' all you bringing polish too
and look like you intend
to make it shine

And we be bringing, each of us
the music of ourselves to wrap
the other in

Forgiving clarities
Soft as a choir's last
lingering note our
personal blend

I will be bringing you someone whole
and you will be bringing me someone whole
and we be twice as strong
and we be twice as true
and we will have twice as much
of love
and everything

Birthday Swim

MARY FELL

i.
I never trusted lake water to hold me up.
Below lay grasping weeds, creatures to suck
the blood of a girl like me, primordial muck.
I swam as if my life depended on it.
In my nightmares, tunnels of dark water ran.

The ocean was another story. Churning
like an old washing machine, it swept the bottom
clean. My feet touched sand. I felt at home
in the maternal pull of tides, strength of breakers,
salty taste of liquid where I first swam.

ii.
I started, green again, in Ireland,
plunged in the ancestral pool.
Meters unfamiliar, the chlorine strong,
I stroked toward an elusive mile.
That rhythm rocked the Coes Pond crib
where I began, where I learned to breathe,
to hold my breath, to turn.

iii.
The safety of the lane, the painted lines
I follow, the end and the beginning clear.
I go up, come back to where I started. Repeat.
My fellow swimmers skim the surface, water
striders. My element is earth,

but I'm courageous here, able to see bottom.
In this liquid, fish don't rise to bite,
no frogs croak or spawn. It's dead
clean. Reassured, I breathe the chlorinated air,
admire my vestigial scales.
Now late September
currents lap the shore, three quarters of a year gone by,
three quarters of a mile. Nine months I've floated
in the chemical brine. This is the day I was born.

Solo Act

CHRIS FORHAN

The moon, the moon put the screws to me
and shut me up. The phoebe trained me
to flutter from the cliff side,
a berry in my beak. No want in me
then, or human friend. I took
instruction from the dolphin:
nodded, grinned, skittered
backward across water.
A man can step from his life
as if from a bus, can settle
for thistle and bird song, wistful
safe elucidations of beauty.
Not for me to bleed
on the razor-wire; fox-like
I crept, would father
no daughter, hazard no son—O
son, I did not mean to lug
love to where you could not live.
Come out with your candle,
lean your ladder
against my branch, lift

a crumb in your cupped hand,
I'm hungry, hungry
enough, I think, at last,
to be defenseless against you.

Valentine's Day, Sixth Grade

HELEN FROST

Yesterday, snow was coming down, big flakes,
and you were writing "Love is like snow"
how it comes down so soft, one day,
but the next day it blocks you in, or it is gone.
Some of you left it new-fallen, tender,
how it should be, I thought, sixth grade love should—
then I remembered sixth grade, how all the girls
wanted a valentine from Steven. He gave us
each one, and we compared them. Two sizes.
Charmagne, of course, got a big one, mine was small,
and when Jane said, "Let's see
your Valentine from Steven," I said, "No."
Then, at the bottom of the pile, a big white envelope,
my name, a second card from Steven Deane.
He was watching me open it. We both knew
I wasn't pretty, he should like Charmagne, would
go on being her boyfriend. But there was
that moment, and yes, it was something like snow.
Its memory blesses me now like your poems,
their honest endings, melting away to nothing,
or turning—Angie's puppy, to care for like love,

Damon's "Love is like football.
I hope I will have a 100 yard run."

Alfonso Street

EUGENE GLORIA

In Sariaya, Quezon Province, where
          my father's people live, bananas and
mangoes in colored cellophane adorn
          windowsills like gaudy evening wear.
In Botong's pastorals, a fluvial fiesta
          litters Laguna de Bay with lighted
tiny boats like a fleet of candled hopefuls.

Elsewhere, a nervous boy measures his week
with good days and bad days like innocents
          walking on pavements wary of cracks.
In Caracas, a swarm of bees attacks a boy.
          His dog shields his body with its own.
The boy lives; the dog dies shortly after.

On Alfonso Street, a kid I knew,
is paraded on a wooden wagon
          with a matronly woman at the lead.
My metal trucks with missing wheels,
          he once coveted. Stateside toys in chipped
reds and blues I got secondhand

from the children of American GIs.
His cart with wooden wheels, and rings
          round his eyes, are gray as metal spokes.
What good are busted trucks to him
          whose brand name toys are always new?
Fiesta prince with a shuttlecock crown,
          fellow heir of bad blood.

In the kingdom of children where
we conjure angels from rain, a boy's
          will could spin and hitch the earth.
Here my wheel-less truck remains.
          An ashen kid, gray and gilded
is trundled by his mom in evening wear.

The Sadness of Youth

MATTHEW GRAHAM

Tonight walking my dog I heard
Several young women call my name
With an enthusiasm I haven't heard in years.
I turned toward their porch with a smile
And almost waved until I saw the kid
Struggling biblically up the sidewalk
With a case of beer.
His long hair and straggly beard could have been mine
Forty years ago when all I shared
With Christ was poverty.
I turned the corner thinking of Elliot,
Of Prufrock, the mermaids and all that
"I do not think that they will sing to me" stuff.
Elliot at his best, I guess, writing about age
Before he got old.
And then what? I thought of my namesake
A fat and vilified tax collector for the Romans
Who dropped everything
To follow that strange young man
Who heard voices in the night.
And then I thought of my name

In the mouths of those girls
One last time.

Restavek*

JANINE HARRISON

His bike met a taptap
in Port-au-Prince.
Your papa met St. Peter.
You were three.

Your manman sold plantains
and aubergines
from a marchés stall
and after the mudslide,
from a blanket laid gently
upon packed gray earth.

Age eight, you returned from
doing wash in the murky river,
wet things, tub, upon your head.
It fell when you found her
lying on the dusty straw mat
on his shanty floor.
He'd fingerpainted her face
with darkness again—
for days she barely moved.

You'd bathe her with rain water,
dip again into the bucket,
let her suck on the red red rag.

When she stood up
started walking toward the village
without a whisper to you
you watched her limp and list,
and wondered,
Will she come back?

She returned before him,
and her whip spider fingers
encircled your upper arm,
yanked you into waning daylight.
"Chantale," she began,
her voice at once
a whimper,
a plea,
and a long, flat plank.
Your arm hair rose,
though you couldn't catch why.

* A restavek is a child in Haiti under age fifteen who is given away by a poor family to a wealthier family where he or she then becomes a servant or slave in exchange for food and shelter. Such children are often abused, sometimes sexually. Prostitution is a common career path for restaveks once they reach adulthood.

Grandmother at the Dressmakers'

MARC HARSHMAN

A bolt of heavy, cobalt gabardine,
     shot with silver and scarlet threads,
     lay across the cutting table.
It was July. The overhead fan threw slow shadows
     upon the patterned, tin ceiling.
The neckline of Grandma's cotton housedress
     had grown dark with sweat.
The street outside, Mulberry, was empty—it was that hot.
Grandma, however, made lists and did not move from them.
A few minutes, that's all.
I did not chafe too much at the familiar words
     heard in grocery, at the neighbor's fence,
     though always
     my hand was tugging at her sleeve.
Bored, yes, but content enough, able
     to wait for the promises: lemonade, ice cream, cookies.
It was to be an elbow's length longer than the yardstick.
There was tracing paper, thimbles, tweezers, bodkins,
     and pinking shears with their intriguing teeth.
I took it all in, bothering and circling the women
     with questions, anxious to know as much here

as I did in the barnyard with Father.
It was not poetry. Not yet. But it was life as I knew it
        and I was keen to know it more, to keep gathering
        as I did berries and stamps and pebbles,
        to see what rarities might show up, sparkle and speak:
                muscled cloth, scissor slash, and how precision
                might be wedded to beauty,
                        to be the kind of gatherer
                        who would not starve
                        even if my clothes grow thin
                        and I can't find much to say for myself
                        other than I am still here,
                        tugging at her sleeve.

Fog
Light

JOSEPH HEITHAUS

That morning
we could see
their breath
the small coffin
between them
like a word of smoke
slipping up
into places
none of us
ever want
to go

You told me once
that the sunsets'
violent yellows and reds
on the beating indigos
are only dust
cut through
by light

There's so little

we really touch
even people
can become ghosts before
they're ever held

I want to be stone
but am only water
I want to be water
but find
I am only cloud

The Mirror and Map of Memory

ALLYSON HORTON

Some folks ain't cut out for indigenous stories.
Mississippi has my grandaddy's name on it.
His mother steeped her calloused heels in its marshy
flesh. Black salt still troubling the waters to this day.

Choctaw Indian swims downstream
with varicose veins visible in the legs
of great-granddaughters.

Her canvas is deep red clay
oiled with black mud. Hair—
bone-straight, thick as blood.

Up close I studied
the carved bones pillared beneath squashy cheek,
the pebbled necklace
rivery eyes,
flatland lips,
hilly breasts
each telling its own history.

The deep-rooted face
is both mirror and map
window and door
I do not see me in her
I see her in me.

Final Bath

MARC HUDSON

Only Saturday, when I squeezed the last
of the coconut shampoo into my palm,
& lathered your hair, you laughed,
leaning forward on your straps. Water
streaming down your chin made a brief
translucent beard.
                            This morning, I borrow
a hospital's wash cloth, dip it in a basin,
& daub your face, the fuzz along the line of your jaw,
your narrow chin. With great care, I trace
the rigid wing of your left arm, while your mother
stands opposite, performing the same silent office.

Saturday's ablutions were under the sign of Top Hat,
Fred & Ginger swirling in the mist, "dancing cheek-
to-cheek again" amid scarlet arpeggios, while we
listened to Casey Kasem's Top Forty—me clucking
at the insipid love lyrics to a surfer boy, you cracking
up at my antics, mocking my aged tastes with your sidelong
squint. I loosened your chest straps & laved your shoulder
blades, a little brusquely perhaps, surprised again

you were no longer a boy, but a lithe young man
with the shoulders & lats of a swimmer, narrow hips,
and, how shall I put it, your virginal male beauty?

       Now I pass the cloth over your chest,
your skin strangely flushed where the blood has pooled
above your heart. (Or is it from the EMT's
frantic lunge at your stillness?)
Now down the relaxed slats of your belly,
along your thighs, marbled calves, lovely
ungainly feet, our cloths sweep
as if, together, we are Christ
ministering to the desert body of Christ.

Under their long lashes, Ian, your eyes appear
half open. Most carefully, they seem to be considering
a difficult equation. Has your breath contrived
somehow to continue without its body,
the way a boat does, when its oars are shipped
and it lifts into the further wave?

Vacation

ANGELA JACKSON~BROWN

Sometimes I checked out
I would literally sign the tab
say thank you for the room
and then I would leave.

I'd rush past the bellman
crashing out of the hotel room
running blindly towards the lobby
dragging behind me luggage crammed with dark secrets
and hidden shames.

And I wasn't checking out to go to a better place.
I went on no extended vacations to exotic locations. I
retreated to back wooded areas—places undiscovered
by human eyes. I built shelter out of kudzu.

I unpacked my luggage and draped myself
in all of the pain it contained. Then I waited
giving the kudzu time to wrap itself around
me until I was a mummified mess. Until

I was so far gone that the screams of my son
sounded like whispers. He'd yell: *Mommy where are you?*

I wanted to answer but I didn't know how. There
were no maps to where I was and even if
there were, I didn't want him to come and
see me there. So at times I'd manage to weakly call
back to him: *Don't worry. Mommy will be back.*

I made it seem like we were playing an elaborate game
of hide and seek. I made him believe that Mommy's
condition was normal. It was Halloween and I
was in disguise. *Shhhh. Let's be quiet and the
Voices won't be able to find us.* He'd play the
game until he'd get tired. *Mommy come back.*

And for him, I would drag myself back.
I'd repack the sadness the bitterness and the shame
back into the suitcases and then I'd unravel the
ropes of kudzu that clung to me like an Anaconda ready to
suck my very life away. Tired and exhausted
I would gather my boy in my arms. *It's okay,* I'd say.
I'm back. Mommy is back.

World without Birds

GEORGE KALAMARAS

I wonder what the world would be like
without birds? she asked. Bring me the soup—
make it hot. I tended to over-worry
about the next incarnation.
Would I have a hound? Could I
sleep through the night? *With* the night as if it were
a knife? I wonder about a tornado
without pale-anemic green. Without the small-flung
bodies of terrified ants. Let my blood into a cup.
The wind. Let the wind in my throat. The full-throated
howl of a hound treeing a coon. Full-bodied mirror
when I've eaten too much. When I've had too much
to bleed. I dreamt a world. I dreamt
a world without birds. All the setters
seemed confused. Irish setters. English setters.
Gordons. All the dogs that pointed birds.
All the spaniels forgave the rivers
without ducks. Can you spot the otter
in the picture of a left hand
trying to scoop soup? The bawl-mouthed
sound of a hound is enough to make me

want to give it all up and live in the woods
again and again. Life upon life
we come into our bodies, half-afraid
of salt. We look to the river. We bend
to the sky. We open our mouths for a cloud
of birds to enter. Half-afraid. Half-afraid
to show us their hollow-boned bodies.
I want to play them like a flute. Cull the air
they've gathered in their bones. The space
from all the wind they've stirred passing through.
Flush them from this crown of thickets and that.
To be so sure of the dark places. To cramp oneself
in a covey of starlight waiting out
the veritable washing of the womb. I wonder
what the world would be like
without setters to track birds. Without hounds
to continuously till the soil scents
of the ground. Blueticks. Treeing Walkers.
Redbones. Whose gangly pups have yet to have grown
into their skin. Old-man wrinkle around
a two-month snout, showing what's young
to be impossibly old. Loose-faced yet smooth.
How we come into our bodies again
and again. Older than what we are.
Scenting the coon we hope to one day tree.
Looking to the sky full of dark
darting spots that show us the wingèd way
we came. The pull of our silken ears
holding us all the way down to the ground.

Assemblage: Lake County

KAREN KOVACIK

Begin with this box, common as a star chart,
and blow into it till something shows up:
maybe the dim clarinets of Standard Oil
with flaming bells, or rows of white
oil tanks like hatboxes for giants, each
with a curvy staircase dangling like a ribbon.

Build boxcars and houses, your grandmother
lurking in the doorway like a witch,
your elfin grandpa painting ducks
on stakes to poke into the lawn.
Add your mother in a red headband,
who just lost a baby, and your father

drinking a shot and a beer, probably bored,
though you wouldn't have guessed it then—
elements you once thought frozen
like the plot of a fairy tale
with death a gory ornament
and not the unhappy end.

Time lurched slow like the freight trains behind the house.
In the Chevy's backseat you'd shut your eyes
over the humming bridges and open them
only at the Sinclair dinosaur guarding the oilfield.
You wanted to run up a staircase like Cinderella
and spin like a weathervane over that concrete forest.

So arrange the black car, white tank,
paper stars on a circle of blue.
Dangle old folks and parents
from a heaven of steel and smoke.
Then paste in seven-year-old you,
all umbrella skirt and kitten face,

now your grandma's age and waving from a different door
as the cars and bikes and children of the world stream past.

Bach in the Morning

NORBERT KRAPF

The children are dressed for school,
we finish breakfast without a snarl,
school bags wait packed at the door.

We have time for violin practice
without the usual rush before
the school bus lurches to the corner.

Daniel and Elizabeth decide to
play a Bach minuet, in harmony,
by heart. The violins are in tune,

one with the other. Daniel takes
the lead on his half-size violin,
big sister Elizabeth plays under

and around him on the heirloom
full-size my brother used over
thirty years ago in Indiana.

Today there is no cacophony, no

conflict between them, or between
them and me. Today I just say

"One, two, play," and sit back
and listen. Some days the notes
come together in just the right way.

Some days I wish my father,
who did not have the good luck
to meet my children, could pull

up a chair in this dining room
where we practice. How can all
eight fingers find just the right

spot on the right string at
the right time? How can both
bows cross the right strings

at the right angle and time?
How can both hearts and both
souls feel the very same beat?

How can we three people have
come together from different parts
of the world in this configuration

in this 1920s Dutch Colonial
house where the sun beams through
the small suspended stained glass

windows on which painted minnesingers
celebrate their love at just
the same moment the snow has

begun to fall beyond the bigger
windows framed by rich chestnut?

And how could a man named Johann

Sebastian Bach who lived hundreds
of years ago have been such a genius
as to make this moment possible?

On Seeing *The Embroiderer, or Mette Gauguin*

NANCY CHEN LONG

After the divorce, I took a class in art appreciation
to occupy my head. We studied Gauguin.
While everyone else was taken in by his use of color
and image after image of nude Tahitian beauties,
I couldn't stop staring at his wife Mette, embroidering.
I'd seen it before, as a painting of a woman
in obedient domesticity.
Now, she was a wife in situ, posing
while her husband withheld the sun

to blot out her face. He rendered her featureless.
She became more mask, a quiet interruption
in the wallpaper. Instead of needlepoint,
I started to imagine that she would have wanted
to leave, stroll down the banks of the Seine,
smolder along the soot-like evening,
reclaiming that textured glow some of us feel
as we fall under the whitewash of summer.

I scarcely glanced at the other paintings,
those fine features of Tehamana—

the Tahitian who became, at fourteen, mother
of Gauguin's youngest son, whom he named Emile,
after his oldest son Emile, who lived in France
with Mette. The day Mette learned of his pubescent
other-bride must have been trauma,

the way it is when you learn of a husband's lover,
the way it is when a girl comes to your home
on a Sunday afternoon in August
while you're outside gardening
and you think it odd
that the dog seems to know her
as he trots up the driveway to greet her,
and the weight of summer humidity
has caused you to be slushed in sweat
and you smile politely as she approaches.

Epidemic

ALESSANDRA LYNCH

Thin women are trooping over hills, through
fields & rivers. They splinter as they stride, narrow
between trees & sparkling. Their eyes harder

than glass, than bone. Women trooping, brushing
against railings & mirrors, you would think their elbows
could cut through iron & glass, but iron & glass are

smarting their calves & thighs & necks & lips.
Even the rain is on parade— delicately tinkling
& cutting the women ever-so-lightly as they troop & thin

en masse over bits of glass & diamonds & caulk, bearing
gleaming compacts & glass jars of chalk. A glimmering
glass set—. How brightly the women thin in the gloss—

poised, swallowed by dumb reflective
surfaces with a sheen that stuns—.
(O Shining Epidemic!)

When the sun

drops low & the women lie safely
abed, their skin covered by glittering gauze,

their hard eyes focus solely
on themselves as things that need
thinning, weapons that will harm.

Map to the Stars

ADRIAN MATEJKA

A Schwinn-ride away: Eagledale Plaza. Shopping strip
of busted walkways, crooked parking spaces nicked
like the lines on the sides of somebody's mom-barbered
head. Anchored by the Piccadilly Disco, where a shootout
was guaranteed every weekend, those gun claps: coughing
stars shot from sideways guns shiny enough to light the way
for anyone willing to keep a head up long enough to see.
Not me. I bought the Star Map Shirt for 15¢ at the Value
Village next to the Piccadilly during the daytime. The shirt
was polyester with flyaway collars, outlined in the forgotten
astronomies of disco. The shirt's washed-out points of light:
arranged in horse & hero shapes & I rocked it in places
neither horse nor hero hung out. Polyester is made from
Polyethylene & catches fire easily like wings near a thrift store
sun. Polyethylene, used in shampoo bottles, gun cases,
& those grocery sacks skidding like upended stars across
the parking lot. There are more kinds of stars in this universe
than salt granules on drive-thru fries. Too many stars,
lessening & swelling with each pedal pump away from
the Value Village as the electric billboard above flashes first

one DUI attorney, then another who speaks Spanish so the sky
above is constantly chattering, like the biggest disco ball ever.

Himmler's Lunch in Minsk, 15 August 1941

BONNIE MAURER

(from his diary and excerpt on the museum wall at Terezin)

What did he eat for lunch
in the Lenin House, the SS headquarters,
at 1400, just after attending the morning
Einsatzkommando squad boys
taking turns to execute Jews near Minsk,
where reportedly brains splashed his face,
and he turned a greenish shade of pale,
and hey! he told the boys there,
terrible it all might be,
even for him as a mere spectator,
how much worse it must be for them
to carry the killing out and
he could not see any way around it.
"And reportedly he came to the view that it would be
necessary to find a more suitable and effective
killing method that would not have
such a disheartening influence on the executors,
particularly with women and children among the victims."
With what relish did he dig in his knife and fork? Was he

ravenous for lunch? With what eureka! This inspection trip—
the moment the gas chambers came into being.
With what hearty hale did he slug back his beer and lick his lips?

When the Stars Go Dark

JIM McGARRAH

There are no stars out tonight
in the alley behind Maidlow's Liquor Store.
Here, Charley Waters used to lean
against another old veteran of WWII
way back in the 60's when I'd come
down the block after high school
civics class and give him my allowance.
"You ain't old enough to drink," he'd say,
buying me a quart of Sterling Beer and himself
a fifth of Thunderbird to quench his guilt.
They'd sip the wine, he and his buddy,
without saying a word, staring upward,
waiting for stars to pop through
the dusk like white kernels of kettle corn.

I'm in this alley decades later to piss
on the whitewashed wall and look
for those same stars. I've done it before,
bought bourbon and snuck out here
always to wonder, going to my car
as those blooms, some ice and some fire,

flowered somewhere in the distant darkness,
what Charley found in the vacuum
of the universe that caused
tears to swell in his blank eyes.

I almost had it once when I first came home
numb from Vietnam, a shadow in the primal brain
forming a vague shape,
gathering substance as it seeped
through me like hot tar,
that connection we've all had and lost
with our one beginning.

Tonight, it's possible to imagine again
when all that's above me is a black
well of nothing hung on nothing.
What connects us is our loneliness
tearing through the endless sky,
arms outstretched begging the darkness
for a glimpse of those same stars
that always made Charley Waters cry.

Country Roads

KEVIN McKELVEY

The oldest roads snake the land. Creeks or landmarks
or the burg they lead to name the roads.
Elizaville, Strawtown, Mule Barn, Holmes Station.
Along Jerkwater Road, locomotives stopped to take on water.
But roads never escape the square-mile grid
that made order and ownership of forests and swamps.
100, 200, 300, 400, East, North, South, West.
The straight roads only ever cross or T, rigid as a circuit judge.
You know every house along your drive. They know you.
At county lines, the roads turn to gravel or just end
and return you where you started. The only way out
the highways or interstates condemned across the grid
to connect cities that might as well be islands. One lane
or two or eight; asphalt, chip-and-seal, concrete, gravel;
the interstate down to one lane and the gawkers.
The road grader blades the washboard smooth each spring.
The grid a mnemonic that locks the past of who
married who, who died and how, of silence for
fatherless babies, murders, drunks, arrests, suicides.
When I pass people I know and they wave two fingers
from the steering wheel, I recoil, startled.

I want to be unknown. But I'll stop and block the road
to roll down my window for unfettered talk.
And if I don't recognize the person, I wave my two fingers
from the steering wheel as welcome, to witness.

Kissing in Madrid

ORLANDO RICARDO MENES

Dance floor of Rex, Gran Vía discotheque,
My first deep-tongue kiss, sloppy, succulent
Like mango, long slurps, giggly burps, my neck
Wet with nibbles, as we grope, grind, vent
Libido, strobes pulsing to Barry White's moan,
Our bodies simmering in slow-burn funk,
She an Air Force brat from the base at Torrejón,
Frizzy blonde, light as a mannequin, I the clunk
In platforms, bell-bottoms tight as a corset,
So I cling to her, swaying in that nicotine fog,
No words to spoil such a gift of spit and sweat
Given to a boy she's just met, shy, bookish, a clog
With seduction, and once the song is done,
We split, lurch, mouths dry, lips like laundry wrung.

Veteran's Affairs

NORMAN MINNICK

Watching baseball with my grandfather-in-law
I study his varied expressions
as he tells tales about good old days
bathed in the blue-green glare of his TV
rabbit ears tin foiled to the east,
the volume turned up for old ears,
his large pale hands streaked with blue veins
draped over his knees like moth-eaten doilies.
"Hell," he says out the side of his mouth
like Clint Eastwood might if he were here indignant
to my company, "Hell, is hearing your buddy scream
and not being able to reach him."
Honestly, all I really heard him say was "Hell." The rest
was garbled. He probably said, "If that woman
don't get home soon with the ice cream..."
Barry Bonds is about to break Hank Aaron's
home run record. The bottom of the fifth.
The count is 3 and 2. A foul ball. Then the hit.
The camera pans to an ecstatic crowd.
Fireworks. Cheers. He watches without expression.
"I'll be damned," he says, which I am sure of.

"I'll be damned," he repeats as colors blur behind
the Giant rounding third base at an easy trot
into the arms of his teammate.

Extremist Sonnet

MARK NEELY

This small world
contains a starfish

pressed on the beach
like a crippled hand,

crumpled baby pictures, the
handsome strangers of the Internet,

and Bin Laden's tiny
television. Pine trees shivering

like addicts on the mountain.
I wanted to tell you about the bees.

I wanted to ask the youth if they are over
being shocking, to say one night

I came home drunk and watched
Daniel Pearl's beheading.

1948

ROGER PFINGSTON

Cookie Taylor, whose given name
I never knew, came strolling out
of the woods, his bare chest writhing
with green snakes, Cookie smiling,
inviting us, younger by four or five years,
to step up and be equally adorned,
Unless, he said, *you're chickenshits.*

To my surprise, I stepped forward
that June afternoon, muddy sneakers
squishing in a rain-soaked field, put down
my catch of tadpoles and crawdads,
frantic in the gray-water slosh of a Mason jar,
and offered a sunburnt arm to Cookie's dare:
emerald green the living flow down my wrist,
smooth, cold, tangling itself between
my fingers, its tiny head erect, tongue
flicking, tasting air but never my skin
as I stood perfectly still, my heartbeat
beats ahead of my breathing as Cookie
lowered a second snake onto my other arm,

iridescent...coiling...uncoiling.

When I slowly turned to show the others,
I saw it in their eyes, how they too would
remember—Simon, Donnie Shaw, tomboy
Madeline Hughes, the bug-eyed Archie
King who came caning across the floor
at the fifty-year reunion to shake my hand:
Snake boy! he'd said, squinting,
trying to read the print on my name tag.

Joining the Community of Ghosts

RICHARD PFLUM

We are friends now and I'm told that I might eventually
be elected to their Board of Trustees if I continue
to work for their interests. What I'd like is that I not
be required to wear a suit and tie at the meetings, that
even a bit of bone or decaying flesh would be optional
depending on my seniority. And I can see myself now
floating through walls and time-traveling to visit various
friends, lovers and historic figures and at times even
appearing again to the living. Giving some sound
advice to those I approve of and scaring the bejeebers
out of those who are obviously jerks. And so I'd win
the ghostly equivalent of medals and awards, maybe
even stipends and special privileges. And, because of
all that light coursing around at the end of the tunnel,
I'd see things I wasn't able to, when alive. Whisper
to my literary critics, the real meanings of my metaphors.
And I'd do the *Danse Macabre* on Halloween nights
with super attractive ghost princesses even though in life
I was clumsy as a log. Since gravity would have no effect,
we'd dance on the ceilings of haunted houses, tap dance
on the tables of mediums to the bright accompaniment

of clacking bones and a ghostly violin. And it will all be
great fun, for in Ghostland we won't have to worry about
any of the constraints of earthly dimensions.

So now, still being alive, I think sometimes I might see
through the veil into an interesting future, with ditsy scholars
pouring over my papers and hard drives, and (with much
difficulty) trying to figure out which word goes where.
Finally asking, "who wrote all of this abstruse and disjointed
stuff? Who was this language criminal anyway?"

Chartres in the Dark

DONALD PLATT

It was almost sunset
when the cathedral rose out of the rolling December farmland,
        fields still green

with winter wheat. One moment there was nothing but horizon
        and muddy sky.
Then its two gray spires appeared as we drove over the next

        hill. I first saw
those red and blue rose windows—muted sunlight flooding through
        leaded petals—

when I was fifteen, the age of our younger daughter Lucy. Because that dark
        light had branded
its afterimage on my brain, I was taking my family

        thirty-seven years later
to Chartres to show them stained-glass sunrise. By the time we reached
        the cathedral after countless

roundabouts, whose small red and white triangular signs said, "Cede
        the passage"
or "You do not have priority," it was dark. We walked the nave. I pointed

to the now black
mosaics of stained glass, tried to describe for my wife and two daughters,
who had never seen them,

the haloed apostles. I failed, stood silent under extinguished
windows in the dim
half-light of the south ambulatory, and had to imagine

La Belle Verrière,
the blue mother holding her rust-robed child while gold censers swung
incense over

their heads and angels bore white candles to light their winding
way. The dark
glass illumined the boredoms and terrors of 12th-century

French peasants.
Somewhere in the central window of the west façade, a mother lay bleeding
on a gold fourposter.

Joseph dozed on a chair. Their newborn cried himself beet-red,
finally slept, watched over
by a drooling ox. I remembered how once Dana and I

came down with flu
simultaneously and lay in bed, sitting up only to vomit into mixing
bowls, while our six-month-old

daughter Eleanor howled in her crib for milk. We were too sick to feed her.
I still discover scrap paper,
stuck in old books, with long lists in Dana's hand, "Right 2:40,

left 5:05," in red pen
to help her keep track of which breast Eleanor, who's now nineteen,
had nursed last.

Right breast, left breast, her mother weaned her. I couldn't find
the window in which Christ,
tied to a post, got beaten by two men, one with a cricket bat,

the other with a flail shaped

like a broom. At sixteen Eleanor had walked with the handsome stranger
        to his top-floor apartment where

he tried to rape her. She ran down twenty flights of stairs. In the starless
        Charlemagne window,
Roland pierced the black giant Ferragut with a silver sword

        through his navel,
the only vulnerable spot on Irongut's body. To the left of the altar my father
        hung crucified on Alzheimer's

cross. My mother and I took him down from that tree, washed his wounds,
        perfumed his body,
stuffed a stone in the open mouth of his grave. For nine centuries Charlemagne

        had gazed at the Milky Way,
cornucopia of God's coronation jewels, and tried to read there
        his fate or fortune

in the next day's battle. I could not see how the three butchers hacked
        at legs of lamb
on a long table. Or how two bakers carried a man-sized wicker basket

        of round loaves
hung on a pole they shouldered. The loaves looked like cobblestones.
        I was condemned to eat them

and shit blood. On our journey from Provence, my internal hemorrhoids
        had ruptured,
turned the water in the toilet bowl—no getting around it—

the same unearthly red
as the stained glass of Chartres, sunset or sunrise, cumulus
        clouds of blood

I flushed. Rose windows, because you showed me in the dead of winter
        how my small life
shone through your blacked-out panes forty feet above me, I knelt

        down in that empty
cathedral. I kissed the old worn stones we walked on. Nothing
        could have been colder.

The Fire Academy

DANA ROESER

I want to be a student
        at the Fire Academy
and not, as in
        my dream last
night, the gassing
        practicum. Why
did we all sit there,
        obediently,
in our detachable
        desks, new carpet
smell, gas seeping
        in, in that
sunken classroom,
        instead of fleeing?
It wasn't until the
        very end that
it occurred
        to me to not
wait for permission,
        to go. To gather
up the high school students

                    in the "gathering
area" and whatever
                    we were, teachers
in training—some
                    version of
                    grad students. One woman
had already
                    escaped. She heard the
lecture, she saw
                    the list, and she
said, Excuse me,
                    uh, I just have to
go do something.

Blue spruce.
                    Like a flash
of fire. Very tall. I forgot
                    to look the
one time I was
                    there since
twenty-five years
                    ago, at the
side yard. There was
                    so much
to look at, my childhood
                    house. Inhabited
by a music professor—and
                    his wife and
the yipping schnauzers. He
                    let me in! (His
wife wasn't
                    home!) He
let me into the
                    "elevator game"
hallway back
                    behind the
kitchen, with its

five doors.
But not upstairs.
        Dreams take
place all around
        there, even near
the split rail
        fence (surely
that's gone) near
        the spruce. A
display of
        Christmas trees.
We got them
        from the tree farm
each year with a
        ball of dirt. Do they
never die?

        Here, there's a spruce
tree back
        behind an
abandoned
        furniture
store—or is it not
        abandoned?
I can't quite remember.
        I know more than
half the retail "spaces"
        in that mall
are empty—
        and there
are cracks and
        exuberant
bursts of weed in
        the parking
lots. Not universally. Just
        in places. My favorite
is when a drive

                  has been built,
a feeder
                  road to some
prospective
                  business, a "pain
clinic," a medical
                  supply store,
an advance-on-your-
                  tax-return-
loan-shark place,
                  paved, organized,
curved and then
                  just stopped,
cut off with
                  a knife after
five or twenty
                  feet. Nix
that project!
                  I saw the fir
tree, I mean the
                  spruce,
on a little slope
                  leading down to
a small ravine, cattails,
                  a slope up the
other side, separated by a
                  chicken wire
fence leading to
                  nothing, leading
to nature, trees.
                  I was in
the "loading area,"
                  orange back
doors
                  for the mall
stores. One
                  lonely car. Affair?

Drug deal?
      Loading something?
The spruce
      was flaming
though. Thriving. Screaming
      of Christmases
past. I don't think,
      though, that some
child and her
      father brought
it out there
      one
holiday-aftermath,
      in its ball
of dirt.

      The Fire
      Academy is
the place for me. High
      school kids
in the country,
      in lieu of
"cosmetology" school,
      the Lafayette
Beauty Academy,
      are training
at the Fire Academy.
      And here
they can practice
      on real fires,
as the crews are
      all volunteer
anyway. (If fire doesn't
      suit them, they
can become
      EMTs.)
Where was

      it I lived
that there was
      a special
fire building
      on the
outskirts
      of town, off
of some four-lane
      semi-main-
drag? Many of
      the places
I have lived
      have been
flyover standouts.
      A four-
or five-story brick building
      sitting alone
by the road
      in some weeds. Used
for staging
      fires, death,
and destruction
      over and
over, and the fire
      students would
scramble
      up and down
the faces the
      staircases
looking for
      dummies, who
were posing
      as smoke-stricken
people or bodies.
      I used
to look at that
      place. Death

and destruction
     headquarters.
Please let me
     not state
the obvious: "If
     only it could
be restricted to
     that, to that
one building." The woman
     escaped, with
a phony excuse,
     a lie. Shall I start
with that? All the lies
     I hear all the time,
every day. There are
     so many lies
in the air, so much
     willful
obfuscation, cheating,
     why bother
looking for
     the breathable
air? As a child, I loved
     people half-heartedly,
already with a
     shield. Only
person in the
     security tent
was me. In the Fire
     Academy all
of that is
     burned off. You may
not be able
     to be heard,
but at least
     what interactions
you have

        can be trusted
to be genuine.
        Save me.
Save him. Save her.
        Get the
child. Get the cat.
        Crawl on your
belly under the
        smoke. I can't
breathe. I love
        you. I'm sorry.
Something's
        strobing
me, stroking me,
        basting me,
some awful
        clean thing
that'll strop
        me like
a razor, right
        against
my skin.

The Sky Turned Orange on the Eastern Side at Twilight

RACHEL SAHAIDACHNY

Scepters of fir descend the mountain
until their edges fade.

I smell of metal—my tin
fingers, silica shoulder.

What are you mountain
what are you chest what are you
breath I can't see yet fills me.

What is this I hold onto
I don't mean to hold onto. Needles
cling to pines.

They plunge in silence
and make a patch on the ground
of silence. As I walk

eyelashes shed on my cheeks.
Follower of leaf prints in a land
without fallen leaves—

I turn my hand over for a whisper
of thunder: a faint thud

in my breast when I undress and don't
want to be seen.

Bringing Things Back from the Woods

DAVID SHUMATE

Each time I wander into the woods, I bring something back with me. Antlers. Toppled nests. Stones smoothed by streams. The mating call of a wren. (Which doesn't seem to work on humans very well.) Sometimes I return imbued with the attitude of a tree and remain stationary for hours on end. Lately the spirits of the forest have begun following me home. Wiping their feet at our front door so as not to scatter their moss about. Flipping our television on. Bumping against my wife's hip as she chops vegetables for a stew. Testing out the type of rain our shower makes. Rearranging my dreams with their lower branches as I doze. I sense they have instigated a rebellion among our wooden furniture making it nostalgic for the forest. One of our oldest chairs is growing back its bark. A beam that spans this side of the house has sprouted a dozen leaves. And just today when I went to move my desk, it wouldn't budge because its legs had taken root.

The Tragedies

KEVIN STEIN

It's best to admire the police from afar,
all that badge glint and the clip-on tie
safe for wrestling guys bad or good
to the unceremonious pavement.
O, sartorial fakery, your dapper clip-on
winged me free of knotted hours' indenture
mirroring my father's sandcastle hands.
In song Jimi Hendrix laments what befalls
all castles made of sand e-ven-tu-al-ly,
waves lapping syllables as they do ankles
in my desktop vacation photo. I'm flaunting
the inflatable canoe my breath made whole
on Huntington Beach before its Titanic
maiden *voyage,* which I first misspelled *voice*
while channeling Jimi's, and those clouds
scudding as Wordsworth's always do,
tranquil above the cop's blueberry-cherry-top's
Tintern Abbey. Allen Ginsberg dropped acid
at the Abbey, so good thing he's not here
to get busted naming what can't christen itself,
say, the Carolina chickadee or my backyard's

budding bleeding heart that I've dubbed Ruby,
or the masterful *diacope* of this cop's baritone
"Your hands, your hands, let's see your hands,"
the phrase echoing Richard III's horse-wish
before a sword punctuated the kingly comma
of his scoliotic spine. Power's not a thing to do
without, being *without* both cause and measure
tin-crowned upon thy head. Power skewers
even our lionhearted, interring what's left
beneath a parking lot not unlike the one
I'm eyeing now, where black hands rise
from the pavement's opaque rhetoric.

This God of My Waking

JESSICA D. THOMPSON

I still had my milk teeth
when I saw him drop

to his knees in the dark
Appalachian dirt,

the serpent severed in half.
Mother running, tearing

at the strings of her apron,
tendrils of hair

escaping her bun, wild
pink and white morning

glories
reaching for light.

She saved him with words
she gave to the wind.

She saved him when
she took fire into her mouth.

Three times she went there,
three times she spat.

Only then did I dare believe
he was mortal,

    this god of my waking
days

        falling to earth.

The Lerner Theatre, 1953

SHARI WAGNER

Elkhart, Indiana

When my mother purchased high heels
at Ziesel's Department Store
and then crossed Main Street
toward a white terra cotta wall
with a marquee that announced,
From Here to Eternity,
it was the beginning of the end.

When she fell head over heels in love,
not just with Burt Lancaster, loping,
bare-chested across the beach,
but with the click of her blue
stilettos on terrazzo stone,
it was the end of the world
as a good Mennonite knew it.

The girl who made a necklace
from safety pins to wear
beneath her dress to school

marveled at the extravagance
of beaded chandeliers. She saw
dancing maids and griffins,
pipes, harps and Grecian urns,
the Turkish screens behind box seats,
the plush gold, pleated curtain.

All of it was worldly.
All of it was good.

Outside, the city was an oven,
but she slouched in a sanctuary
cooled by the river's pumped water
sprayed as fine mist into fans.

She loitered with hundreds of other sinners
in a dome of darkness
where she could see distinctly
the complications
a romantic life could take.

There she was: on the deck
with Deborah Kerr, tossing
her lei upon Pearl Harbor,
watching a wave, like a cursive swirl,
sweep the flowers out to sea.

Myth

ELIZABETH WEBER

Tonight I am creating
the killer of my brother.
I am reading a *Smithsonian* article
on Vietnam and looking at a picture
of a freelance photographer
on the shore of Hoan Kien Lake in Hanoi.
Five blurred men surround him
and only he smiles.
He could be my brother's age,
thirty-nine. He could have been
in Chu Lai on February 12, 1968.
He could have waited with a gun in a tree
near a rice paddy and watched
a line of stupid Americans
walk into view on a dike.
He could have aimed his gun at the one
who carried the radio
and seen not a man like himself
with fears and loves, but
a radio, a gun, an obstacle and
thought *radio, kill, fire!*

All day this man has worked by the lake
and stopped tourists who look
at the dun-colored water
or lean against the trees
to rest and look at what they've bought.
He's made 1,000 dong
and watched fifty people
feed bored ducks.
He walks home through gritty streets,
the day cool with a slight drizzle.
Hawkers call to him
to buy American TVs,
radios—dreams
he can't afford. He walks
and feels the earth go automatic
under his feet.
Home, a daughter comes to greet
him after her bath.
Her skin wet on his skin
and clothes as she
climbs into his lap
and he holds her.
He has won this moment
with his daughter in his home
where no bullets stir the leaves
in the ginkgo trees outside.
He has survived.
I want to ask him how it was that day.
I want his daughter to listen
to him explain how the bullets entered
my brother's body
and exploded, and how what we hold inside
is torn irrevocably apart.
I want this, and I don't want it.
I want his daughter in his lap.
I want the trees outside still.
I want him to pick up a book

about the creation of the world.
I want her to fall asleep
to the sound of his voice,
telling how near a high plateau
over the Muang Ten River,
the Moon became the wife
of the Morning Star, and they gave birth
to the human race
whose dead children become stars
and how glorious it was
on the first day on this earth
in the beginning.

Taking Aim at a Macy's Changing Room, I Blame Television

MARCUS WICKER

No chain link fences leapt in a single bound. No juke
move Nike Commercial, speeding bullet Skittles-hued
    Cross Trainers. No brown skin Adonis weaving trails of
Industrial Vaseline down a cobblestone street. Heisman-shucking
    trash receptacles. Grand Jeté over the little blue recycling bin,
a prism of clouds rising beneath his feet. Nobody all-fucked in
    boot cuffs wide enough to cloak court appointed tethers.
Or slumped over, hoodie-shrouded— *sheepishly scary* according to one
    eye witness. Definitely not going to be your Louis V
Sweat Suit red carpet fashion review, coming at you live from E! & Fox
    News outside of the morgue. No chance for homeboy
in the peekaboo boxer shorts. Homeboy with the frozen
    wrists. Iced. Homeslice with the paisley, Pretty Flacko Flag
flying by the seat of low-slung denim— no defense
    attorney gets to call me *Gang Related.* Tupac
in a mock leather bomber. No statement taken
    from the Clint Eastwood of your particular planned
community, saying he had the right to stand his ground
    at the Super Target. Because my flat-billed, fitted cap
cast a *shady* shadow over his shoulder in the checkout line. No, siree.
    See, I practice self target practice. There is no sight of me

in my wears. I bedecked in No Wrinkle Dockers. Sensible
        navy blazer. Barack Obama Tie, Double Consciousness-
knotted. Stock dandelion pinned to the skin of an American
        lapel with his head blown off.

fiction

The Spirit Stone

MAURICE BROADDUS

IT'S BEST TO LEAVE SOME things forgotten.

Lord have mercy on my soul. Have mercy, have mercy, have mercy. I don't know why you want me to talk about all this in the first place. This here's a spirit stone and I come out here to make sure it ain't been covered up. Things need tending to.

OLD man Marse Chapman was always away on business. He left the young Marse in charge. Used to be that we had a colored overseer, Uncle Moses, running the field coloreds. Though black like the rest of us, with a little bit of authority he forgot who he was and where he came from. But young Marse Chapman was coming of age and was eager to prove himself. Told Uncle Moses he was too soft on us and took over. Young Marse was generous with the bull whip.

"What you staring at, nigger? Don't you go on get no ideas about running off." Young Marse Chapman would say to me when he caught me staring off at the hills. Then he'd crack that whip. Let it land right next to me to give me a start. I was the same age as young Marse Chapman. He had a special hate in him, even then. I tried to stay away from him in case his hatred was a-catching.

I did little jobs to help the field coloreds: toted brush and bark, rolled up little logs, carried water around to our men folk, and swept the yard. Mrs. Annalynn, old man Marse Chapman's wife, took a shine to me early on and I spent many a day on her lap. With my thick braids of hair and my knobby-kneed li'l self sticking out of the burlap sack that passed for my dress, she said I was the smartest colored in the Ohio River Valley. Few of us coloreds had anything to do with no reading or writing as there weren't no schools for us back then. And I wasn't one much for figuring anyhow. My smarts were in keeping my eyes and ears open and my mouth shut. Sometimes I wondered whether Mrs. Annalynn was trying to make herself feel better by taking me on. Owning other folks twisted a body up inside as much as it twisted up those you owned.

WE called everyone aunt and uncle out of respect, but Aunt Clara really was my kinfolk. After Mammy was sold, she watched out for me. When I asked her about the mole under my left eye, she said it was a black tear drop. "You cried for all of us," she said.

The field coloreds called Aunt Clara a conjurer.

One time, Uncle Moses tied her up to be beaten. There she was, all spread out for everyone to watch. Even those who resented her light skin didn't want to see her whupped. They feared for anyone who had to face the whip. But I saw her eyes. She weren't scared none. She just stared all boldly at him, practically daring him to whup her. Then Uncle Moses turned and walked away, like he forgot where he left her. No one was allowed to touch her.

One day, a cough settled in old man Marse Chapman chest. A fever burned him up dead. Folks said he became a haunt, swore they saw his spirit walking about the shotgun houses. All I know was that Aunt Clara's eyes weren't so bold after that.

I opened the gates for Mrs. Annalynn, then rode into town with her to buy supplies. Afterwards, she wanted me to sit with her in the kitchen. That turned a few heads, because field coloreds never was allowed in the house, and house coloreds never worked in the field. But Mrs. Annalynn said that I had "special dispen'sion."

I think I was like a doll to her, someone safe for her to tote around and be her friend, who didn't talk back, but could keep her company. I was still surprised when she asked me "Do you want to live with me in the big house?" She had an odd, dreamy sort of look in her eyes, as if she were already lost in special plans. Or hopes.

"I want to be with my Mammy." I don't know what got into me. My Mammy had long been sold off. I couldn't even remember her eyes.

Mrs. Annalynn grew red-faced, like I'd slapped her. Betrayed her worsen if I stole her prize cow and sold it to the neighbor she feuded with next door. Something cold replaced the light in her eyes. I knew that look from Uncle Moses' face. That was the last time she asked me anything.

I couldn't hate her though. She just wanted a child to call her own again. No shame in that.

Only hurt.

MOST days blurred into the next. Lying in my pallet on the floor, I slept until the guinea fowls woke me up. An old bell donged on some plantation up the road a ways, then more bells added to it, like the clanging was on a morning stroll up the road. By four in the morning, young Marse Chapman straddled his horse, a big, monstrous, wild-eyed beast that had a devil in him. Riding down to us, young Marse Chapman picked ham out if his teeth with a long shiny goose quill pick. The rising wind carried the smell of sow belly frying past the shotgun houses. The smell of hoecakes and buttermilk soon followed. The kitchen from the main house had different smells coming from it: cakes, hams, chicken, and poke, taters and good egg and pone bread. Most times I was lucky to get li'l pieces of scrapback each morning. We worked from sunup to sundown in family groups, that way we could help each other when someone got behind.

YOUNG Marse Chapman's big mean self studied me. Not like he watched the other coloreds, but like I was a flower that he waited for the right moment to pluck. One night, not long after dark, he came around the houses. The door to our shotgun house creaked open, waking all of us. We all knew what the midnight creak meant. Now, he saw me, with that look men got when they were heated up. He stood over my pallet. The other women rolled away, turning their backs and closing their eyes. He crawled on top of me, all pawing hands, his weight pinning me as he grabbed at me. I clawed and gave him what for. He came away from the houses, like a scalded bear. Folks whispered about it all through the night. But all I could think was that if you wounded a bear, you better kill them.

Lord Jesus, have mercy on this poor old soul of mine.

HILLS bumped up all around the Chapman house and the land stretched on far as the eye could see. A creek, cold and bubbly, crept through two caves before it passed through the property. It separated the row of shotgun houses the coloreds had from the rest of the estate and emptied into the river. My favorite place was where the creek passed through the caves. It was near dark, but I wasn't worried none. I was supposed to be fetching water, but folks knew I had a way of lingering whenever I went. Whispers carried on the breeze. I tell you what, my heart pounded so hard I thought it was going to jump out my chest and swim upstream. I knew they could only be one thing: patrollers.

Sometimes we called them buskrys, poor white folks who had no slaves of their own, but who tracked runaway coloreds. Iffen they caught a lone colored out by themselves, with no pass—cause you had to have a permission slip to be off or away from your Marse's property—they would catch you and whup you or just sell you to a trader themselves. Iffen they returned you to your Marse's, he'd turn around and give you a proper whupping for running off.

So I held my breath and crept along.

I listened carefully, trying to figure out where the voices were coming from, then I heard this woman speak with a slow, deep voice that made you snap to attention. I recognized her voice, which boldened my steps to find out who she was meeting with. I crept and I crept, not noticing the drop off til I was already tumbling down.

"Land sakes, Viney." Aunt Clara wanted to yell at me, but afraid of being heard, it came out like a stern whisper. "You gave us a start. We thought them patrollers had us for certain."

As I dusted the leaves and dirt from me, a round-faced little boy crouched behind her.

"It's all right, Frederick, it's just Viney. She's clumsy and noisy, but we're safe. Me and Frederick were trying to figure out how to get this here paddle boat cross the river. Think you could get him to the other side?"

"That li'l thing. I rowed bigger'n that for Mrs. Annalynn. I'm stronger'n most men after working in the field for so long."

"His mother's waiting for him over the river."

Frederick's big brown eyes would haunt my dreams forever iffen I said "no."

The current was strong, but it hadn't rained in a spell, so we weren't in for too much paddling. My skinny little arms trembled every time I set my oar to water. It wasn't the cold that sent a shiver up me and gave me goose flesh, it was the whupping I knew young Marse Chapman waited to give me should I get caught. Too scared to dare whisper to Frederick, I locked my eyes on the near-ing shore, focusing on what Aunt Clara told me to tell them when I got there.

As soon as the boat bumped the shore, I started praying. Frederick clutched the back of my dress, wrapping up in the folds as if they were curtains. The dark had a funny way of pressing in on you from all sides. Even tree limbs seemed stark and unfamiliar in the gloom. I knew I wasn't alone. Hands reached down and started to pull me up. I swooned, nearly dead from faint.

"Menare." I yelled what Aunt Clara told me. She said it was from the Bible. "Menare. Menare. Menare."

"Shh, girl," the bushes whispered with urgency. "We heard you the first time. Who else would be out here?"

That was when I first saw him. Zias.

He was a great big buck of a boy. No scars ran along his fine, dark skin, near as I could tell. And his soft brown eyes had a sparkle to them. Full of hope. And freedom. Weak as I was, I slumped in his huge strong arms.

"You hungry?" he growled. His gruffness held a gentleness in it, like he didn't know how to sound tender. But he tried.

"Yes" was all I trusted myself to say. I trembled as I ate. I don't know why. I wasn't cold, and I no longer feared young Marse Chapman's bullwhip.

After that night I rowed poor colored across the river, most every Saturday afternoon and Sunday night, just to see Zias.

AUNT Clara taught me lots of things about men and women. Told me that some Marses handed out permission slips for colored to get married.

I only knew Zias once. It was beautiful and I didn't need no Marse's permission for it.

YOUNG Marse Chapman, not so young by then, was quick to stop men. "Whose colored are you?" he'd always ask. Iffen the slave was reedy or sickly looking, young Marse Chapman would say, "You can't see my gals. You ain't good stock." Zias belonged to Marse Chapman's Uncle Silas, who started sending him around to the farm. Marse Chapman took one gander at Zias, tall and husky, like he was bigger and stronger than a horse. Normally he'd have planned to use him as breeding stock, studding him worsen a horse. But Marse Chapman didn't like how Zias and me snuck glances at one another. His eyes got full of the devil whenever Zias came around.

EVERY colored in the field knew that Marse Chapman was a thunder cloud waiting to break wide open and rain anger on us all. His eyes followed me everywhere, burning worse than the noon-time sun. One day, without warning, he spat and cussed something fierce, yelling about how we coloreds have forgot who was in charge. Leaping down from that big horse of his, he went after Zias. He didn't care that Zias wasn't one of his own. He was property and Marse Chapman could always settle up what he owed. All the ruckus drew Mrs. Annalynn and Aunt Clara from the house.

Uncle Moses brought his arm up high and held his bullwhip there. All the field coloreds gathered around. We'd recognized that delighted glint in his eyes, like a preacher caught up with the Spirit. He waited until he had our full attention, and let that whip fall hard on Zias' back. The first stroke was always the loudest, the one that made everyone jump. Lord Jesus, that first lick. He let loose a soul scream, crying out for all of us. His skin split open, a busted seam along his back, sputtering blood like a gutted hog.

His back arched, drawing away from the bite of the whip. His knuckles turned white as he gripped the air. Tears rolled down his face.

Marse Chapman whupped him with the passion of a man knowing his wife.

Some turned away, they knew how things usually went: the thirty lashes, rubbing salt over his wounds, throwing the poor colored in the stock house, maybe chain him up a couple days with nothing to eat iffen the punishment was to be more severe.

Two words formed on Zias's lips. "Pray, Marse."

Young Marse Chapman paused when Zias murmured that. Then he said, "You coloreds have forgotten how to work and I aims to teach you."

He hitched Zias to a plow. Slipping a bit into his mouth and jerked him about by it, he worked poor Zias like a mule, beating him bloody and sore. Suddenly his big body slumped. Zias was dead.

Marse Chapman told us to leave him where he lie, as an example, and iffen we moved him, he'd do the same to someone else. So no one touched him.

LORD have mercy on my soul.

TO hear Aunt Clara tell it, when the universe was created, powerful stones soaked up the magic of creation. Like lightning striking the earth, they fell, bringing with them sparks of magic. Life and spirit fused, things of power. Aunt Clara taught me about them. No, a spirit stone wasn't like a head stone, though sometimes it feels like a grave marker. A spirit stone kept a part of a person's spirit so that they were bound to whoever owned the stone. Lord, how she'd hunch over one of her chosen stones, painting it, doting on it like it was a baby. I wanted her to help me make one not too long after Zias died. It was a way to capture a piece of a person, to always remember them. I asked, "How do you know which stones have power?"

"You'll know. It's like the stone chooses you," she said.

THE midnight creak didn't send a shiver through me. I'd snuck out like I was due to help someone across the river. Instead, I went to the big house. Aunt Clara let me in, but didn't meet my gaze. I slinked up to young Marse Chapman's room. He snored lightly beneath me, wrapped in his privilege of being born a Chapman. He'd known birthdays, his Poppa, his Mammy. He'd never tasted a bullwhip. He might find a love and have a child and be able to know them in peace.

He was allowed to dream.

The stone grew heavy in my hand. I smashed it down on his head hard as I could. Marse Chapman raised up out of bed, his arms flailed in his sheets like a ghost flapping in the breeze. I brought the stone to bear again, but the light had gone out of his eyes. He tumbled forward, toppling off the bed, bashing his head against the night-stand.

I was certain he went to hell, even though I didn't know how the devil could stand him.

I waited all the next day for them to come round me up. I prepared myself to cross the Jordan and meet my Lord. But no one came. Mrs. Annalynn found him. Told everyone that he had a spell and fell out of bed.

NO, I don't know how I felt. Sometimes you were better off not feeling. Feelings could grind you up, leaving you nothing. But I feared the hate. I feared that hate might one day eat me up. The truth had a way of coming out, no matter how long you let a lie settle into you. So I vowed I'd always remember how easy it was to hold a life in your hand and what not cherishing life could drive a body to do.

MY spirit stone chose me and I chose Marse Chapman. It was Zias' grave marker since Marse Chapman wouldn't allow no proper grave. So now he watched
over Zias.

Lord Jesus, it was an awful business belonging to folks body and soul. Then
one day, one of them Union boys, all tired and pale, came up to us.

"You're free," he said.

Lord, how we sang and danced. I wanted to move across the river to put the
plantation behind me and explore the world. But the Chapman house was all
I knew and I was afraid to leave it behind. It had broke and bowed everyone.
They never walked the same, a bent to their spirit as if they'd never be quite
whole. At night, low moans and cries might snap you fully awake, each sob
picking a scab on your soul. Just cause some law said we weren't a slave no more
don't mean everyone obeyed it.

So I left. But once a year I return to that place, to minister to my spirit
stone. A memory kept for safekeeping. A pain so deep, it lost all meaning. A
bit of Marse Chapman's spirit bound to it to remind him that he was bound to
me. Kept. Owned. In the cool of night, I could still feel the heat of his hate, but
that was all right. I brushed the leaves from him and let him rest.

The Close Calls

CHRISTOPHER COAKE

I.

THE FIRST TIME, CARL WAS ten.

His mother was driving the two of them from Fairfax, Virginia to south Florida, cutting downward across the south in the middle of the night. His mother's mother had suddenly begun to die in a hospital in Hollywood *(No, honey, not that Hollywood)* and goodbyes had to be said. His father had vanished three years before, but Carl still felt too alone, traveling with his mother, both of them exposed and small. His mother smoked with the window down. The wind lulled him as he lay across the back seat; he woke only to his mother's occasional sobs, to the thumps when big southern bugs hit the windshield like fists.

He held it as long as he could, but in the middle of Georgia he finally told his mother he had to pee. She stopped at a McDonald's. The only other vehicles in the parking lot were big rigs.

The lights inside the bathroom flickered. The tiles were cracked, uneven, the color of his grandmother's teeth. The mirror was a piece of polished steel, and Carl's face in it was warped and clouded. Someone had carved the word

FUCK into the metal, which startled him; he should not, he thought, be seeing a word like that alone.

Nobody who'd used them seemed to have hit either of the urinals, and this offended him; he placed his feet carefully between the puddles before unzipping. But he couldn't go. Right before he started a man emerged from a stall—he didn't flush—and began washing his hands at the sink.

Carl kept his head down, waiting for the man to leave, but he didn't. He stood beside the paper towel dispenser and dug in his pockets. Carl could feel the man looking down at him. His cheeks grew warm.

"Now what's a little fella like you doing here, this time of night?" the man asked.

Carl didn't answer.

"What's your name?"

Carl zipped himself up without peeing. He went to the sink. He was compelled to. He wanted to run, but his mother always checked his hands; she'd be angry if he didn't wash. He didn't want to explain why he hadn't. What if the man came out of the bathroom and overheard?

"Why don't you want to tell me your name?" The man stood behind Carl, visible in the mirror, a cigarette hanging unlit from his lips.

"I have to leave now," Carl said. His voice sounded honking and stupid and weak.

The man—old, gray, his cheeks loose and stubbled—glared in the mirror. The reflection of his eyes touched the reflection of Carl's. The man's eyes were blue, bloodshot and desperately angry.

"You didn't have to be scared," the man said, when Carl was opening the door. "It ain't like you're pretty."

II.

THEN there was the time when he was sixteen.

This was a Friday evening in September: the beginning of the first weekend of Carl's life during which he would have both a car and a legal license to drive. Carl and his mother lived in Ohio, then. His high school was out in the sticks, but that night he was driving into Cincinnati, to a concert. Even better:

he was in the car with two girls—the Davis sisters, Marie and Dora. He liked Marie, who was in his grade. Dora, one year younger, liked him. They were both smart and pretty and he could make them laugh. Several of their friends were headed to the concert, too, but the girls had chosen to ride with *him*. He could not predict how the night was going to go, but for the first time in his entire adolescence, he felt any possible outcome was going to be one he'd like.

But then Carl got them lost, trying to navigate a back route through the suburbs into downtown. The sky was growing dark, and the concert would start soon; he grew angry, flustered. Finally Carl turned the wrong way down a one-way street. A car honked, roared past them; he jammed on the brakes. Marie laughed. He put the car in reverse. A group of black kids standing on the sidewalk began to laugh and jeer him, and he felt himself reddening. No black kids went to his school, and he was afraid of these.

When he'd turned the car around, another had pulled in behind him. It honked, loudly.

Carl didn't think. Or, maybe, he did. Maybe he was thinking he was grown up; maybe he was thinking he needed to seem tough in front of Marie and Dora, in front of the black kids on the sidewalk. Maybe he was too angry, at himself, at the girls who'd started complaining about his driving. He put his hand out the open driver's side window and flipped the car behind him the bird.

As he did this, his foot slipped off the clutch, and the car stalled.

He tried to start the engine, but it wouldn't turn over. Tried again and again. "Carl," said Dora—and when he looked up, a man, this one white, was standing beside the car. He bent down and looked into it, first at Carl, then at Marie in the passenger seat and Dora, sitting behind Carl. He looked like a biker—he was massive, bearded, and his bare arms were covered with tattoos. His breath smelled like cigarettes, and his eyes glittered.

Carl was holding his breath, and he could feel the Davis sisters holding theirs, too.

"You just flip me off?" the man asked. His voice was surprisingly high and reedy.

"No," Carl said, stupidly.

"Oh god," said Marie.

The man looked at her, at Dora in the back seat.

"Yeah, you did," the man said. "And you flooded the engine."

"I know, sir."

That last word hung for a while. All of them listened to it, considering.

The man looked up, around. Carl didn't think the kids on the sidewalk were there anymore.

The man was wearing a Bengals cap, and Carl wanted to babble to him about how they both liked the Bengals, that everything was okay. But then the man reached behind him, and then he was holding a large pistol. It rested on the doorframe, its barrel only a few inches from Carl's chest. The man's finger was on the trigger.

"Boy," the man said, "do you have one of these?"

"No," Carl said, his tongue made of cement.

The man looked at each of them again. "No *sir.*"

"No sir."

"Do you know what kind of fucking day I'm having?"

"No sir."

"Think I got room in my life for some little faggot like you?"

"No sir."

"I could take you out. I could take your girlfriends back to my place and show them something."

Dora screamed, a short burst of fear so intense and painful Carl was sure he'd been shot, that being shot in the chest must sound like a scream.

"I know," he said.

The man nodded. He lifted the gun and placed it heavily against Carl's temple. A long second passed. "Bang," the man said. Then he took the gun away. He stood and slapped his hand against the roof.

"The fuck out of here."

Carl turned the key. He was sure that if the car did not start, the man would kill him.

But the car started. He pulled forward, working the clutch steadily, carefully. The man's form fell away in the rearview mirror. By the time Carl had steered the car back onto the main road, he was hiccuping sobs.

"I'm sorry," he said, to both of them.

"Let's just go home," Marie said then. She was holding Dora's shoulders, but she spoke to him gently, kindly, as though comforting a child.

III.

THEN there was the time when he was twenty-four. Carl was living in an apartment in a redneck neighborhood on the south side of Indianapolis. He had just finished an M.A. in literature at Purdue, but had no job. He was getting fat off fast food. By Friday night of the second week in August he had just shy of a month's worth of rent in the bank, and no groceries in his refrigerator. Carl had moved into the apartment a year before with a woman he'd met at school, but she'd left him, suddenly, in May. She'd never been able to communicate a reason, but now, looking back, Carl understood pretty clearly: she was gone because he was unemployed, fat, and unperceptive.

That night, as he gathered up his laundry and a miraculous handful of spare quarters, he decided that the world was unjust if it expected him to do his laundry sober. His ex had given him a flask for Christmas, as well as a bottle of nice Scotch—though she'd drunk half of it before leaving him. What better time to take care of the rest? He filled the flask and tucked it into his laundry basket.

The apartment complex's laundromat was a small concrete-floored room lit with overhead fluorescent bulbs that made it easy to check for stains. It smelled of detergent and spackle. No one else was inside, which was fine by Carl; the dramas of his neighbors all seemed to be worse, far more base, than his own. The laundry room was not air-conditioned, and his skin immediately sheened with sweat. He kicked off his shoes and threw the socks he was wearing into the wash. He had brought a book, but he didn't open it. Instead he sweated and drank quite a bit of the Scotch and watched the clothes slosh in the washer. All of this was better than reading a bad novel.

"The problem with you," his ex had told him, over the phone, "is that you—"

She hadn't finished. He'd asked her, twice: "The problem with me is *what?*"

She'd never answered. Carl had come to suspect he'd offered her too many choices.

A young woman—Chinese, and very pretty, and single, he thought; he'd seen her around—opened the door, a basket under one arm. She glanced at him, then down at her basket, then backed out of the room; the pneumatic door sighed shut behind her. He waited for her to return with whatever she'd forgotten, but she did not. He stood, unsteadily, and walked to the door. Outside the asphalt parking lot was still emitting heat, the overhead lamps humming and beset by clouds of insects. Not a soul was visible. Most of the windows of the surrounding apartments were dark.

The woman had looked inside, seen him, and decided she would do her laundry another time.

He drank the rest of the Scotch. He put his wash into the dryer and then walked, still barefoot, out and around the laundromat, to a grassy slope that dropped to the shore of a small artificial lake, fifty feet across. The lake was a pool of water, nothing more. The impoverished, unimaginative, Carl-fearing residents of Homewood Estates didn't use it for anything. Ducks sometimes paddled around it. The end. No novelist could imbue this lake with any meaning beyond the fact of itself.

He had wanted to marry Laura, his ex. Yet even in the early days with her, back when he must have radiated some promise, he'd never looked into her eyes and seen any love. Lust, sometimes, sure, and that had compelled them forward, until he'd gotten so big. But maybe that wasn't it. Laura had told him once how afraid she was to be alone. Maybe he'd been counting on this fear, to keep her close. To keep *him* from being alone.

Tonight—this—was what loneliness was really like. They'd been right to fear it.

The shore of the lake was fudgy and smelled of rot. He waded into the water, which was bathwater-warm. He had no idea how deep the lake was, or if anything lived in it. He kept going and going. The water cupping his balls, climbing his belly and breasts, was as erotic a sensation as he'd experienced in a long while. Then the lake lifted him off his feet.

As a high schooler, taking swim lessons, he'd learned he was good at diving to the bottom of the pool to collect the handful of pennies his teacher had dropped. A useless compliment had made him unduly proud: You have mighty big lungs, kid.

He filled them now and then dove, deep, the water silky, heavy, heavier.

The descent seemed to take a long time. It seemed, frankly, unreal; he was doing an illogical thing, and some part of his brain insisted that it was not happening. And yet his lungs began to burn, and panic began to shine in his stomach, and his eardrums hurt. His eyes were shut, but he doubted he'd have seen anything with them opened. He reached out and clawed against the water, pushing himself down and down. Then his hand caught the lake bottom, furred with algae. He hung there, compacted, invisible.

There, his ears pounding, his fingers twined into the silt, a voice spoke in him:

Open your mouth. Breathe.

He kicked toward the surface, heart rabbiting. Shambled, dripping, out of the water, up the slick and treacherous mud of the shore.

But not right away.

Down at the bottom, he thought, *Breathe.* The water trying to force its way through his clenched eyelids, his sealed lips, his cuts and crevices. He was a poor vessel, most systems near failure anyway. Why not let the water in? Then the trouble would be over.

For a long moment this all made sense to him. And then he fled for the air.

In his apartment, showered, damp, his laundry folded in its drawers and Letterman on the television, Carl lay awake, mulling what might have happened. How it would have appeared in the papers. What Laura would have thought.

Local Man Drowns in Lake. Or would that take up too much space? Would he deserve any detail? No. *Man Drowns,* it would say. Beneath the headline the article would list his name, his age. Unemployed, single, *survived by his mother Dolores.*

He imagined Laura reading the article. Telling her friends, I really dodged a bullet.

You should have done it, he thought, his teeth clenched. You coward.

IV.

IT's funny, how all this comes back to him now.

Carl is thirty-six years old. He is, to outward appearances, doing all right for himself. He is the manager of a bookstore on the north side of Indianapolis; he lives not far from it, in a small, neat, brick house. He works out every day, eats right, dresses like he knows what he's doing. For the past two years he has been married to a baker named Meredith. The love of his life, he has told their friends, and has always meant it.

All of this is a fraud, of course.

Meredith has been living with her parents for weeks; they struggled for months before that, in a fashion that Carl found horribly familiar. Today, without fanfare, she sent him divorce papers. Carl walks back and forth in his socks across the tiled kitchen floor, unable to stop looking at them. The papers sit on the countertop, incandescent beneath the hanging lamp.

Ever since Meredith moved out, Carl has been thinking about the close calls.

Not the accidents, not those. Not the time when he was nineteen and blind drunk and fell down the dormitory steps, when he was lucky to have broken his arm and not his neck. Not the time when he was seven, and developed a fever so bad his mother submerged him in a tub full of cold water and ice. Not the two car accidents, either—not the one when he was twenty, when a drunk t-boned him at an intersection, bruising his ribs, nor the one he was in two winters ago, when he hit a patch of ice on the interstate and flipped over into a ditch; he'd broken his collarbone. (Meredith hurried to the hospital that night, her face gray with worry, her hands jammed in her pockets; how he'd loved her for coming to his side.) Not the countless slips in the shower, or on wobbly ladders, or the too-quick steps off the curb.

No. He's thinking of the other times. The ones that haunt him. The ones that would not have been accidents, when someone—when he—had nearly forced the issue.

They shame him, reveal him to himself. They always have.

He's never told Meredith about any of those stories. Would it have mattered if he had? Would she have cheated on him? Left him for her parents?

Weeks ago she'd told him, "I think I was trying to hurt you. Because if I could hurt you, that would mean you were someplace I could reach. It would mean we at least lived in the same world."

She'd said, furious, crying. "Say something. At least fight with me. It's like you've given up."

But what could he say? That she'd been his last, best hope? That when she took his ring, he felt, for the first time in his life, a kind of safety? That, at last, he could hide the worst of himself away?

He told her, "I'm sorry."

"You and your self-pity," she said.

He thought about telling her: I actually died in a fast food bathroom; I died on a Cincinnati street. I drowned at the bottom of a lake. I should never have made it this far.

If he'd told her, I should never have been here. I should never have given you the hope that I might be.

He thinks of the lake bottom. A metal gun barrel against his temple.

Carl goes out for a drive, and cannot admit to himself why.

No, not a drive. He'll go to a bar. He will not be alone, not again. He tells himself he is engaging in a hopeful act. He doesn't look so bad, these days. He can tell a joke or two. He will prove Meredith wrong. He will.

As per usual, he drinks too much. Once several beers are in him, he asks a woman with red streaks in her hair if he can buy her a drink, and it's as though he's watching himself talk from a few feet away, embarrassed for himself. He can feel the flicker of his own confidence sputter out well before he's finished speaking. The look in the woman's eyes when she says no is nearly sobering.

He fights that impulse. Two hours later, when he stands up to leave, he's swaying, his throat swollen, his eyesight blurred.

He's thinking now about his Acura. About the handgun in the glove compartment. He bought the gun after Meredith moved out, and has been afraid to bring it into the house, no matter how the thought of it consumes him. He's thinking about how he's parked in a corner of a garage where no one will see him or stop him.

He's thinking that he's been living a life he should never have had. He's thinking that it's about time.

What happens next will preoccupy him for the long remainder of his years.

He's hurrying as fast as he can down the cold downtown streets toward the garage. It's two in the morning and the air in his lungs is painful; his cheeks feel scraped. He staggers from streetlight to streetlight. He's nearly alone out here, and he starts to laugh, because he's hurrying as though he's afraid someone might mug him, as though someone might hurt him, and it's almost as though this irony summons the man in the windbreaker and stocking cap, who rises up out of a recessed doorway and grabs Carl and turns him around and slams him down on the sidewalk. Before he falls Carl catches a glimpse of the man's eyes, bloodshot and full of a fury Carl has never felt, and he remembers them; then he feels cold metal against his temple, and the man is saying, "Don't you fucking move," and Carl shrieks, and the man kicks him in the ribs and says, "Quiet."

He's digging for Carl's wallet, tugs it out. He turns Carl over. "Gimme your fucking phone," the man says. "Don't fucking look at me."

Carl is stammering, his words in time with his heartbeat; he digs for his phone and hands it over. The man looms over him, young, white, his face gaunt.

"I said don't look at me!"

The man holds the gun to Carl's face. Carl holds up his hands and cries, "Wait!"

The man does not shoot Carl. Instead he kicks Carl in the stomach, doubling him over. Then a bright light blooms behind Carl's eyes.

The police come almost immediately, summoned by a passing pedestrian, when Carl is still struggling for breath. His tears and his spit have frozen his cheek to the sidewalk. Easy, the policemen say, easy. Soon EMTs are kneeling beside Carl, and the air is full of light. His head throbs and sings, and he's surprised to learn that he was not shot. The man kicked Carl in the temple, he's told, but he barely remembers this. People are fussing around him, shining penlights in his eyes. Their gloved hands poke at his scalp and come away bloodied.

In the hospital a doctor tells him he's concussed, but not too badly. His skull is not broken, and his scans are all right. "You're lucky," the doctor says.

"I've seen blows to the head like this kill people."

The policewoman who takes his statement says, "I wouldn't take it personally. For most of these people it's just a matter of opportunity. You were there at the wrong time, is all." She smiles at him. "You were just unlucky."

Well, he wants to ask them, which is it?

They keep him overnight. His head pounds and they give him painkillers and water. Soon his body recedes from him. The nurse keeps checking on him, and apologizing, and he keeps saying, No, it's all right, I'm glad for the company. He's floating inches above his bed. He will hurt tomorrow, but he does not hurt now.

It is nice, not hurting. He is reminded of being a boy, sleeping in front of a box fan on hot summer nights, the sheet rippling over his skin.

Beside his bed is a phone. Late in the morning he calls Meredith's cell. She does not answer, but he is comforted by her voice saying, *Leave a message.*

He tells her the story, aware that he's drifting in and out. He tells her a lot that he suspects he shouldn't. He smiles as he talks, the pain at the center of his skull bobbing as though suspended in water.

He doesn't tell her he's sorry, because he remembers that makes her mad.

Don't worry about me, he says.

I just wanted you to know, he says.

Before hanging up, he laughs and tells Meredith the funniest part:

They say I nearly died.

Go Back

KAREN JOY FOWLER

I SPENT THE FIRST ELEVEN years of my life in Bloomington, Indiana, but I don't remember it as eleven years. In fact, I couldn't tell you in what year or in what sequence anything happened, only in what season. It is as if in my mind my whole childhood is collapsed into one crowded year. And me, I grow, I shrink; I am three years old, ten, five; I am eight again and it is summer.

In the summer the tar on the streets turned liquid and bubbled. We popped the bubbles with our shoes on our way to the pool and came home smelling of tar and chlorine. In the evenings we chased fireflies and played long games of Capture the Flag. I was fast and smart and usually came home covered in glory.

The Rabinowitzes, our next-door neighbors, had a brief bat infestation in their upstairs closet. Stevie showed them to me during the day, hanging from the rod, sleeping among Mrs. Rabinowitz's print dresses. You could see their teeth, and the closet smelled of moth balls. At dusk the bats streamed into the sky through an attic grate, which Mr. Rabinowitz then screened over. You might have thought they were birds, except for the way they shrieked.

Above the Rabinowitzes' bed hung a star of David made of straw. Mrs. Rabinowitz's wedding ring was of tin. They came from Germany and spoke with accents. Mrs. Rabinowitz was much calmer than my mother would have been about the bats.

Stevie Rabinowitz was my best friend. He moved in next door when we were both four years old. Stevie could already read. He learned off the sports page. He would come over in the morning for toast and juice and to tell my father the baseball standings. We played Uncle Wiggily and he read both his own cards and mine. When I played with Stevie, we drew cards I never drew with anyone else. After I could read for myself, the cards were ordinary again. But when Stevie read them, Uncle Wiggily said that he would play for the Pirates when he grew up. He went ahead two spaces. I would play for the Dodgers. I would be the first girl to bat leadoff in the majors. I went ahead three spaces. Uncle Wiggily said Stevie would have a baby sister and his parents would pay her all the attention. He went back three spaces. Uncle Wiggily said I was too bossy. I was supposed to go back three spaces, but I wouldn't.

"Sometimes going back is better," my mother told me when I complained about it to her. "Sometimes it only looks like you're losing when really it's the only way to win."

Uncle Wiggily said that we would meet movie stars, and in the summer Jayne Mansfield came to the Indianapolis 500. We went to the airport to get her autograph. She signed pictures of herself, dotting the *i* in Mansfield with a heart. Her husband was furious with her, but it probably didn't have anything to do with us. She looked like no woman I had ever seen.

In the spring my brother entered the science fair with a project on Euclidean principles in curved space. He took second prize. Spring was the season for jacks and baseball. My father bought an inflatable raft for fishing trips. When I came home from school, it was fully inflated, filling our living room. "How did I get it in here?" my father asked, tickling me under the chin like a cat. "It's a boat in a bottle. How did I do it, Yvette? How will I get it out again?"

In the winter he bought us skis, although there was nowhere in Indiana to go skiing. One snowy morning I looked outside and saw a blue parrot in the dogwood tree. My mother went out to it and coaxed it onto her finger. We put an ad in the paper, but no one ever called. My own parakeet was an albino who could talk. "Yvette is pretty," it said. "Pretty, pretty, pretty." And sometimes,

"Yvette, be quiet!"

In the winter we went sledding on Ballantine Hill. When we came inside again, the heat would make our fingers ache. There was an ice storm that closed Elm Heights Elementary for a whole day since no one could keep their footing. I stayed home with my mother and brother and father, as if it were Christmas already.

Uncle Wiggily said the Kinsers' house would burn down and this happened in the winter. One Sunday morning, my mother answered the door. She was already up, cooking breakfast; I was lying in bed waiting for the house to get warm. I couldn't hear what she said, but the tone of her voice made me get up and I met my brother in the hallway. The five Kinser children were crying in our kitchen. They were all in their pajamas, their slippers wet with snow, holding toys and books in their laps.

There'd been a fire in Meg's closet, Barbara, the oldest, said. Barbara found it and then she had to hunt for Meg, who was hiding under her bed and didn't answer for a long time. And then her mother wouldn't let her go back and get Tweed.

"Where is the dog?" my father asked.

"She sleeps on the back porch," said Barbara.

We could hear the sirens coming now. "I think you should wait," my mother said, but my father went into the snow, his pipe in his mouth, sending streams of smoke around his face. We all watched him from the kitchen window.

He passed the Kinser parents, who were standing in the street watching for the fire trucks. They spoke to him briefly. The Kinser adults didn't like my father, who didn't go to church. The rest of my family didn't go to church either—my brother and I considered it a great gift our parents had given us, our Sunday mornings—but my father drank and was noisy about it. Bobby Kinser, Stevie Rabinowitz, and I argued religion. Bobby's family believed in God and Christ, Stevie's in God but not Christ; my family didn't believe in either one. Also, my father wouldn't go to the local barbershop, because they wouldn't take black customers. The barber was a friend of the Kinsers. My father went up the steps of the Kinser house and in through the front door.

The fire trucks arrived and began unrolling the hoses. My father did not come back. Flames were visible through the glass of the upstairs windows. A net curtain burned, browning and curling at the edges as if it were newspaper. The glass cracked and black smoke came out, thick as oatmeal. The firemen spoke to the Kinsers; there were gestures and shouting. The ladder went up. And then, finally, Tweed bolted into the front yard with my father behind her.

My father had burned his hand, but not badly. The firemen were very angry at him. "You're not just risking your own life," one of them shouted. "Someone has to go in after you. You have children. Did you think about them?"

My father hardly paused. He came through the kitchen with Tweed. Tweed checked for each of the Kinser children in turn. My father went to my mother. He was still smoking his pipe. She put his hand under the water faucet. "You're proud of me," my father said to her. "You might as well admit it."

"I shouldn't be," she said, holding onto his hand, smiling back at him. "Sometimes I just can't help myself," and suddenly, just like that, I was in love with fires and storms, thunder and wind. I can remember a lot of fires and storms in Indiana when I was growing up, but what I remember is that they were never big enough. No matter how much damage they did, I was never satisfied.

In the spring there was a green sky and a tornado watch. "A tornado sounds like a train," our teacher, Miss Radcliffe, told us. "But by the time you hear it, it's too late for you."

"Then how do you know it sounds like a train?" asked Stevie. When the tornado came it picked up a horse trailer and carried it seven miles, dumping it finally in Bryan's Park just six blocks from where I lived.

In the fall the Imperial Theater was struck by lightning and set afire. I'd seen *Ben Hur* there and *Old Yeller*. Stevie and I biked over. We were unlikely to get permission to go to a fire so we didn't ask. This was my first fire in the rain. The insides of the theater were gutted, but the outside was untouched. The police wouldn't let us get near enough to see anything.

In the fall Elm Heights held a Halloween carnival. I wore a red cape with a hood and carried a basket for treats. My brother bought me a cake I wanted with his very own money. There was a booth where you could win a goldfish

by throwing a ring over its bowl, and I won at this, too. Barbara Kinser organized all her brothers and her sister to spend their money at this booth. By the
end of the evening they'd won thirty-three goldfish, all of which boiled to
death in the winter when their house caught fire.

In the spring the nursery school where my mother taught held a picnic at
Converse Park. Converse was forty minutes out of town, heavily wooded and
big. It contained the Tulip Tree Trace, a twenty-two-mile hike my father took
me and my brother and the Kinser and Rabinowitz children on in the summer. We weren't very old, but we all made it, even Julia Rabinowitz, Stevie's
little sister. I remember my mother sitting on the hood of the car, waiting for
us, smiling and waving when she finally saw us all walking in.

My father didn't come to the nursery school picnic. He was fly-fishing on
the Wabash River. He was camping out. He was to be gone the whole weekend. Stevie came to the picnic so I'd have someone my own age to play with.

Stevie said if we walked down the trace, but not all the way down to the
sycamores, if we took a turn off to the right and went downhill again, there
was a cabin his father had shown him. We went looking for it. My father was
a botanist at the university and had been teaching me the names of trees and
wild plants. I walked and named things for Stevie.

It took us awhile to find it and then it wasn't really a cabin, just the remnant
of a cabin. The front door was gone, if there had ever been a front door. Weeds
grew up around the windows, blocking the light. Inside was ghastly, a webby,
musty place with one dim little room, a jumble of bad-smelling clothing on
the floor, plates and cups and silverware for four on the table. The plates were
of tin, the clothes old-fashioned. There was a black dress with a bustle.

"They left in the middle of dinner," Stevie told me. "Without packing or
anything. They left everything."

I thought there must have been something awful to make them leave like
that, something that really frightened them, but Stevie said no. It was gold. A
wagon train came by and told them there was gold in California, and they left
without even eating their dinner. The food got cold and spoiled and bugs ate
it and eventually it just dissolved away, leaving only the chicken bones on the
tin plates.

"The historical society keeps the cabin up," Stevie said, but it didn't look kept up to me. My mother's parents lived in California. My grandfather was a dentist and he put gold into people's teeth. Stevie didn't have any grandparents at all.

It started to rain. We had about twenty minutes back down the trace to the picnic. The rain was light at first, then so heavy it was hard to walk in it. Water streamed down the trace over our feet, up to our ankles.

The nursery school party was gathered by the picnic tables, which were sheltered and on a hill. I found my mother. She dried my face with a paper napkin, never really looking at me, looking instead down to the gravel parking lot where we'd left our cars. Water covered the lot, deep and deeper. While we watched, our cars began to move, only jostled at first, but then lifted. They floated away, fifty, sixty feet downhill and piled up on each other in a big metal dam.

The city sent a bus and some firemen to pick us up. They stretched a rope across the gravel lot and carried the children, including me and Stevie, across the water. The adults and my brother came next, holding on to the rope. My mother was worried about my father, out on the Wabash in his inflatable boat.

He didn't come home that night, but he did manage to call. My mother spoke to him and told my brother and me to go to the Rabinowitzes and tell them we were having dinner with them. Mrs. Rabinowitz made me a peanut butter sandwich, because she knew I didn't like fish. She talked to my mother on the phone and said my brother and I were to spend the night.

In the morning it was still raining. I went home before anyone else was up. My mother and father were in the living room. My mother was in her robe. She was crying. My father was drunk. "I love her more than I ever loved anyone," my father said in a strangled, slurred voice. "Nobody will believe it because nobody wants to believe it. They prefer it ugly."

"How can you say that?" my mother asked. She was holding his hand. "Tell me how you have the nerve to say that to me."

"I just can't help myself," my father answered. He saw me and his voice rose. "Go back to the Rabinowitzes. Do as you're told."

By the time I got back, I was crying hard. Mrs. Rabinowitz heard me. She came down from the bedroom and held me in her lap. Mr. Bush, the milkman, came to the door. He had just been to my house. He spoke to Mrs. Rabinowitz in a whisper while he handed her their milk. "Cynthia Marciti drowned," he told her.

"I know," Mrs. Rabinowitz said.

"Her parents thought she was at a slumber party. She was out on the Wabash."

"I know," Mrs. Rabinowitz said. Cynthia Marciti baby-sat for me occasionally. She was a student of my father's. My brother and I stayed with the Rabinowitzes for four more days.

On Friday, my mother came walking across the lawn, dressed in a black dress. "No one expects this of you," Mr. Rabinowitz told her. "You don't have to."

"She was eighteen years old," my mother said. "Do you think I could blame her for any of this?"

Stevie told me that my father paid for the gravestone. He said it was very big and had an angel on it. I didn't see how this could be possible. My father didn't believe in angels.

The Rabinowitzes drove my mother to the funeral. I hadn't seen my father in four days. When I tried to talk to my brother about the angel he told me to shut up. "I wish everybody would just leave me alone," he said, which was unnecessary because pretty much everybody was.

Stevie and I got out the Uncle Wiggily board. I couldn't read my first card, because of the tears in my eyes. "Read it to me," I said, handing it to Stevie.

"Uncle Wiggily says you are moving to California," Stevie said. "Go ahead three spaces."

I put the card in my pocket. At some point I must have used it as a bookmark, because seven years later I found it again, stuck in a book in my grandparents' house, in the bedroom my mother had slept in as a child, which was now my room. There were no seasons in California. In seven years I had had to learn to remember things differently.

I had been eleven years old the last time I saw Stevie. Now I was eighteen, the same age as Cynthia Marciti.

The card had Uncle Wiggily's picture on it, a rabbit gentleman farmer in a top hat, collar, and cuffs. "Uncle Wiggily says you will marry a man who is a lot like you are. You will have two children, a boy and a girl. You turn out very ordinary," it said. "Go back three spaces."

Ruin

MELISSA FRATERRIGO

N O ONE SEES HER SLIP out back wearing one of Daddy's shirts as a
nightgown. They think Luann's in bed even though there's much to
do. Pulls the wagon best she can, her doll, Tracey, inside it. Maneuvers around
a busted footstool, plastic milk crate, things spit from the sky three days past.
Tracey won't sit upright on purpose, doesn't want to be here, keeps toppling
over, air full of smoke, rot. Luann finds a bodiless Barbie face down in newspaper, yellow hair neon in fading light. Tries to hide it from Tracey but it's no
use. Tracey begins to shake, demands they return home. Luann picks her up,
looks deep into her fear-globed plastic eyes. It won't happen again, Luann tells
her. Tries to soothe her voice. Repeats what her daddy has said, that a storm
like this only happens once a lifetime.

Tree fell on the train crossing now the bell rings constant, three days since
it struck. Piles of boards, collapsed fence, uprooted trees. Has to bump bump,
stop the wagon. Dented cans of pineapple from Welmann's, a busted birdcage,
arm chair with its price tag still affixed. Nothing they could afford but now
it's theirs. All of it. Anything Luann wants is for the taking. Daylight has giv-
en way to that blue plumy color. Things underfoot snap and crackle. Tracey,
never fond of the dark, pleads for them to turn back. Aren't supposed to be

here, she is saying when Luann notices a furrow in the river grass, gouged up trees, cardboard heaped in a sudden clearing.

She sees a twisted hand. Thinks she hears a voice. Bends down, lifts the cardboard. That first look of him sucks her breath away. Grass stuffed mouth, blue-tinged face lifeless and still. Tracey buries her face in Luann's shoulder, howls.

Let's go back, Tracey pleads through her unmoving mouth. Be quiet, Luann says. And then the boy speaks. It's okay, he says, words coughed out like pebbles. Don't need to be afraid.

Leave him, Tracey says. There'll be trouble.

Hush now. Quiet. Luann repositions Tracey, pivots her legs on her hip. Give me think, Luann says, and knows these are her mama's words. Rubs her lips so they'll stop. Doesn't want to consider her now.

Help me, says the boy.

Tracey's the one who is confused. But he's dead, she says.

MOMENTS before it struck the cows grazed in pasture. Horses in the barn. Her daddy put halters on them and then opened their stalls, all the interior gates. Would have remained in the barn if Grandma had let him. Go on, Go! he yelled.

They huddled in the root cellar just off the basement and listened to it all roll down and hit. Screams pierced the ground, everything toppling. Luann's breath coming uneven, jittery. Beets jellied purple, shivering in their jars. Not quite fear inside but curiosity. Steady lowing of the cows, her dad's face stony. Hands breaking open and shut. Knew if it were up to him he'd lead as many of them as he could into the basement. But it's Grandma's house and Grandma's rules and no matter how often he spoke of them getting their own place again Luann knows now that will never happen.

It was not just the tops of houses but cars and trees, tractors, combines. Red Arrow Bridge snatched up, its pieces scattered like toothpicks on Route 26. Luann imagined the sky whirling with everything she could dream up; even after it stopped all that whupping rushed on. While her grandma cried Luann waited for the cellar roof to crash, bury them. Never saw her grandma cry. Now not sure she'll ever stop.

All day her daddy heaved loosened boards into a pile, started a great fire in the pasture. Mr. Sparkman and a few other men came over day after the tornado, tied bandanas over their mouths, dragged the cows and horses, the ones that didn't make it, into one fly-swarmed pile. Found one of the horses ten feet up in a sycamore. Took two of them more than half an hour to get it down. Her daddy steels his face. There is work to be done. Daddy adds more wood. There is plenty of it from the busted machine shed. Now the fire burns and snaps, black smoke rises. The stench bites her nostrils. She's supposed to stay away.

Stuff that's never had a smell stinks. Rots from the inside out. Her great-grandmother's Windsor chair, dresser from her daddy's room on the second floor is without drawers and backside up on the front yard. The mattress from her own bed is lodged in the window frame, bent like a hook. Walter Sparkman said they were lucky, said nearly twenty people died in Pruewood, where it first touched down. Ingleside was already flat, he said. Tornado just further that.

The people from church brought food, blankets. Daddy didn't want to take it but Grandma said they had no choice. Don't be stupid, she said, already wearing a donated Mickey Mouse sweatshirt despite the heat, unseasonable for spring. Luann stood there, listened to them, traced the kitchen table with two fingers. Someone gave them a tent and blankets and her grandma set it up in the living room, on top of the rug. Refused to go outside. Darkness puddled her eyes. Cried and cried, hands trembled her face. Said they are forsaken.

Crying won't help, Daddy said, We need to focus on rebuilding, cleaning up—

Grandma threw back her head, spoke the most words she's said in days— You're crazy, Teensy. Bulldoze the whole thing. If you don't, I will. Her grandma's been sad forever. Hates Ingleside despite being here so many years. Waited until Teensy went outside before speaking again, this time to Luann. What do you care? She said, jutting with her chin. Isn't your house. You don't like it go back to your own.

Luann's reflection deepened in the old woman's cataracts. She waved her hand manically, that old person smell wafting off her as she shuffled to a cabinet of broken dishes, began to wipe the inside door with a rag. Winter grass pushed flat. Corn stalks tilled to the ground. Rotting smell. Train crossing bell in the distance.

SHE doesn't favor either of them right now, which is why she and Tracey snuck out. Land chalked with things. A hairbrush, books from the public library, a boy's biked curled up like a potato chip. Desk miles from school. Everything suddenly spilled out on their land, handle on the wagon crooked but wheels moving just fine. It's like the whole world has been shaken and turned upside down. Smoke rises, burning stench masks air.

He's not right, Tracey says about the boy. Maybe he's even diseased. And Luann who has had things building in her for days says, Enough! Takes Tracey with both hands and sets her firm in the wagon. Get me out of here, she screams, pounding her feet.

I am the big person, Luann announces. You'll do what I say or I'll throw you away like all this other junk, gestures at the land.

Tracey quiets and Luann leaves her, lifts the boy from his cluttered grave. She cradles him like a baby, although he's not, he says; legs dangling over her arm, much heavier than he looks. She stumbles beneath his weight, clears the grass from his mouth and carries him to the river. Water beats white and restless, churns with torn branches and garbage; a lawn chair does cart wheels farther downstream. Cups water and lifts it to his lips. So cool. Go on, she says. Drink. His hair fritters in the breeze, smell of ruin; she combs the hair with her fingers, soft and fine as rain. Something scurries across her foot.

I need to get home, he says, and his words seem to tilt, slant sideways. She holds him steady, and while she does so he speaks. Tells her how the wind burst in the apartment, blew the door off the pantry where they crouched, snatched him from his mother's arms, that dizzy grey choking light ripped off his clothes and he saw a car lifted hundreds of feet in the air. Screams bore his bones, body battered by glass and heavy moving things. The pop of power lines caught his breath—slit of his rump cupped air—tasted damp wool and old milk, whimpered hot and cold all at once, heard screaming in the wind, everything swirling, growing thick, smothering his face. He threw up his arms, tried to find her, hit air and jagged things—bones buckling beneath, cardboard draping him, black pressed flat. Those screams, he says, were mine.

She feels his tears; only they live deep, deeper than the space on his face, the eyes that remain open, glazed. It's over now, Luann whispers. How rough he's been worked. She pets his hair real nice. Water rushes past. Tells him to cry all he wants, wobbles as she rocks him. Tracey in the wagon waving her fist in the air, pounding her feet on the hollow wood, yelling for Luann to pick her up right this minute, to take her home goddamnit! And then she says what Luann already knows: the boy has begun to smell unkind. Still, she swings him in her arms. Daubs his face clean with the hem of her daddy's shirt. Thinks of his mother ranting the loss. Wonders what that must be like. Knows it does her no good to think of her own mama, the one in the ground, so she considers the one who birthed her, the one she knows nothing about. If Luann missed her hard enough she wonders if she might return, claim her. Thinks of this as she rocks the boy. His loneliness, his stillness. Does anyone even know she's here? I'm not going anywhere, she promises. He cries and she holds him. Moon brightens up high. Smoke scrolls the distance, her daddy's work. And this, this holding on, hers.

Love and Mono

BRYAN FURUNESS

August 1989

I WAS CONVALESCING ON A cot under the red oak in our backyard when I asked for a story.

Mom seemed surprised by my request. "Really?" she said. "You sure, Revie?"

This was late in the summer before my ninth-grade year. There was a cool breeze that smelled like it had come through a mile of clean laundry and she had just returned from the house with a blanket to drape over my legs. I think we both knew a story might not be the best idea. If Dad had been around, I wouldn't have asked her. But he was gone, off at practice with his high school golf team, and I was laid up on a cot while mono beat my ass into the ground.

If you've never had mono, it might help to imagine all your blood replaced with forty-weight motor oil. Blinking wears you out. The simplest tasks become Herculean. Like eating: all that knife-cutting and fork-lifting, the endless chewing, it's exhausting just to think about, you don't know how anyone does it. In two horizontal weeks, I had lost enough weight to walk clean out of my shoes. Not that I was doing much walking. In fact, if there had been a magic cure-all pill on the back deck, I could not have summoned the energy to walk over and get it.

But there was an upside.

Take away the tedium, the bedsores, the crippling fatigue, and what's left was a kind of tranquility. There was no real pain to speak of. All my responsibilities had been lifted away and replaced with a small bell, always within reach. Mono was languor, *ennui,* malaise, it was how I always imagined being French. I took baths. I began to ask for sandwiches without crust. I was a child again.

I said, "How about something from Holyghost?"

WHEN I was younger, Mom made up Bible stories. She had the Lost Episodes of Jesus Christ. She had the Thirteenth Apostle, about Justus, the guy who lost the vote to replace Judas. But my favorite ones were about Holyghost, which she pronounced as one quick word, like Superman.

Holyghost had my sympathies. He was the original third wheel. He was always left out of the real action by the other two, followed by promises of next time, next time, don't worry, your time is coming, come on now, don't be like that, of course you're important to us, we didn't forget about you, I said you could get the next one, didn't I?

I imagined God and Jesus as overworked, stressed-out, while Holyghost sat by his phone, trying to look busy.

"Oh great," sighs Jesus. "Here comes another batch of Lord's Prayers. Haven't heard that one before. Delete, delete, delete. I wish they didn't take me so literally. When I told them that one, I just meant, like, this is one example."

God says, "Tell me about it."

Holyghost Lysols his phone quietly.

As a boy I imagined I was the only one in the world praying to Holyghost. I asked if he could read minds. I asked if he would tell me the day I would die. I said, "Holyghost, protect me."

I lay on my bedroom floor and listened for his voice in the distant wail of trains. I put my hand on an old alphabet puzzle and waited for Holyghost to move the pieces around like a ouija board. While Mom played records and Dad watched the television down in his workroom, I stared at the patterns the passing headlights made on my wall.

"IF your dad asks," Mom said, "we were talking about your future or something, got it?"

"I'll tell him we were having The Talk," I said. "That'll keep him from asking any questions."

Before she left us four years earlier, Mom loved stories, games, anything to do with imagination. A particular favorite was Charades, which sometimes ended in weeping. She transcribed made-for-tv movies for us to perform as dinner theater, reading the lines over half-frozen/half-broiling Hungryman platters. There were a thousand ways these games could fall apart, and near the end we saw all of them. She took things too far, she got stuck in character, she brandished dangerous props, and finally, when she was swallowed by her imagination, she fled to California for a life in the movies.

It had been four years when she came back that summer, but time alone couldn't account for how she appeared to have changed. Out were the cocktail parties and kaffeeclatches she used to stage with Dad and I; in were casseroles, culottes, *Reader's Digest*. Her hair, which used to look like Barbara Eden from *I Dream of Jeannie,* was now a little brown bowl. She used coupons at the grocery store, though she handed them to the checkout girl as though they were an incomprehensible pile of foreign currency, here, *you count it out and tell me what it's worth.*

She said, "Remember Juke? Al Djukic the sales guy?"

I started to nod, but I hesitated. I knew her characters like other kids remembered Pinocchio or the Big Bad Wolf. But in that moment I realized I was pulling Pandora's Box out of storage. Telling this story, there was a chance that all the madness would come rushing out on bat's wings.

But in the end, I had mono and I could get anything I wanted, so I nodded. I said, "I know Juke."

"SO Juke is working late, copying a proposal for the boss when the copier jams. It's a bad one, deep in the machine. He sticks his hand inside, deeper and deeper, searching for the mangled scrap of paper, until he's in up to his armpit. Just as he's about to pull out and reassess the situation, he feels something flutter against his fingertips, so he gives one big last shove. There's a groan of bending metal and something clamps onto his hand."

"Juke tries to wrench his hand free, but that sucker is *in* there. Like it's trapped in a steel mouth. He chuckles to keep himself from panicking, then makes a fist and rattles the whole machine, but it doesn't budge. He tries to make it small and sneak it out. He coaxes it, talking in a soft voice. He kicks the machine, but not too hard; he's in enough trouble at work without damaging the copier.

"With his free hand, Juke drags over a footstool and sits down to think. The copy room's hot as hell and he's sweating pretty good now. He remembers a guy in Ottawa who got himself into a similar situation with a vending machine, but he can't remember how the guy got out of it. Or if he did. Now that he thinks about it, the vending machine may have fallen over and crushed him. But getting crushed isn't what Juke's worried about. He's a little worried about his hand, and what'll happen if he has to go to the bathroom, but mostly he's worried about his job. His sales numbers are in the toilet. His boss provides him with constant updates on the thinness of his particular ice. 'Crack, crack,' he says, the a-hole. 'Danger, no swimming,' he says. If Juke's sitting here in the morning *sans* proposal with his hand plunged into a machine that costs more than his car, he's history. In a spasm of desperation, Juke looks up to the acoustical tile where there is a water stain that vaguely resembles the profile of Abraham Lincoln. He says, 'I could use a little help here, Lord. Or Abe. Whoever's available. A miracle would be nice, but I'll take a sign, whatever you got.' He sprinkles in some language that God likes. He says, 'Showest thine mercy upon mine hand, and upon mine job. Amen.' Then, feeling a little silly, he closes his eyes to give the miracle a chance to work.

"When he hears the fluorescent bulb flicker and buzz, he opens his eyes. He looks around, but nothing has changed. His hand, still stuck, is going numb. He moans a little," and here she moaned, an oddly comforting sound, "and leans up against the machine to rest. And that's when the copier starts up again."

I have a picture of my mom at a pool party from when I was two years old. She is in the center of the picture, a little blurred, her mouth a wide circle of lipstick, arms spread like a bird. People on both sides of the picture are bent in various poses of hilarity. My father is in the background with a smoky, amused look on his face. In her telling, she is giving a one-woman play of an episode of *The Love Boat*.

But this was not the reason she would bring out the picture, nor why I've hung onto it for so many years.

The picture was Mom's prop to tell the story of The Miracle. "You fell into the pool," she would tell me. "You drowned, Revie. Your father rescued you."

Tears would come down her face and she would embarrass me with terms like *resurrected* and *we almost lost you*.

In Dad's version, which he only told when I begged and begged, and then with clear discomfort, he said I awoke from a nap in a bin of towels and toddled over to plop into the shallow end of the pool. He said he didn't realize I had gone in until some woman screamed.

Here he would add: Sorry about that.

Everyone jumped into the pool at once, he said, it was impossible to say who picked me up from the bottom, where I was laying calmly, "eyes wide open, bubbles coming up in a stream. We slapped you on the back a few times and you kind of puked and started bawling."

Here he'd stop and look thoughtful for a second. It was his pattern to end a story with a re-cap or a moral or a reassurance. "So you were fine."

I still bring out this picture sometimes to hear their stories and to remember perfectly who my parents were when I was young.

They became different people the summer Mom came home. Dad was as strange and unrecognizable as her. Where he had always been distant, he became attentive to the point of suffocation. He skipped golf practice to be around her, essentially turning the high school team over to assistant coach Fredline, who was fine with ballwashing and disciplinary matters, but swung a club like a lumberjack. Every day Dad gave me a dollar to go down to Sherwood Pool so he could have her all to himself.

Then I got mono.

"JUKE feels a sudden crushing pain when the machine starts up and then he feels nothing. He jerks on his arm to see if anything's been severed, but it's still stuck. Copies begin dropping in his lap. Juke picks one up. It's a picture of his hand.

"Well, that is just perfect," Mom said. "Juke looks up at the sign that says NO PERSONAL COPYING and has to laugh. Just freaking perfect. The machine keeps dropping copies of his hand into his lap until Juke gets the sense that he's waving himself goodbye."

I snorted and turned to look at her. She was sitting on the ground, kneading the grass with her toes. I wondered what she would be doing if I didn't have mono, if I was off at the pool, or riding bikes, or shooting Roman candles at my friends. Probably continuing their second honeymoon, as Dad called it. I felt a squirm of pleasure at having her all to myself, even as I recognized this as the feeling of a child, a baby.

"By this point," she said, "his hand isn't looking so hot. The fingers are going every which way and it looks squished pretty good. *Great,* he says to the box of tax documents 1986. *Shit on me,* he says to the microwave rimmed with exploded raviolis. By now Juke is pretty sure he's going to come out of this room jobless and handless and probably responsible for the cost of a new copier. It's only a matter of time before he becomes a humiliating paragraph in newspapers around the world, the man who needed the Jaws of Life to rescue him from a Xerox machine.

"But then," she said, pausing until I rolled my head to the side to look at her, "miracle of miracles, he sees the copies of his hand taking on different shapes."

She held a finger up as a car came around the corner, both of us waiting to hear if it would pull into our driveway. If it was Dad, the story was over.

The car accelerated down the street with a whoosh. She lowered her finger.

"On one copy," she said, "he sees a thumbs-up. On the next one, it's the okay sign. Then he's giving himself the bird. Pretty soon he's laughing his weary ass off in there, it's so ridiculous, until he relaxes to the point where the hand falls right out of the machine. 'Oh!' he shouts. It's white as a dead guy's hand, it's swollen and floppy like a rubber glove filled with Jello, but he manages to complete the presentation with the other hand before dropping all his personal copies into the dumpster and driving himself to the emergency room, thanking God for automatic transmission."

She stopped there, like it was the end of the story, but I knew it wasn't. I knew she was teasing me, wanting me to ask what else happened. This was an old habit of hers. Someone would tell a joke, a story and she would listen eagerly and when it was finished she would say *And then what happened?*

The question was jarring to most people, but it never stopped her from asking. She wanted to know what was left out or held back. She believed there was always one more secret to tease out of a story, if you only asked.

ONE day that summer I was on my cot in the kitchen watching *What's Happening Now?* on the portable TV when Dad walked in dressed in a crisp white shirt.

"You look nice," I said accusingly, looking around for Mom.

"We're going out," he said brightly, opening the refrigerator for a jar of green olives. He popped two into his mouth and seemed to be dancing to a piece of music in his head until he looked at me. "Not for long, though," he said, his tone now sober, almost apologetic. "Just a little bit. For dinner. We'll bring you back something."

Mom came out in a dress and heels that clicked. She seemed to be having trouble clasping her necklace. Either that or she was going through contortions to avoid eye contact with me. Just a moment before, she had been out here doing crossword. I thought she had gone to the bathroom.

I sat up with great effort, more effort, to be honest, than necessary. "Oh, you don't have to," I said to Dad about his offer to bring something back. "I'll just make a sandwich. I can't taste much of anything, anyway. Heh heh."

Mom looked at me nervously, then turned toward Dad. "Can you help me with this, Tim?"

I went to the cupboard and pulled out the bread. I found the ham and mayo in the fridge, then laid my head on my arms on the counter and waited for her to notice.

I admit I did it to make her feel guilty. I admit I took full advantage. I admit I was greedy for her. But she played into it too. I think both of us were trying to make up for lost years. No wonder it didn't last.

She helped me back to my cot and made my sandwich before changing out of her dress. I heard Dad from the bedroom saying, "No, hey, it's all right. No problem here," but he sat around glowering in his good clothes all night.

"OKAY," I said finally, after we had grinned at each other a long moment. "I give. And then what happens?"

She acted reluctant, but her eyes were shining. She said, "Well . . ." and waited until I said *Mawwwwm*. Then she laughed and kicked her feet in the grass.

"So. The doctor's holding the x-rays up to the light and Juke's telling him the story, but the doctor stops him. He says, 'Look, son, I don't mean to call you a liar, but why don't you tell me what really happened?' And Juke's like, 'What do you mean?' The doctor says, 'Son, your hand is pulverized. Your bones are gravel. There's simply no way you could have made all those hand-signs.'"

She paused a beat to let it hit me.

I said, "You mean?"

"That's right," she said. "The hand of Holyghost. And the kicker? The next day, when Juke went into work and opened his drawer? He found a single copy of the hand, giving him the thumbs-up."

Now she smiled like it was over, a triumph of a story, everything revealed at the right moment. I had to smile back to keep from bursting.

A few weeks later, after I couldn't pretend any longer that I couldn't walk or make sandwiches without growing faint, she left. The last I saw of her, she was backing down the driveway in her brown station wagon, calling out the window how sorry she was for making such trouble, all she did was smear the pain around, while I stood on the porch believing that something was going to stop her in her tracks and make her come rushing back. I whispered, "Holyghost."

That story ended up doing more harm to me than to her.

She did stop, as it turned out. A line of cars came around the corner and held her up. She turned her head and lowered her visor, I guess so we wouldn't see her crying. A weak black line of mascara appeared on her cheek, I could tell that much. The falling sun illuminated the car and I could see her chin wasn't trembling like mine, it was set and fierce and beautiful in a way I had never noticed before. The cars kept coming and the moment stretched on until it seemed like time had slipped into neutral, the way it had when I lay under the oak and imagined this as a life, the cot, the mono, the attentive mother with no secrets left to shake out. It was a rare, expansive moment, one that is possible only in a summer of youth or infirmity, and even then, only until there's a break in traffic, and then it's gone.

Double On-Call

JOHN GREEN

God is weak and powerless in the world and that is precisely the way,
the only way in which he is with us to help us.
—Dietrich Bonhoeffer

THE CHAPLAIN IS JUST A boy, just a shock of unwashed hair and a pair of glasses and a poorly tied tie. He's been awake for a couple days.

If the door to the meditation room were not glass, then he would lie on the carpet and sleep. He would lie alongside the diagonal *qibla,* a yellow arrow dyed into the thick shag of the carpet, pointing towards Mecca. Mecca is mostly east, a tad South. He would lie in the direction of Mecca and leave the pagers outside somewhere and sleep. He gazes across the chapel at that glass door, praying fervently that the force of his stare will render it opaque.

But the door is glass, and besides, the chaplain has company.

The man across from him is all biceps, rippling as he clenches his fists, all clear tears dribbling down the clear skin of his face. He hunches forward in a chair, facing the chaplain. The chaplain's best attempts to correct his bad posture in pastoral situations are failing with the onslaught of fatigue. The man is whispering, praying.

The chaplain tries to remember what to do. He sees his supervisor, a Unitarian who believes deeply in absolutely everything. He sees her in the way people see apparitions, the way they see the faint reflection of the Virgin Mother in a parking lot pool of motor oil. The chaplain is well acquainted with visionary hallucinations. He has studied their importance, from peyote-induced spirit quests to Paul's vision on the road.

"She didn't fall," the man says. His name is Joseph, and his fists clench and unclench, his biceps undulating like pond water in an earthquake.

The chaplain lived the previous summer, the last summer of college, in Alaska with a girl. He had seen pond water ripple in an earthquake, as if a sudden gust of wind came from beneath the water's surface, and then the ground shook lightly beneath the A-frame gift shop where he worked alone. It was the chaplain's first earthquake, and he ran for a doorframe, but it was over before he got anywhere. A woman came into the gift shop a minute later, and the chaplain said, "Did you feel that earthquake?"

"Is that what it was?" the woman replied. "I thought it was something."

The baby, Joseph's daughter Z, had a fractured skull. It was fractured in three places, a triangle of fault lines that came together in the upper left part of her head, just behind the temple. The area of the triangle—that piece of skull was gone. When she came in, alone, ahead of her family, red-gray matter was visible, bulging from her skull. Her brain leaked out of her little head. It pulsed like a tiny heartbeat, like hummingbird wings. The chaplain thought, for some reason, that it might explode, that it might blow onto his powder blue chaplain jacket and that he would go home the next morning and hang up his jacket and crawl into his girlfriend's bed and she would say, "Is that blood?" and he would say, "No, it's *brain*." But it didn't happen like that. It never did.

"We're really fucked," Joseph says. "I mean, we are *really* fucked."

"You must be feeling pretty scared." That is his job, to name the feeling. Say what the person is feeling, validate it, and allow them to feel it.

Joseph begins to cry very hard, and the chaplain knows he has nailed it. Joseph is letting the grief in, acknowledging his fear with tears.

He killed his little girl. Two years old, with beautiful pale skin as clear and perfect as her nineteen-year-old daddy's. The women—mother and grandmother—had gone off to Church, and he had stayed home to look after the baby.

He was not much for Church, Joseph. Never made him feel any better.

The story comes out from Joseph in bits and pieces, staccato gunfire. He told the paramedics that she fell out of the high chair. He told the Mom that she fell out of the high chair. But everyone knew that she had not fallen. Clearly, he is fucked.

He cooked breakfast. An omelet with just cheese. And the baby would not stop crying, screaming for her Mommy. The baby never wanted anything but the mother. She had breast fed the baby for too long. She had never given Joseph enough time with the baby, and the baby didn't like him, didn't give a shit about him.

He picked the baby up. He sang to it. To *her*. He put the baby back in her high chair. Still, she cried. "Fine, Z," he said, "Fine. Just sit there and fuckin' cry. See if I give a shit." He left the room, watched TV, came back, held her, played horsey with her, bouncing her up and down in his immensely safe arms. She cried. He sat her down, and she wailed. Mommy. Mommy. Mommy. And so he picked up the frying pan—still hot—and he smacked her.

The cops come, as they always do. It takes them a bit, even after all this practice, to find the interfaith chapel on an administrative wing of the hospital's third floor.

"I don't want to interrupt," one of the two says, interrupting. "But we need him as soon as you're done. We'll be outside."

They stand a foot outside the chapel's door, effectively ending confidentiality. The chaplain whispers, "I don't suggest you talk to them without a lawyer."

There is a brief prayer. The prayer part is not the chaplain's specialty, and he only does it when asked, or when compelled by the drama of a situation. He is Episcopalian, and Episcopalians pray from the Book of Common Prayer. They do not extemporize. Still, he comes up with something. He says, "we" a lot, and "Joseph" a lot, as he's been taught to do. Make your presence felt, Lord. Bring comfort where there is fear. Bring hope where there is despair. Nothing new. He should offer to sit with Joseph for the questioning. He should give unqualified love and support to this suffering man.

But the poor chaplain is tired. He thinks that perhaps it would be nice to have a cigarette before anyone dies.

Baby Z has other family members in the hospital as well. There is a mother who stands to lose a daughter to brain trauma and a husband (three months they've been married) to a life sentence. A live-in grandmother, the baby's primary caretaker. Aunts. Great-Aunts. Cousins. All women, and all wearing large hats, having come to the hospital directly from a Saturday morning Church breakfast. Their vigil is now sixteen hours old. When the mother came in, the chaplain had to restrain her, because security was elsewhere and the woman was trying to get at the bed in the trauma room. He pulled her back to the doorway. The hospital believes it is important for parents to be present for all phases of a child's treatment, but not too present.

The mother asked, "Is she going to have to spend the night?"

And though he was not supposed to give medical information or advice of any sort, he said, "Yes," because he had seen the little girl's brain.

"Is she going to die?"

He copped out on that one. "I don't know."

BEFORE his cigarette, the chaplain drops by the PICU to check on the nurse caring for the baby.

"Hey," he says. She is Irma, married to a man who used to have erectile dysfunction something serious but now pops an effective, if expensive, blue pill twice a week. She recently had breast reduction surgery and you cannot imagine how painful it is, how long it takes to recover to the point where you can raise your arms over your head to hook an IV bag. She is very talkative, and his job is to listen, so he has learned a lot about Irma.

"How is she doing?" he asks.

"Z?"

"Yeah."

"Oh, you know. She may die before they do the brain function tomorrow."

"Mmm."

"Her heart rate is dropping. Drops like this—hmm—keeps dropping like this I'd say maybe 7:30?"

"Okay. And the brain function test tomorrow?" the chaplain asks.

"Yeah, in the morning. If she gets there."

"Right. Okay. Thanks, Irma."

"What time you get off?" she asks.

"Eight," the chaplain says.

"Hope she makes it for ya." Irma makes a thin lipped expression. A smile of some kind.

"Me too," the chaplain confesses.

"Long night?"

"No. Well. Yes. Yes, really. Yours?"

"Not so bad," Irma says. "Just this one. I have two others, but both very stable. So it's just this one. Get some sleep, kid. You look like you just saw a ghost."

"Call me if I can be helpful," he says.

"Sleep."

"Yes,m," he says.

He turns, so his back is to Irma when she says, "Oh. Hey. Happy Easter."

He swivels back toward her. "Oh, right. Yeah. Well, officially I guess, it is. Happy Easter."

He slams his fist against a blue button. The doors open, and he jogs down the hall, forgetting his cigarette break. There is no stopping him now. A minute later, he sits in a small room, the sleep room. The bed, sheets, and blanket are all hospital issue. The alarm is set for 7:42. Four hours. Eighteen minutes. He throws jacket, shoes, and pagers on the ground. He lies down over the sheets, so he will not have to remake the entire bed, and pulls the blanket over his head.

He is thinking that he should perhaps loosen his tie when he falls asleep.

There are two pagers. The trauma pager goes off when a child is coming to the hospital with serious injuries. The chaplain and the social worker take care of the families while paramedics, nurses, and doctors work to stabilize the patient. Down there, in the Emergency Department, the name of the game, for chaplains and neurosurgeons alike, is stabilization. The chaplain pager goes off when someone wants him specifically, for a baptism or a prayer or a death. All things being equal, he prefers the trauma pager, because it is more melodious, playing a song that sounds an awful lot like "Dixie." Also, the trauma pager is some sort of walkie talkie, so he gets information on the situation. The chaplain pager usually just has a phone or room number. Neither pager portends particularly good news. They never call him to have a look at a beautiful, healthy baby growing up in a deeply communicative and functional family with an abiding religious faith that sustains them in times of trial. One night out of seven, usually, he spends 24 hours in the hospital with the pagers. But this night is his second in a row. The dreaded double on-call.

It's beeping. *Well I wish I was in the land of cotton,* and he is awake. "Level two. Fourteen year old male. Nine minutes." 3:56. Asleep for half an hour and, if anything, more tired. Nine minutes. If he hurries, he can smoke that cigarette he's been meaning to bum, and he will smell like smoke, but they won't notice. They never notice. Jacket, pagers, shoes back on and a quick glance in the mirror to diagnose and treat a wicked case of bedhead. Down stairs, two at a time. I am still so young, he thinks. My knees are still so good. These knees can take anything.

"Doog!" Lynn cries out. The social worker. Lynn, the late 20s, pre-burnout social worker with hair in tiny tight dreadlocks. Lynn, who hates chaplains but likes him, because the chaplain himself hates chaplains. With Lynn, he acts as he does outside of the hospital, like a recent college graduate who sometimes has unprotected sex with his girlfriend, to whom he is neither married nor engaged. There is no pretense of ministry, of pastoral care.

"Hey, Lynn. Do you have a cigarette?"

"Of course. Doogie Howser, boy chaplain, smokes?"

"Tonight he does."

"Rough with the high chair kid?"

"Yeah."

"Chillin' with the Dad?"

"'Till the cops found us."

"Shame about how he's gonna die in jail," she says gleefully.

"So what's this Level II?"

"Oh, whatever. Humpty Dumpty had a great fall, losing consciousness only briefly. God, Doog, you look like a train wreck."

"I'm on a double."

"How's your girl?"

"She's good. Good. Her eyes are getting bluer. How's yours?"

"She's okay. She wants to move in. Bluer eyes?"

"Yeah. They're green. I mean, they've always been green. But they're start-ing to turn blue. Very strange. You want her to move in?"

"Dunno. I've never had a live-in ... whatever. Partner."

"Me neither."

"Either."

"Right. Yeah."

"Go to bed, Doogie. I'll get this one. The kid is fine. He's fourteen. He'll cuss when they put the catheter in and that'll be the extent of it."

"Sold! Call me if you want me."

The chaplain lets his cigarette fall to the concrete and steps on it to put it out. He steps on like he imagines James Dean doing it, although he has never personally seen a James Dean movie.

Back in the sleep room, he realizes why the pager went off. In his rush to bed, he had failed to take the necessary precautions. This time, instead of throwing his jacket and shoes and pagers willy-nilly around the room, he is careful.

The shoes go perpendicular to the bed, the left one on the right and the right one on the left. The jacket is folded into quarters, and laid on the small end table. The pagers, trauma on the left, chaplain on the right, are aligned par-allel to the alarm clock, about four inches behind it. The alarm is set to radio, not buzzer. This is the routine, and the routine needs to be followed.

The routine arose the one night that nothing happened. Twenty-four hours on call, and no child died, no child needed an emergency baptism, no one wanted prayer or healing. He woke up to the radio at 7:42 in the morning, with eighteen minutes to dress and fold the blanket. He looked around the room and memorized the precise location of everything. *A Grief Observed* on the nightstand, beneath the chaplain jacket, which was folded into quarters. The shoes, arranged backwards, halfway down the bed.

You are either religious, the chaplain likes to say, or you are superstitious.

It did not work, of course, because neither superstition nor religion works.

They are not *intended* to work. But it had worked once, and so the chaplain honored that night with his every on-call.

HE is not an Easter chaplain. He's more of an Ash Wednesday or Good Friday chaplain. For him, the only season is Lent and the only gospel Mark. And not the canonical version either, with its Hollywood ending tacked on a century after the gospel's first appearance. The oldest versions of Mark do not end with Jesus' triumphant ascension into heaven. The original gospel ends with three women running from an empty tomb, as scared as anyone would be who's just seen a ghost. The *real* good news according to Mark ends with the word "afraid."

The first gospel in chronology, Mark is an important source for both Luke and Matthew. And John, well John is no gospel at all to the chaplain's mind, because gospels bring good news, and John brings only Baptists.

For him, the last words of Jesus were not "it is finished," (John) or "Father, into your hands I commit my spirit," (Luke) but rather, *eloi eloi lama sabach-thani,* the only untranslated Aramic in the entire New Testament. For the chaplain, they are the only wholly true and accurate words of the historical Jesus. My Father. My Father. Why have you forsaken me?

HE is no Easter chaplain, and yet it is very nearly Easter morning. The chaplain mourns as he sleeps, grieving the loss of Lent. He wishes that every day might be Ash Wednesday, that he might walk for the rest of his days with an ashen thumbprint of a priest on his forehead. But as he sleeps, Easter approaches. Peter Cottontail hops down his bunny trail. There is no Easter Sunday service at the hospital. They tried one for a few years, but they were badly attended.

Seven forty-two, and he wakes to a sweet, soft voice of the American Midwest introducing some adult contemporary love song. The chaplain folds the blanket, smooths the sheets, and walks to the pastoral care conference room. He brews a pot of coffee, although he does not drink coffee. He waits.

Gary is coming. It is Easter Sunday and Gary will come and take the pagers and pour himself a cup of coffee, and Gary will be chaplain for a while.

The chaplain will go home and sleep. He will lie in bed with his girlfriend, a woman who loves him very much but may not love him for very long. He will wake up around noon, and perhaps watch television. He will read, maybe. Check his e-mail.

Gary comes at 8:04. Not bad, for Gary.

"The Lord is risen!" Gary greets the chaplain.

"There's a braindead girl in the PICU," the chaplain says.

"Sweet," Gary responds, sarcastic. He is much older than the chaplain, but tries to speak in the boy's vernacular. Gary is very concerned for the poor chaplain's soul. They sit down across a conference table from each other, the chaplain leaning on his elbows.

"Her father killed her."

"On purpose?"

"Is there another way?"

"Lord mercy."

"Yeah."

"Did you pray with him?"

"Yeah. I did."

"I don't think I could do it. With a murderer. I should, but I don't think I could wish him peace."

"I didn't have to." The chaplain slides the pagers across the table, feeling vaguely like he has stolen something, and wishes Gary a happy Easter. He walks down the stairs, not skipping any this time, and walks outside, shocked by the warmth of the day. He gets into his car, find a single stale cigarette, and lights it. He pays a machine three dollars for parking, turns the radio up loud, and begins his long drive home east, the risen sun too bright in his eyes.

Rings

LUCRECIA GUERRERO

IT IS A BALMY LATE afternoon in early October 2000, and you are in Manhattan to present a media arts lecture, "The Murals of Portsmouth, Ohio: Mystery and Tapestry." You are particularly fond of the artist's superimposition of the faces of present-day Portsmouth citizens on the bodies of historical figures. Someone once told you that *all* artists are obsessed with time. The rain has let up and, on impulse, you walk toward Casa Brasil, the restaurant where twenty-three years ago you caroused with friends, your last night out as a bachelor. You are two blocks away, standing at the corner of 53rd and 3rd, waiting for the crosswalk light to give you the go-ahead.

The concrete pulses through the soles of your shoes. The city inhales, exhales, blowing its halitosis of soft pretzels, lamb seasoned with oregano and garlic, hot dogs, sauerkraut, something sweet and fatty, and beneath the heady bouquet, an undertone of decay. But your thoughts are not on decay. The city is alive. You are alive. You are *you*. Not husband, not father, certainly not grandfather. Your only daughter—your little princess—recently gave birth to your first grandchild. Your best friend teased you and called you *grandpa*. You didn't realize you were scowling until he quirked his eyebrow. You explained: It isn't being a grandfather that bothers me, it's thinking of my daughter as a mother, that's what I can't get used to. He nodded but said nothing. He is your best friend.

The light changes and you enter the crosswalk. In the distance thunder rumbles. More rain tonight, probably. Your hotel room looks out on 45th and Broadway, and you will be able to watch the umbrella parade of theatergoers if you want. You are alone in New York. You can do as you wish.

My ring, a woman calls out from the curb across the street from you. Her hair is red, a jungle of curls. She stretches out a model-thin arm and points to the rivulet that runs along the gutter. Inches from the drain, a glimmer of gold catches your eye. You dash across, swoop up the ring, and offer it to her. She is young and her gaze is soft, yielding. Your fingertips graze her palm. There is a connection. You feel it; you see it in her eyes of velvet-blue.

Thank you, thank you, she says. And for some reason you both laugh, which makes you both laugh again. I'm Jennifer, she says.

You offer your name, your hand. When you pull away, her heat lingers. Is she always so warm? Jennifer is beautiful, a dream realized. You are a dragon, an eagle. No, you are a dancer of Samba. You are *you*. Your feet tap a tune, leave the ground, dance high, up into the tangle of her hair, catch in the ring-lets of fire, higher, higher, into the abstract and away from the concrete.

One of a kind, a keepsake, she says, and holds up the solitaire diamond in the old- fashioned setting. She glances at your left hand, the gold band grown tight with the ten pounds that have crept up on you over the years in spite of the jogging, the racquetball.

Her eyes quickly return to yours, linger.

Can I buy you a cup of coffee? Anything? she says. She is young, your daughter's age. My ring's irreplaceable, she says, my grandmother's, family, you know?

Your grandmother's, you repeat. Irreplaceable. You smile sadly. A cool breeze chills you, and you slip your hands into your pockets to warm them. Sorry, you say (and you are sorry). There's someplace I should be.

You don't look back even though you feel the blue gaze following you. The Casa Brasil isn't far now, you are thinking, just as you spot the pile of rubble. You pull the saved matchbook from your pocket, double-check the address printed beneath the half-moon of dippered stars. You stare at the rubble. You cannot see your memories in the broken pieces before you. As you walk away, you try to recall the happy beat of Samba in your step. In the distance the thunder rumbles.

The Secret of Cartwheels

PATRICIA HENLEY

THE WINE SAP TREES ALONG THE road were skeletal in the early evening light. I stared out the school bus window and cupped like a baby chick the news I looked forward to telling Mother: I'd decided on my confirmation name.

"What's nine times seven?" Jan Mary said.

"Sixty-three," I said. Joan. That was Mother's confirmation name, and I wanted it to be mine as well. She'd told me it was a name of strength, a name to carry you into battle.

"I tore my cords," Christopher said. He stood in the aisle, bracing himself with one hand on the chrome pole beside the driver, who wore a baseball cap and a big plaid mackinaw.

The bus driver sang, "Don't sit under the apple tree with anyone else but me." I knew we were nearing our stop, the end of the route, whenever the driver sang this song. We were the last ones on the bus. Although the heater was chuffing hard, frost in the shape of flames curled along the edges of the windows.

"Sweet dreams," the driver said, as we plodded down the slippery steps of the school bus.

Aunt Opal's pale green Cadillac was parked at an odd angle near the wood-shed. I knew something was wrong—she never drove out from Wenatchee to visit in the winter. I remembered what our mother had told me the night before. Before bedtime we all lined up to kiss her good night, and when my turn came, she'd said, "There are signs in life. Signs that tell you what you have to do. "Her voice had frightened me. I didn't want to hear what she had to say.

Jan Mary said, "Who's that?" Her knit gloves were soggy, her knees chapped above slipping down socks.

"Aunt Opal," Christopher said. His voice was dead and I knew he knew and understood.

Our breath came in blue blossoms in the cold, cutting air, and a light went on in the living room. I didn't want to go in, but I kept trudging through the snow.

Inside, everything was in its place, but our mother was gone, which made the house seem cold and empty. Four-year-old Suzanne stood on the heat register, her grubby chenille blanket a cape around her shoulders. Her hair had been recently brushed, and she wore plastic barrettes, a duck on one side, a bow on the other. When I remember those years at home, this is one of the things I focus on, how nothing ever matched, not sheets, not barrettes, not cups and saucers, not socks. And sometimes I think the sad and petty effort to have matching things has been one of the chief concerns of my adult life. Aunt Opal perched uneasily on a ladder-back chair with the baby, Laura Jean, on her lap. Laura Jean, eyes roving, held her own bottle of milk, and when she saw me, her look latched on to me and she stopped sucking and squirmed and kicked. Her plastic bottle clunked onto the floor. Aunt Opal's white wool pantsuit stretched tightly across her fat thighs. Her teased hair stood hard and swirled. Ill-at-ease, she shifted her weight gingerly as though she might get dirty. I thought I saw pity in her eyes, and I looked away. Christopher and Jan Mary hung back by the kitchen door, Christopher banging his metal lunch box softly against his leg.

"Where's our mother?" I said, scooping Laura Jean away from Aunt Opal.

"Now I hate to have to be the bearer of bad tidings," she began. "I know this will be hard on you children. I don't know what your mother was thinking of." She got up and stalked over to Suzanne, her spike heels dragging on the linoleum.

"Just tell me where she is." The baby stiffened in my arms. This was the first time I'd ever issued a command to a grown-up, and I felt both powerful and worried. Without our mother there, I was suddenly older.

Aunt Opal took a few seconds to adjust one of Suzanne's barrettes. "At the VA hospital," she said. "She's sick. Surely you must have known? She needs a rest. She's gone away and left you."

Christopher and Jan Mary went meek as old dogs into the living room and turned on the television. I snugged the baby into her high chair, wrapped a receiving blanket around her bare legs, and began peeling potatoes for supper. Suzanne sat in her miniature rocker, holding a Dr. Seuss book upside down and mouthing the words she knew by heart. I remember thinking if we could just have an ordinary supper, do our homework, fold the laundry, say our prayers, then it would be all right with mother away. We might feel as though she'd just gone through the orchard to visit a neighbor, and that she might return at any moment.

"You'll have places to go, of course," Aunt Opal said, lighting the gas under the stale morning coffee. The sulfurous smell of the match lingered.

"Places?"

"Christopher can stay with Grandma and Grandpa. Janice will take the baby."

"We'll stay here together," I said.

"Roxanne," she said, pouring coffee into a flowered teacup. "You can't stay here alone with all these children."

I remember feeling small and powerless then, and I saw that I still needed to be taken care of—in fact, wanted to be taken care of—but I did not think I would be. I had no trust in anyone, and when you are a child feeling this way, every day becomes a swim through white water with no life jacket. Many years went by before I allowed myself to wonder where my father was during this time.

"How long will we be gone?" I said.

"It's hard to say," Aunt Opal said, sighing. "It's really hard to say."

I was thirteen, Christopher twelve, and Jan Mary eight. We went to St. Martin's and rode the public school bus home, aware of our oddity—Christopher's salt-and-pepper cords instead of jeans, the scratchy scapulars against our chests, the memorization of saints' names and days and deeds. The week before our mother went away, I had stayed home from school twice, missing play auditions and report card day. She had written excuses on foolscap: Please excuse Roxanne from school yesterday. I needed her at home.

Our father worked in another state. The house was isolated, out in the country; our nearest neighbor lived a mile away. During the summer I loved where we lived—the ocean of apple blooms, the muted voices of the Spanish-speaking orchard workers, the wild berries, like deep black fleece along the railroad tracks. Winters were another story. We heated with wood, and the fine wood ash smudged our schoolbooks, our clothes and linens, our wrists and necks. The well was running dry, and we children shared our bath water. By my turn the water was tepid and gray. Our mother fed the fire, waking sometimes twice in the night to keep it going, and her hands and fingers were cracked, swollen. I wanted to cry whenever I looked at them. The loneliness was like a bad smell in the house. In the evening while the others, the younger ones, watched *I Love Lucy,* she sipped Jack Daniel's from a jelly glass and told me her secrets, plucking me from childhood's shore. Very late, when the others had gone to bed, she'd curse our father in a whisper. One night, when she had filled that jelly glass for the third time, and wanted company, she told me about her true love, a woman she'd known in the WACS during the war when they worked together in the motor pool in Dayton, Ohio. You can learn too much too soon about your mother's past. The weight of her concerns made me turn from her and wish that something would save us from the life we shared with her. I couldn't make the wish while watching her split and bleeding hands light a cigarette. But later, lying confused and rigid in the double bed I shared with cuddling Jan Mary and Suzanne, I wished that our mother would go away.

ALL of the moving took place at night. Aunt Opal drove Suzanne, Jan Mary, and me up the Entiat River to Entiat Home, a place local people called the orphans' home, but in truth the children there were not orphans but children whose parents could not care for them. The frozen river glittered in the moon-light. The fir trees rode in dark procession along the far bank. I sat in the front seat, a privilege of the oldest. The car was vast and luxurious and foreign. Most of the way, no one spoke.

Finally, from the cavernous backseat, Suzanne said, "Where's the baby?"

Don't ask, I thought, don't ask. I tried to send this silent message to Su-zanne, but she didn't get it. Blood beat in my head.

"Laura Jean might need us," she said.

"Laura will be fine. Fine, fine," Aunt Opal said. "She's with your cousin Janice, who has another baby for her to play with."

Her jolly voice made me feel as though someone was hugging me too hard, painfully. When we'd left Christopher at Grandma and Grandpa Swanson's I'd felt sick to my stomach, not because I would be separated from him—no—but because I wanted to stay there too. I wanted to cling to Grandma Swanson and say, Take me, keep me. But I was the oldest. I didn't cling and cry.

I would miss Christopher. We had fallen into the habit of sitting in the unfinished knotty-pine pantry, after our baths and the dishes were done, lis-tening to the high-school basketball games on the staticky radio. We knew the players' names and numbers .Together we had anticipated the mystery of going to high school.

Aunt Opal turned slowly into the uphill drive, which was lined with bil-lows of snow. The dark was my comfort—I didn't want to see everything at once. We parked in front of a red brick house with two wrought iron lamps beside the neatly shoveled steps. Silence leaped at us when Aunt Opal shut off the engine. The place seemed a last outpost before the black and convoluted mountains, the Cascades, which, I imagined, went slanted and ragged to the sea. Then quickly, nimbly, a man and woman came coatless down the steps and opened the car doors, greeting us as though we were their own children returning home. The woman was thin and wore pearls and a skirt and sweater. The man had hair as black as an eggplant. Their voices were cheerful, but they kept their hands to themselves, as though they knew we would not want to be touched by strangers.

One moment we were in the dark, the car, the winter mountain air; the next, all three of us were ushered into the blinding white room, which was like a hospital room, with white metal cupboards, white metal cots, and everything amazingly clean and shiny under the fluorescent lights, cleaner even than Grandma Swanson's house. We sat on the edge of one cot without speaking to one another. Snow dripped in dirty puddles from our saddle oxfords. The floor was black and white like a checkerboard. In the hallway, out of sight, Aunt Opal spoke with the man and woman—"well behaved," I heard her say—and then she departed with all the speed and indifference of a UPS driver. Through a tall window in the room I watched her headlights sweep across the cinnamon bark of a ponderosa pine. From someplace far away in the house came Christmas carols, wreathed in pure recorded voices. My body played tricks on me; my head hurt; my stomach knotted in an acid snarl.

Suzanne growled in a baby way she had when she was tired or angry. I pulled her onto my lap and she sucked her thumb. Consoling her was my only source of reassurance. Jan Mary stamped the dirty puddles with the toe of her shoe. "How will we get to school?" she said.

"We'll go to a different school."

"I don't want to."

"We don't always get to do what we want," I said, shocked at the way I parroted our mother.

The woman in the pearls came into the bright room and leaned over us, one arm around Jan Mary's back.

"I'm Mrs. Thompson," she said. Her words were stout with kindness, which seemed a warning to me, as though she could hurt me, and she smelled good, like flowery cologne. She's someone's perfect mother, I thought.

"You'll need baths before bedtime, girls," she said. She strode to the oak door across the room and opened it, then switched on the bathroom light. "You have your own pajamas?"

"Yes," I said, nodding in the direction of the cardboard Cream of Wheat carton, which held my clothes. Each of us had packed a carton with our best things.

"You can help your sisters bathe, Roxanne," she said. "Then I'll check your heads for lice."

"Our mother wouldn't allow that," I said.

"What did you say?"

"Our mother wouldn't allow us to have lice," I said. My voice seemed inordinately loud.

"It's just our policy," she said. "Now get moving. It's late."

We bedded down the first night in that same room, on the single cots made up with coarse cotton sheets and cream-colored wool blankets with a navy stripe around the edge. The light from the hallway bridged the high transom of the closed door, and I didn't sleep for a long time. Our presence there rebuked our mother, and I felt that humiliation as keenly as though I were she. I kept thinking, We'll be better when we go home—we'll work harder, knock down the cobwebs more often, check Jan Mary's homework, throw out the mismatched socks. Keeping domestic order was, inexplicably, bound up with being god-blessed. The fantasies that lulled me to sleep were of cupboards packed with thick folded towels, full cookie jars, an orderly abundance like perpetual fire against the night.

The next morning I lay there, warm but wet, with the covers up to my neck. Suzanne and Jan Mary were still asleep. A cat meowed urgently in the hallway. The windows were long and divided into panes of wavery old glass. Outside it was snowing; the dry, fine net of winter. There was an old cottonwood tree in the yard that had been struck by lightning some time ago.

The split in the main trunk had been girdled with an iron band; it had healed, and now the scar tissue bloomed over the edge of the metal ring. I wondered what time it was and what would happen next. The procedure of moving, being dropped off like a litter of kittens, had been bad enough, and now I had to admit I'd wet the bed. I dreaded telling someone, but wanted to get it over with.

I thought of Mary in *The Secret Garden* and the way her spite protected her. I remembered the places I'd read the book: on the school steps at recess in second grade, under the cooling arms of a juniper tree when I was eleven. My own spite and anger could not protect me. They were repulsive thoughts I couldn't bear to admit to myself, because then I'd have to admit them to the priest. I'd told him once that I'd wished our mother would go away. I'd wished it for my birthday, which seemed to magnify the sin. He did not understand the power of wishes, and for penance he gave me a mere five Hail Marys. And now our mother was gone and I tried to imagine her inside the VA Hospital, but I could only picture the rusted iron bars, the flaking pink stucco walls. It was down by the Columbia River. The summer I was ten, a male patient people called a crazy had deliberately walked into the river and drowned.

The door opened, Mrs. Thompson peeked in, and Jan Mary and Suzanne sat up in their cots, their choppy hair all askew, eyes puffy with sleep.

"Time to get up, ladies," Mrs. Thompson said. She wore a robe of some soft peach fabric.

"Snow," Suzanne announced.

I threw back the covers, and the cool air sliced through my wet pajamas and chilled me. I forced myself to slither across the floor.

"Mrs. Thompson," I said officiously, as though I spoke of someone else, "I've wet the bed."

"Oh?"

"What shall I do?"

She stepped into the room and closed the door. "Does this happen often?" She walked to my cot, with me close behind.

"Roxie wet the bed, Roxie wet the bed," Jan Mary sang.

I flung her a murderous glare, which silenced her at once. "Sometimes," I said vaguely. By this time I had no feelings in the matter. I'd killed them, the way you track down a mud dauber and squash him.

Mrs. Thompson quickly jerked the sheets from the bed and carried them into the bathroom, holding them at arm's length from her peachy robe.

"Please," I said. "Let me."

She dumped the sheets in the tub. "Run cold water on them. Add your pajamas. Rinse them good. Ask your sister to help you wring them out and then hang them over this shower curtain. When they dry, we'll put them in the dirty laundry." I felt I'd depleted whatever good will there'd been between us.

The entire six months at Entiat I followed this routine. I managed to keep from wetting the bed four times in that six months, by what miracle I could not tell. I tried prayers and wishes, not drinking after six in the evening. Nothing worked. I lived in the Little Girls' House, though my age was borderline—they could have assigned me to the Big Girls' House. And every day all the little girls knew what I'd done when they saw my slick and gelid sheets hanging like Halloween ghosts in the bathroom.

Mrs. Hayes, the dorm mother of the Little Girls' House, had two immense tomcats, Springer and Beau, whose claws had been removed. They lived like kings, always indoors. Everyone called the dorm mother Gabby Hayes behind her back. She was in her fifties and smelled of gardenias and cigarette smoke. Her lipstick was thick and cakey, the color of clay flower pots. She prided herself on her hair—it was coppery and resembled scrubbing pads we used in the kitchen. If someone broke the rules, she would announce to the group at large. "That's not allowed here." The chill in her voice always arrested the deviant.

Life in the Little Girls' House was orderly, neat, regulated. Before school in the morning we did our chores, young ones polishing the wooden stairs, older ones carting the laundry in duffle bags to the laundry building. Some were assigned kitchen duty, others bathrooms. Everyone, down to the four-year-olds, had work to do. I was impressed with the efficiency and equanimity with which work was accomplished. I wrote letters to our mother, in my experimental loopy left-hand slant, suggesting job charts on the refrigerator, new systems we could invent to relieve her of her crushing burden.

There were twenty-three of us, Jan Mary and Suzanne naturally gravitated toward others their age. They slept away from the oldest girls in a drafty long hall near Mrs. Hayes's apartment. Our family ties were frayed, and I was genuinely surprised when I met Jan Mary's musing blue eyes in recognition across the dinner table. She seemed to be saying How in the world did we arrive here?

The first day at the new school I was issued a faded blue cotton bloomer for PE. At St. Martin's, PE had meant softball on the playground. At the new school the locker room was my personal hell: the body smells, the safety-pinned bras, the stained slips, the hickeys, the pubic hair growing wild down our thighs. Sister Michael had always told us not to look at ourselves when we bathed, to be ashamed and vigilant. In the locker room we girls were elbow to elbow in the narrow aisle beside the dented pink lockers.

"What is your problem?"

"The F word. That's all he knows these days."

"My mother won't let me."

"Bud's getting a car for his birthday."

Their conversations shimmered around me like a beaded curtain. We couldn't help but see one another—our new breasts, our worn underwear—but the talk kept us on another plane, a place above the locker room, where we could pretend we weren't totally vulnerable, absolutely displayed.

Georgia Cowley, a squat freckled woman, ruled that class with a cruel hand. When I entered the gym for the first time, she waved sharply in my direction and I went over to her.

"Name?"

"Roxanne Miller."

"We're tumbling, Roxanne Miller," she said, writing something on her clipboard. "You ever tumbled?"

"No, ma'am." I looked at the girls casually turning cartwheels, blue blurs, on the hardwood floor. My hope of fading into the wrestling mats for the hour fluttered like a candle in a storm.

"Come out here with me," she said.

I followed her to the sweaty red mat in front of the stage.

"We start with forward rolls. Squat down."

I squatted, glancing desperately around to see if there was someone I could imitate. All motion had wound down, and the girls were gathered in gossip knots, chattering and watching me with slitted eyes. I remember staring at Miss Cowley's gym shoes; there were dried tomato seeds on the toes.

"Tuck your head. Now one foot forward, hands on the mat."

She gave me a little shove to propel me forward. I fell sideways, my pale thigh plopping fishlike on the floor. The girls giggled and hot tears swelled in my head. The seconds on the floor expanded, seemed to go on forever.

"Get up," she said. "Sit over there on the bleachers for a while and watch. You'll get the hang of it." Then she blew her chrome whistle, and the girls lined up to do their forward rolls.

On the bleachers, a Negro girl from Entiat, Nadine, slid next to me, sighing hard. "Got the curse," she said. "I'm sitting out."

"You can sit out?"

"Sure 'nough." She scratched her skinny calf. "You know the secret of cart-wheels, Roxanne?"

"No," I said; interested, thinking there might be some secret I could learn from her, some intellectual knowledge that I could translate into body knowl-edge.

"Catch yourself before you kill yourself," she whispered, as she retied her sneaker. "Catch yo-self." And then she leaped up and turned a few, flinging herself in to them with her own peculiar flick of her pink palms above her nappy head.

"Jefferson," Cowley barked. "Sit down and keep quiet."

For the rest of gym period, Nadine and I wrote messages on each other's backs, using our index fingers like pencils through the scratchy blue bloomer blouses.

At Christmas we were farmed out. I do not know how these decisions were made. Certainly I don't remember being asked where I would like to go for Christmas. Suzanne went with Mr. and Mrs. Thompson. Jan Mary was taken by Aunt Opal. I went to stay with the family of Darla Reamer, who had been our neighbor for five years. Darla was two years older than I was. When I'd been in fifth grade and Darla in seventh, we rode the school bus together and wrote love notes to one another using a special language we'd developed, lisp-ish baby talk in writing. Later that year she chose another girl as her best friend and left me miserable. Going to spend Christmas with her and her family, en-during their charity, was like an arduous school assignment I had to survive to attain the next grade. Her mother gave me a Shetland sweater and a jar of Pacquins hand cream. Her father took me out in the wind-crusted snowy field to see his apiary. We went to church, and those brief moments kneeling in the oak pew and at the altar, with its star-like poinsettias, were the only familiarity and peace I experienced. Darla spent many hours on the telephone with Julia, the one who'd taken my place. I was relieved when Mr. Reamer drove me back to Entiat on Christmas night. Many girls were still away and Mrs. Hayes let me stay up late. I drank hot chocolate alone in the dining room and wrote our mother a letter of false cheer and fantasy about the future.

IN the older girls' sleeping quarters, after lights out, under cover of dark, some girls took turns revealing fears, shames, wishes expressed as truth. When this talk began, their voices shifted from the usual shrill razzmatazz repartee about hairstyles, boys at school, and who'd been caught smoking. They spoke in church whispers.

"My mother tore my lip once. I have five stitches."

"My father's coming to get me on my birthday."

I didn't participate in this round-robin, but instead lay on my stomach, my pillow buckled under my chest, and watched the occasional gossamer thread of headlights on the river road.

It seemed there was so much freedom and purpose—a will at work—in night travel. Their talk was sad and low, and I, in my isolation, dreamed of going away, of having the power, the inestimable power, to say I'm leaving. Boys could somehow run away and make it, survive. But everyone knew that a girl's life was over if she ran away from home, or whatever had become home, whatever sheltered her from ruin.

Some nights, if we heard the rush of Mrs. Hayes's shower, we would sing in our thin voices a maudlin song that was popular at the time—"Teen Angel." One night the community of singing gave me courage, and after the song faded, I said, "I saw my mother hit my father with a belt."

As one they sucked in their breath. Then Nadine said, "No wonder your mama in the hospital, girl."

And the others laughed, a false, tentative snicker. I hated Nadine at that moment and felt heartbroken in my hate. I'd always tried to be nice to her, because our mother had said they were just like everyone else inside.

On Valentine's Day, we received a crumpled package wrapped in a brown grocery sack and tied with butcher twine. Inside was a cellophane bag of hard candy hearts stamped BE MINE and I LOVE YOU. Our mother had enclosed three penny valentines and on mine she wrote, "I'm home now with Laura Jean and Christopher. See you soon." She was home! I'd given up on mail from her, but I'd kept writing. I tried to imagine her there with Christopher and the baby, without me to help her, and the thought made me feel invisible, unnecessary in the world. Don't think about it, I said to myself, and I began then the habit of blocking my thoughts with that simple chant. Don't think about it.

IN April, we were allowed to go home for a weekend.

"Your neighbor's here," Mrs. Hayes whispered in my ear, early that Saturday morning. "Help your sisters dress. I'll give him a tour while he's waiting."

I had a great deal to be excited about: seeing Christopher, going to our old church, being with our mother. Our mother. Her life without me was a puzzle, with crucial pieces missing. I had high hopes about going home. Our mother was well; everyone—Mrs. Hayes, Mr. Reamer—said so.

We met him by his pickup truck. His khakis were spattered with pastel paint; he said he'd been painting his bee boxes. We fell into silence on the drive home. The thought surfaced, like the devil's tempting forefinger, that though we were only an hour's drive from our mother, we hadn't seen her since that morning in December when we went to school not knowing life would be irrevocably changed by the time we returned home. Did she know that morning that she wouldn't see us for four months?

Spring was alive down in the valley. The daffodil leaves were up along the driveway, though the flowers were still just pale shadows of memory, curled tightly and green. Mr. Reamer parked his pickup truck and sat hunched, arms folded across the steering wheel, waiting for us to get out.

We were all shy, bashful, and I hung back, urging Jan Mary and Suzanne forward with little pushes on their shoulder blades.

Jan Mary flinched and said meanly, "Don't push."

"Don't spoil it now," I said.

And we three walked forward in a solemn row down the gravel drive toward the house. We wore our next-best dresses. Mine was a taffeta plaid with a smocked bodice and a sash, and I'd worn my cream-colored knee highs, saving my one pair of nylons for Sunday morning. I hadn't wanted to go home in nylons—they were a new addition to my sock drawer and I was afraid our mother would say I was growing up too fast. The house looked the same, sagging at the roof corners, the gray paint blistering along the bottom of the door. It was a sunny day. Darla Reamer's cocker spaniel came yapping out the drive, flipping and bouncing the way cockers do. As we drew near the house, I saw that Darla was sitting with our mother in that small patch of grass in front of the house. Someone had put a wooden cable spool there for a table, and Darla and Mother sat near each other in lawn chairs. Darla was painting Mother's fingernails.

"Here come my girls," Mother said, waving her free hand.

Music was on inside the house and we could hear it through the open window: you made me love you. I didn't know what to do with Darla there. I'd imagined our mother embracing us, welcoming us, with significance. My heart shrank in disappointment, a rancid feeling, everything going sour at once. Suzanne, being only four, went right up to our mother and slipped her little arms around her neck and kissed her cheek. Jan Mary said, "Will you do mine, too, Darla?"

Laura Jean started crying from somewhere in the house. Mother, startled, rose partway from her chair and then sank back, waving her wet fingernails and looking helplessly at Darla. There was a raw, clean smell about the yard, like cornsilk when you go outside to shuck corn in the summer dusk. Darla looked older, in a straight linen skirt with a kick pleat in the back. She had on slim flats and tan-tinted nylons. Her hair was in a French roll.

"I'll get her," Darla said, and she went in the house, letting the screen door slam. Suzanne was close on her heels.

Mother pulled me near, her arm around my waist. "How's my big girl?" she asked. She'd had her black hair frizzed in a permanent wave and her nails were painted fire-engine red. With one hand she shook a Lucky from the pack on the table. A glass of whiskey and melting ice was on the ground beside her chair. Her knuckles looked pink, but the cuts and splits were healed.

"Fine," I said.

"Darla's been helping me,' she said.

I held my breath to keep from crying.

I felt exhausted, not the clean exhaustion of after-dark softball but a kind of weariness; I was worn out with the knowledge that life would be different, but not in the way I had imagined or hoped. I didn't want to forgive her for being the way she was, but you have to forgive your mother. She searched my eyes and tried to make some long-ago connection, sweet scrutiny, perhaps the way she'd looked at me when I was a new baby, her first baby. I looked away. Jan Mary gnawed delicately at her cuticles. Christopher came around the corner of the house swinging his Mickey Mantle bat, his leather mitt looped on his belt. The new spring leaves were so bright they hurt my eyes.

The Woman with No Skin/
The Woman Who Was a House

SARAH LAYDEN

THE WOMAN WITH NO SKIN

FAR AWAY OR UP CLOSE, she appeared just like anyone else, a young woman with pale arms and legs and a milk-face unblemished by a single freckle or pimple or blotch. Only when she turned a certain way did it become clear that what rested atop her muscle and bone was not skin, but a kind of permeable membrane that anything could pass through. She could not sit outside in spring, for the pollen would swirl in the air and attach itself to her very insides, moving in such a way that suggested her body was not even a barrier, that it was barely there at all.

Clothing helped, but sometimes the fibers lodged deep. And she did not want to completely cover herself. She wanted air. She wanted to let the world in. But the problem with the world was that it wanted to be let in all the way.

Her friend was a scientist and designed for her a special eco-friendly brown polymer suit. He had the garment specially fitted, yet it sagged at the waist and suggested the figure of a doughy gingerbread woman. She wore it to the mall. Teenagers with vulture-like scapula asked, "What's with the jumpsuit? Do you, like, drive a racecar?" For once their comments didn't travel directly through cardiac muscle, or wend their way around chutes of gray matter. The words stuck to the suit. The young woman felt cautious elation. She spent free evenings wandering the city in blank bliss. Within weeks, the polymer carried so much text it looked like a newspaper.

Curiously, she wanted to read her body, so she returned to the mall to stand before the three-way mirrors. She couldn't discern the crowded words stuck to the left shoulder, so she unzipped the suit, just a little, at the neck. Suddenly the flood of voices and words inched inside.

I adore you. Don't make this any harder. While your piece has obvious merit, it's simply not right for us. Please come in immediately to discuss your blood work. You're stunning. Cruelty-Free Chickens, $4.99/lb.! We regret to inform you that your brother...

But she didn't know who was speaking, she didn't know when the words had latched on. She grabbed the zipper, which stuck, so she yanked downward to loosen the teeth. Soon the brown polymer gaped open and she could see the membrane, the un-skin, pummeled by the accumulated gusher of words. An ocean in her ears, like listening to a conch shell attached to headphones with the volume on high. So loud she could hear nothing.

In the mirror she met her own eyes. The suit hung loosely around her waist, the zipper finally freed. Her body a bruise. She held the metal pull-tab lightly between two fingers. She silently asked her reflection a question, then watched and waited to see what she would do.

THE WOMAN WHO WAS A HOUSE

THERE WAS A WOMAN WHO was a house.

Not as big as. Was. A house. A vinyl-sided exterior coating her limbs, a sloped roof over her head. Her insides made of wood paneling, framed dusty pictures hanging on the wall of her chest cavity. Clinging to the back of her pelvis, a collection of Civil War-era spoons, family heirlooms.

A projector shone its light from her lungs, powered by her breath. The projector played home movies and vacation slides. Kodachrome past lives. A version of herself that she scarcely remembered, a clapboarded teenager ambling stiffly along the beach on a family vacation. Back in her cottage days. Now she stayed put, having grown into something closer to a Victorian.

Her attic brain stored forgotten things nobody wanted anymore. Wardrobes filled with her parents' mothballed clothes, decades of polyester and lamé. They'd taken the Civil War uniforms. Her little brother Abe's tricycle, unused for decades. Boxes upon boxes, black-markered "Memories" in her mother's scrawl, filled with photo albums, scrapbooks and postcards. All the old newspaper clippings about her, with screamy, bold headlines.

All the lives lived in this house. Her family, sheltered for free and saving on mortgage payments, now come and gone, migrating to the Caribbean without her. "You can't exactly move a house," they said. "Here. Have these spoons."

She'd seen houses moved before: power lines lowered as a loaded flatbed trailer inched down the pike. She imagined the warm-belly feeling of a family still inside, a fire in the fireplace and smoke snaking up the chimney, though of course that would be unsafe. The family would be driving behind the flatbed in a station wagon. The fire would have been extinguished the night before. Her own family had burned many fires in her fireplace, esophageal soot that still rose up, now bitter.

Probably you could move a house on a boat, down to a Caribbean island. Maybe. "But how would we pay for that?" the family asked. "Be reasonable."

"We could sell the spoons," the woman suggested.

"Those spoons have been in the family for years! You should display them in your house with pride!"

And so she did. They clinked when she shifted and settled, reminding her that she was not particularly interested in Civil War history. Her family planned the first underwater reenactments; Abe had gotten SCUBA certified. The island had no re-enactors, no connection to the Civil War, up until now. Which made the gifting of the spoons all the more poignant.

Home alone, she breathed and ran the projector. Her parents smiling beside the heavy artillery cannon, Mama in her petticoats and Papa in his blue uniform and cap. Abe as a baby, the tickle of him scooting across her wooden floorboards. She saw herself, growing taller each year, adding square footage alongside the flaming red maple. For years her house-proud parents had stepped outside to film her. Now she could only imagine the projector light pouring from her windows, which nobody filmed, nobody saw.

Shuhua's Suite

BRIAN LEUNG

I.

DON'T READ THIS FIRST PART.

Shhhh.

No one will know, and you might not get it anyway.

THEY *have not forgotten about the babies sliced in thirds, the disemboweled women, the Yangtze running thick with bodies and blood, prisoners buried waist deep and torn apart by attack dogs, men suspended by their tongues, heads of the living dowsed in gasoline and set on fire, women raped and raped again. No Chinese anywhere has forgotten.*

The men were toys. Thousands transported to the edge of the city and shot down with machine guns. Some were tied to poles and used for bayonet practice. Others buried alive. There were slaughter contests to see how many men Japanese soldiers could kill in one day. Heads of the decapitated were kicked like balls, lined up like prizes. Some say the men had it easy.

The women were trophies. Many were stripped of their clothes and forced to pose for pictures next to the soldiers who raped them. Some were strapped naked into chairs, their hands tied down, their legs spread wide and bound to the armrests. This happened all over the city. It happened to thousands. Consider the women gathered for military prostitution, those whose breasts were cut from their bodies for sport while they were still alive. Think of the woman lying outside, prone, her dress flapping up over her face, exposing her mutilated body, a Japanese sword plunged into her vagina and through to the ground. Think of women hiding in rooms. Think of any woman stepping onto the streets of Nanking after December 13, 1937.

II.

SHUHUA woke to the sound of gunfire and breaking glass. She sat upright on her floor-mat. The room was completely dark except for small flecks of yellow light showing through the covered windows. Now she heard explosions, still more gunfire, and the sound of men running and yelling—soldiers. Shuhua remembered her father's words not to look outside or make any unnecessary movements no matter what. She wondered if he'd returned but she could not see into the rest of the room and the noise outside was too loud to listen for his breathing.

It was still daylight when he left to see if he could find food. They were hiding in a small burned out building near Chungshan North Road because their own apartment was too close to where the Japanese were trying to break into the city. Shuhua squinted into the darkness again to see if her father had come back. "Papá?" she whispered, but there was no response. He had told her to rest and when she was sure she could not, he gave her a tablet of brown sugar laced with sedative and she fell asleep. Now, in the darkness, she didn't know if he had returned or not.

Shuhua reached her small hand into the blackness to see if she could touch her father but she felt nothing. "Papá," she said again, a little louder this time. She thought maybe he was keeping watch at the door. Despite his warnings not to move, Shuhua started slowly on her hands and knees toward the fragment of light that marked the entrance. Outside, the yelling continued and at every new explosion, the places where light got in flashed with pinpoint brightness. Shuhua froze in place nearly every time, trembling, then continuing tentatively through the sooty floor. She had stopped thinking about the charred dust and broken glass she crawled over. It was a fact of existence. After their first day of hiding, she and her father were almost completely blackened.

When Shuhua had almost reached the door she was sure her father was there, leaning against the wall, sleeping. She paused, thinking she did not want to wake him and make him mad that she had broken her promise not to move. He would tell her that she could not act like a frightened child. But she knew he would not stay upset for long. Just yesterday he had given her a small piece of foil-wrapped chocolate for her fifteenth birthday. They were sitting in the dimness of their hiding place when he took it from his pocket.

"Where did you get this?" she asked.

"I've kept it since we left home, Jong yú," he said, smiling, his teeth looking so white inside his blackened face. She liked it when he used this nickname, Goldfish.

Shuhua reached forward to wake her father. She touched the sleeve of his arm, which was strange to her because it felt like he was wearing wool. Where had he gotten such clothes? "Papá," she said, giving him a slight shake.

The figure jumped up, startled, pushing Shuhua backward. "Who's there," he said. Shuhua was silent. It was a strange voice, a young man's. "Who's there," he said again.

"Don't hurt me," Shuhua said.

"Are you alone?" the man whispered.

"Yes."

"Don't worry then, I'm just a soldier come to rest. I injured my arm."

Shuhua backed up, sliding slowly across the floor. "But shouldn't you still be fighting?"

"No," the soldier said. "We're in retreat. The army is trying to cross the Yangtze now." Shuhua heard the man walking slowly across the room toward her. The soldier's boots scoot across the floor, scraping over bits of wood and glass. Shuhua backed up as far against the wall as she could. "What are you doing?" she said.

"I just want to see you." Outside there was the largest explosion yet and the soldier flattened himself to the ground, sending dust and the smell of old fire into the air. The soldier coughed. "I don't think this is going to be a very safe place to hide," he said. "We should get out of here."

Shuhua thought the soldier sounded young, almost her age and she was less afraid. "I have to wait for my father," she said. "Besides, you are a soldier. Why are you hiding?"

The soldier sat up but did not move forward. She was sure he could not see her, but he talked in the direction of her voice. "I have family in Nanking," he said. "And the army is drowning in the river. They've been overloading barges all day and now everyone is just trying to save themselves."

"The Japanese will kill you if they find you."

"I'll steal some clothes." The soldier was quiet for a moment before speaking. "You should be more worried than me. I hear things about how they treat women."

Shuhua sat up on her knees. She'd heard stories too, but her father told her not to listen, the Japanese were not all bad people. They had bad leaders. "Papá will take care of me," she said.

"My arm needs attending. I have to go," the soldier said. "Can I see your face just once before I leave? Are you sure I can't take you somewhere safer?"

"I'm sure Papá will return soon," Shuhua said, but she was becoming frightened. She didn't want to ask this soldier why he thought this place was unsafe.

"My name is Ling," he said. "Maybe we'll meet again." He walked back to the door and when he opened it, dark yellow light flooded the room and over Shuhua in the very back, shining on her blackened skin. He offered a small bow and carefully made his exit.

Ling, Shuhua thought to herself. He seemed brave to her. He was staying in the city. She began writing the character in the dirty floor next to her even though she couldn't see it. As she finished, the sound of gunfire rose again outside. She wondered if her father was safe, if Ling was. What did the Japanese want with Nanking anyway? She felt a small pang in her stomach and realized she hadn't eaten or had a drink of water since the day before when her father gave her the chocolate. Maybe it was just too dangerous for him to return. It was better that he waited until things were safe.

Shuhua sat against the wall listening to the fall of Nanking. All night she heard the rumble of the war outside, great flashes of light shooting into the room, then leaving everything dark again. The air smelled smoky and sour from all the fire. Occasionally she heard someone run by and each time she was afraid the Japanese had finally overrun the city and they would burst into the room. She remained like this until she fell asleep, curled tightly into one corner of the room.

When Shuhua woke, it was morning. There was still little light, but she could see her father had not returned. Maybe he was hurt or captured. Maybe he had fallen and he was lying on the street somewhere in need of help. She stood up. Her knees were sore from being bent tightly to her body all night. Shuhua heard the rumbling sound of engines in the distance, but the morning was remarkably still. She walked to the door and opened it slightly. Debris lay everywhere, and far off there were plumes of black smoke. All Shuhua could think of was her father. She needed to find him. She didn't care how dangerous it was or what might happen to her. Besides, she thought, they would never hurt a girl as young as herself. Someday, she was sure, she and her father would look back and barely remember any of this.

Shuhua knew she should not take another step. For her father, she knew she must. It is just another room, she told herself, a room with an almost blue ceiling. She listened to the percussion of aftermath and named it music, a suite of rescue. Shuhua opened the door all the way and gathered her long, black hair out of her face, pulling it back behind her shoulders. With a confident breath, she stepped onto the street and out of her prologue.

III.

BUT you want a happy ending. Shuhua makes it to the United States. You need not read further.

THE man buys a latte. *Skim milk, please.* A small stack of books sits on the table next to a cranberry scone. The books are about China. The woman pulled her recommendations off the shelf for him because he is *fascinated by the history and culture.* That, and he likes black hair, Mao red, and the idea of dragons.

The Great Wall coffee table book is exquisite. *Such an ingenious people.* The women of Shanghai are lovely. *So modern.*

Sucking cranberry skin off a molar, he picks up the book with the orange spine. It falls open to black and white photos in the center. Jesus. The young Chinese woman is naked and strapped to a chair. The man reads . . . *raped* . . . *tortured* . . . before snapping the book shut. He tosses it behind him onto the table littered with pink rectangles of artificial sweetener.

Why would she fucking recommend that? The man returns to the women of Shanghai.

Shuhua is shelved.

Elvis Presley Visits His Red Harley

SEAN LOVELACE

ELEVEN MINUTES LATER I'M SITTING on the diving board waiting for somebody to come out and try to calm me down and Priscilla comes out of the house, walks a full circle around the pool and slaps me in the face.

I just sit there, confused.

She goes inside and I go into the garage and crank up my red Harley. People are always asking about my favorite kind of Harley, talking about pistons and cams and cylinder heads, and I always say, "The red ones."

I don't like when people try to misunderstand me. People used to call me Elvis the Pelvis. They like to talk about the Jungle Room. That's not me. They say I got angry when the Army cut my hair. I didn't. Hell, hair grows back.

I don't like being slapped and I sit in the garage, gunning the engine, filling it with smoke and noise and anger. The slap keeps hitting my face and I try to feel it, inside, our bodies reflected off the shimmering pool, her arm, hand, flying out, not the outside pain, the inside, the thoughts behind the actions, the motives, the blame, the sighs and glances and mumbled phone calls that lead to that—a slap.

I take the Harley down highway 78, past the cotton fields and the mud fields and the farmhouses and the shacks. The wind whips cold and the clouds take on a runoff edge, brown and silty, eddying, gathering. I shiver and curse and wish for my leathers.

One hundred miles I take the Harley, at one hundred ten miles per hour. Tupelo.

My father built the house with $180 of boards and nails he got on credit. Sure, it's a shack, but still standing tall and sound. Somebody poured a foundation, paved a drive, but really it just sat on top a jumble of rocks, to let the spring floods run beneath. We never had a curtain or a rug.

I stand a moment, filling my lungs, watching the house. Turning back to Memphis, I speed away even faster, taking pleasure in the juices flowing, asphalt purring by in a white-striped blur, escape in the best way, flying, strong and alone and in control, feeling myself, myself, what it's like to go full out, no fear, shooting through life with nothing but the thrill of the humming tires and the wind screaming and the heart inches away, bursting away, pulling up a dark drive, a muffled roar, silence, ticking engine, crickets in the azaleas by the pool.

Priscilla sits on the diving board, a slender leg dangling. Chlorine fills the air like a secret, and those crickets, a sawing. She's been waiting. She's hugging herself, gooseflesh; her skin looks like pebbled gold in the pool lights. I don't know what to say. I finger my key chain, a Harley Davidson eagle, rubies for eyes. It cost two thousand dollars. We were thrown out our Tupelo house; Dad couldn't make the payments on the loan. Priscilla gave me the red Harley; it's true. I finger the key chain and toss it into the pool, the deep end. It twists in the water. It sparkles as it falls. I don't know why. Lots of times I don't know why.

Contributor's Note

MICHAEL MARTONE

M ICHAEL MARTONE WAS BORN IN Fort Wayne, Indiana, and went to the public school there, attending North Side High School during the years they took to renovate the old building. The construction went on all four years of Martone's time in high school and the students worked around the workers who closed first one wing of rooms then the next, sending classes looking for a new space or reclaiming a room now rewired or freshly painted or floored with new terrazzo. The electricity for the master clock in the principal's office had been cut early, and all the clocks in the hallways and classrooms found their own separate times. Most stopped. Some sped up, swept ceaselessly, or stuttered in place as if it was now impossible to move to the next second or the next, sticking with each tick, mesmerizing Martone with a cruel montage of what was now becoming his lost and wasted youth. The period bells, the commencement and dismissal bells, had quit ringing months ago, and the space of time when the students changed classes marked in gritty silence. A rudimentary PA system had been jerry-rigged, tinny speakers and exposed wires, and each morning the Guidance Counselor squeaked that the official North Side time was whatever it was. Everyone set his or her watch, regulated for the rest of the day, shuffling through the debris and drop cloths in the work-light lit hallways. It was here Martone first studied chemistry in the 50-year-old laboratories on the 3rd floor east wing that would be the last to see repair. He still has his slide rule, Army surplus, in its leather case. The hairline cursor embedded in the sliding glass indicator, he realized, was a real hair. He learned to manipulate the contraption in the oversubscribed extra credit slide rule seminar after the regulation lab session. There, too, in the chemistry labs, he saw, for the first time, his teacher perform the Old Nassau clock reaction. He mixed the solutions in the big Pyrex beaker to first produce a pumpkin orange precipitate as a mercury compound settled out and then, after several seconds, the bright orange suddenly turned to a liquid lamp-black as the excess iodine left-over transmuted to starch and turned on its color, a black black curtain dropping instantly. The demonstration was meant to astound with its alchemy, and Martone was astounded, asking to see again the chemical logic of it, how benign soluble concoctions created a product that became a new reactant that then was ready to react. He liked both the anticipation and the rapidity of the transformations, the visual demonstration of whole moles being stewed in their own molecular juices, the quick switch and then its double-cross. It was called a "clock" because of the predictable ticking of the bonding and unbonding that timed-out perfectly, a collection of ionic seconds spinning on their own internal clocks. This led to this and that to this. The equal sign is replaced by arrows in a chemical reaction, one thing after the other. Years later, when he was a senior in organic chemistry, Martone asked the teacher if he could, in his spare time, work on constructing a new clock reaction that would, this time, express itself in North Side High School's colors, red and white, not out of any school spirit but mainly out of an urge to tinker with the watch-works of cooked-up nuclei and electron shells. After all, the class he was taking spent its time knitting together long compounded chains of carbons and hydrogens and oxygens, matrices of esters and ethers, another kind of ticking, the proteins twisted into the worsted zipper of a gene undergoing mitosis, another two-step through time. In that lab, too, he set a girl's hair on fire with the Bunsen burner, the flame eating up the long straight strands of her long brown hair like a fuse, another illustration of time. The burned hair, turning to ash, flaked, crumbs of a rubber eraser, spilling to the floor as the stink of it, the hair burning, rose in almost visible solid cartoon waves of wavy stench, the glow of the actual burning peeling now in the nape of her neck, the instant chemical reaction of it, giving off its own unique rainbow of bright colors. They had been performing primitive, spectral analysis, igniting unknown compounds held in little wire loops over the lip of flame, reading the combustion's signature through the slit of a cheap prism tube. The tip of her hair sparked as Martone tipped the burner toward, what turned out to be, a sulfuric something or other. Martone damped down the crawling flicker with his hand, his fingers flouncing the hairs that wove themselves into a now ratted cap, a nest, and for a moment it seemed that the whole canopy would ignite, enriched by the addition of fresh air. Martone was left holding this halo of fire, a hat from hell, a melodrama of oxidation, when, just then, the teacher pulled them both in to the emergency shower where they were doused and, just as suddenly, engulfed in wet smoke and sodden hairy ash. Martone never did find the combination of compounds to create the clock reaction in his school colors. He remembers poring through old manuals his teacher gave him with pages of tables listing reactants and products and their shades of colors, valences and radicals, ions and elements, metals and base. He wandered through the old laboratory's closets looking for odd specimens in ancient glass bottles stopped up with moldy cork or decaying rubber stoppers, the forgotten chemicals undergoing their own unsupervised and unrecorded experiments, reactions oxidizing into clumps of rusty rust, bleached stains, inert crystalline sweating salts, the paper labels foxing, the beakers mired in viscous goo, and the wood racks gnawed at by some now long gone acidic lick. Helping to clean out the closets in anticipation of the renovation, Martone garnered extra credit to offset the disappointment and possible average grade for his disappointing independent study. In the mess he found the apparatus used through the years to create the famous Old Nassau clock reactions for succeeding classes—the tinctures of iodine, the compounds of starch, the granules of potassium, and the etched graduated cylinders set to deliver the proper quantities of chemical ingredients for the demonstration of time all that time ago. Years later, Martone is on the phone to his classmate from those years whose hair he set on fire during an experiment meant to identify certain chemicals by the spectrum of light they emit when set on fire. Martone has taken to looking through his past lives, has found many of his former classmates by employing the emerging electronic technologies on line. He lives now far away from Fort Wayne, in Alabama, and finds it difficult to return home for the sporadic reunions, and when he does, others from back then now live even farther away or seem to have disappeared altogether. He thinks of it as a reconstitution, as hydration, this telephoning, and admits that his efforts redoubled after the collapse of the towers in 2001. That collapse seemed to be a kind of boundary, a membrane, a demarcation as narrow and fine as the hair fused in glass on his slide rule, of before and after. He found her, the woman whose hair he set on fire in his high school chemistry lab, living in New York teaching organic chemistry, of all things, at Columbia University there. The irony was not lost on them. She explained to him that she now was attempting to isolate low-molecular-weight chromium-binding substance in human urine. It had something to do with diabetes and insulin and iron in the blood. It was late at night and they had been talking on the phone for a while about the past and chemistry and what they had both been doing separately at the same time during all those years when suddenly Martone heard band music. It was past midnight. The music, even diminished by the telephone, was distinctively brassy and rhythmic, shrill and thumping. Martone identified it as "The Horse," a favorite of their own high school's pep band years before. "Oh that," she said. "It's Columbia's marching band. A tradition. They spontaneously appear on the night before the orgo final and march around the Upper West Side." No one will believe this, Martone thinks. After all these years, no one will believe such coincidences of time and space. He learned long ago in the sciences classes of his high school that there were these things called constants. Gravity was one. The speed of light, he remembered. And time—time was constant too.

Jubilee

SUSAN NEVILLE

Nothing matters, and what if it did.
—John Mellencamp

WE SPENT THE SUMMER LOOKING for John Cougar.

I don't know what I'd do if I saw John Cougar, I say to Jack. I think I'd die.

We'll see him, Jack says to me, by the end of the summer. We'll make it a hobby to search. Why not? John Cougar moved back here from some place glitzy. We listen to his songs to see how we're doing, like doctors with a stethoscope listening to our own hearts.

John Cougar wants to see us, he says, as much as we want to see him.

Jack unwraps the new tape exactly like a pack of cigarettes. He puts it into the deck. They say you can see him sometimes in the drugstore. We drive by. There's one old pharmacist, no John Cougar.

Oh, I can think of John Cougar and glide. His hair as brown as maples. His voice a night-time field of dry beans, husk on husk.

We drive around two hours with the windows open, listening to John Cougar's voice, hoping to see him on the back roads.

We tell each other second-hand stories about his house. A family farm, with rooms added on. A studio in the barn. I read in a magazine that there's a room for watching movies, a full-size screen. I imagine him singing as he climbs over fences. I see it in slow motion, like a cowboy movie. He has this sort of sad look like he knows things and has come home. It makes me feel good to know I never left.

Now and then we think we see him, and we speed up. But it's never him.

Will you always love me? I ask Jack.

There are some questions you can't answer, he says, and shouldn't try.

Like how we could live ten miles away from someone like John Cougar and be the only people in town who haven't seen him.

At any moment we might see him, I say, riding his bike on the road, hear his real voice, his knock at the door, asking to borrow a cup of something, like any neighbor.

IT was a strange year. It was like all your life you'd counted on things and then you couldn't. In the spring there was this plague of locusts. They coated the tree branches. There was this ringing sound all day like bells, it wasn't pleasant. Sometimes they'd all rise and then squeal down like bombs on old movies. They left their dried shells on the ground, and when you walked outside they flew in your face.

Then there was the ice storm. It was beautiful, every bit like diamonds. But all the wires snapped and even some of the old oak trees were uprooted. And that April snow where the flakes were so thick they looked like slices of Colonial.

Two of my friends had miscarriages when the corn tassled.

And then the summer, no rain for three months. It made you want to stop thinking. It made you want to look for John Cougar. We spent the summer looking for John Cougar, and we would have headed on right through the fall.

But in August, there's this sale on cars, in town where the buildings are falling in. The dealer was moving to the strip by the highway. So he puts up flags and colored lights like a garage sale. Someone sets up a corn dog trailer, polish sausage with peppers, and lemonade. It was the last business to leave from that block. Everyone else had left, a couple of bars moved in, but they strike like a match and just as soon fade.

For a few weeks there's this festival feeling. In the center of the lot was a tent with white lights beading the edge. Underneath it was a new white car. They were going to have this contest. The contest was why we stopped looking for John Cougar. Jack stands outside the tent, his eyes filled with that car.

It's one of those nights I look at him and I know how young we are. He's tall, but his body is a boy's. I want to touch him, but he won't have it, not here. He moves away from the tent and sits on a stack of tires, waiting with his friends. They put on these James Dean faces. The strip of grass on the road is dry and white. Jack spent the last week waxing our old car so he can sell it when the new one comes. He has faith.

The dealer motions to the boys on the tire. He picks up a big bullhorn and announces that it's time for the New Car Jubilee. Thirty or so men come forward, a few women. They all lay their hands on the car like something holy. A few of the men who weren't as fast are kneeling on the ground, their hands on a hubcap or a fender. The dealer takes all their names. They'll keep their hands on the car for days. If they lift them off at any time but the scheduled breaks, they're out of the contest. The last one holding on will win. The white car, it glistens on their faces.

Jack's wedged in sideways but has a good spot in the center. He can lean on the roof without bending. He's pressed his body tight against the car so no one can get underneath and make him lose his balance. He looks at me and smiles. This is it, the look says, our life is starting. Watch out John Cougar. Last year the winner stuck it out for three weeks. He's cleared it with his boss. They say they'll hold his job until the day he sails into the parking lot in that big white car.

The wives and girlfriends stand outside the circle of the tent. We're ready with pillows and thermos jugs of coffee, home baked pies and sandwiches. During the breaks, some of the wives are as smooth and well-trained as pit crews.

He's brought a lawn chair for me and set it up where I can watch him. The night is close. The plastic webbing sticks to my skin.

Several men drop out, laughing, within the first hour. They make jokes about why they're leaving. They laugh too loud, wish the others well. The bars across the street are filled with yellow light. Hours pass and after each break there are fewer bodies touching the car, someone lying stretched out on a sleeping bag saying Oh God I can't do it, this feels so good.

I stay through the night. I talk to him and wipe his face with cool water. He tells me to go home during the hot part of the afternoons. I leave him with a thermos of shaved ice. My dreams are busy, full of lakes and water.

After the first day, only the committed are left. There are eleven of them. We went to high school with several. There are a few older than us, not many. For most of them, this is the only way they'll ever have a new car. That's probably true for us, though my husband is convinced he would someday have the money.

One of the men ran for mayor in the last election. Like that, this is something to do with his time. He talks to everyone now, has that politician's smile. He acts like he knows things. He has five children. His wife lives in a van, driving them to lessons. He wears a regular cloth shirt with a button-down collar. Everyone else wears t-shirts. When the talk turns to the weather, he smiles. Oh yes, he says, it's the end, it's all over. Everything's ruined. But me and my husband, we're just starting, I say. He waves his hand, no matter.

The other men laugh and say come on, if that were true, we'd see it on television.

Twice a day his wife drives by and brings him food. He waves to his children through the van windows before they drive off.

NO one thinks the contest will last as long as last year's because of the heat. But days pass. Some nights it's quiet on the lot, some rowdy. When the nights are cooler, and on the weekend, it seems like everyone in town shows up. I get tired from all the talk. In the middle of the night men stumble out of the bars and have slurred conversations with those holding onto the car. Their voices begin to slur as well. They start to look pale, like this is something they wish they hadn't started. One night the politician passes out, and an ambulance is called to take him home.

I read in the paper that John Cougar is giving a concert at the fair, in the city, an hour away. The day of the concert I go to the grocery in the afternoon. I make a special dinner and pack it in an old basket I find in the garage. I line the basket with a soft blue cloth and put another cloth over it like a pie. I spend a lot of time on it, making it right.

The lot is quiet when I go there at night. There are only six men left. They all look drowsy, leaning on pillows. None of them are talking. They've told their life stories, every joke they've ever heard. One man sits on the ground, his arms wrapped around the fender. I put my hand on my husband's arm. He jumps when I touch him. His eyes look glossy. His face is flushed, his white shirt wet and transparent as a boiled onion.

He tells me this crazy dream he had, about all our bodies breaking apart into glitter like *Star Trek,* our spirits turning into rainbows and shooting into the sky. I put my hand on his forehead. It feels clammy. Don't you see, he says, we're snared in a difficult time.

One of the wives looks over at me from where she's been giving her husband water. He's hallucinating, she says, delirious. It's been happening to all of them.

It's all energy, Jack says, nothing is real.

It's the old Endtimes thing, another woman says. They should call this whole thing off, give them all a car to drive around in for a couple of weeks. It's too hot for this.

Jack is looking at me like he thinks I'll fly apart. Shh, I say. I start humming.

You're hungry, I tell him. I give him food. I give him chicken, a chunk of cheese, a glass of cold sugared tea. I feed him cherry cake and chocolate cookies. I buy him popcorn from the stand. Nothing fills him up.

At eight o'clock the sky turns milky hazy blue, the sun red and close. The lights come on in the lot. The stars are hidden behind a haze.

I look around. Everything seems shabby. The concrete is cracked and laced with spikey weeds, windows covered with grime. A brick wall that used to be one side of a furniture store has fallen in and no one bothered to fix it. The sidewalk in front of the store is embedded with purple quartz. Most of the pieces are missing. No one walks over it now without trying to kick another one loose. The air smells like burned grease.

An hour before the concert, there's a breeze. The bar across the street opens its doors to let in the air. They're playing one of John Cougar's songs, distant and tinny. The men around the car try to sing along.

We hear this roaring. Dust rises in the street. I see a tired face in the window of the bar. God damn, someone shouts, it's sure enough him.

John Cougar! John Cougar! we all yell, just like that. We run out to the street and cheer.

Forty thousand waiting to hear him sing, the Midway lit up like popsicles. Part of me wants to race him to the city, demand he look at me, and tell me what he knows. Part of me sinks close to the earth's spin, still believing he'll see me in his own good time.

We head on back to the car lot. The six men are holding onto the car for dear life. Tell us about it, one of them says, tell us what you saw.

A History of the Ghosts of Judy, Tennessee

MICHAEL POORE

VONDA STEWART STANDS BETWEEN RAILROAD tracks, and says a secret word three times.

Her fourteen-year-old body quivers in the November chill. She stares down the tracks, east into twilight, waiting. When nothing happens, she stomps off into the woods to smoke a half-smoked cigarette snatched from her mother's ashtray.

After a while, she is joined by her friends, Ashley and Jill. Ashley and Jill have taken the long way around, crossing the tracks behind the Starvin' Marvin because they're afraid to go near the underpass. Vonda is the only kid in Judy, Tennessee, who crosses there, because the underpass is where Odie Clark got killed. If you cross there and say the secret word three times, you can see him, a headless mist in the dark.

Ashley and Jill bring hot dogs from the Starvin' Marvin. The three of them share the half-smoked cigarette before they eat. In their bellies, supper is transformed.

The hot dogs, Ashley says, will give them strength.

The onion rings, says Jill, will become magical powers.

Vonda says the ketchup, red like a heart, will be the perfection of love.

When Vonda Stewart thinks about Odie Clark's ghost, she gets the shivers a little, but not as much as when she thinks of Odie alive.

In fifth grade, Vonda remembers, Odie Clark was this smelly kid with a huge band-aid over one eye. The band-aid was meant to force the other eye to work harder, grow stronger. If you walked up on Odie's left, or if a kickball bounced up on that side, Odie would cock his head around like a chicken, so that he seemed always to stagger sideways through the halls of Hoke Jackson Elementary School.

His stock was further lowered by a tendency to fall asleep. He'd fall asleep in the middle of Spelling, in the middle of kickball, in the middle of peering around to see if anyone was sneaking up on him.

Sometimes, back in fifth grade, Vonda and Ashley and Jill used to have a great time going to the library to look up all the things that were wrong with Odie Clark, and then teasing him with fancy words.

"Narcolepsy!" they'd shout, running up on his left side, at recess. "Narcolepsy Boy!"

And Odie's head would peck around like a chicken, and his wandering eye would do space-loops in its socket.

Odie Clark's eyes are one reason Ashley and Jill won't cross the railroad tracks by the underpass. They could stand to see a ghost, they say, but a ghost with a lazy eye was more chilling, somehow. If the ghost of Odie Clark walked up to you and pulled away the giant band-aid over his good eye, what would you see?

"Something deeper than deep," whisper Ashley and Jill, and they go around the long way, drawing crosses in the air.

JUDY, Tennessee has other ghosts, too.

Zion Calder, who according to Ashley is the ghost who haunts Judy's drinking water, is the oldest.

Back in the Depression, says Ashley, Calder was the most stubborn man who ever lived. He lost an eye in a sawmill accident, but wouldn't admit it. He stuffed the socket with a cottonball and went around for the rest of his life that way, one eye normal, the other a flash of bad lightning. When Renfro County exercised its right to build a road across his property, Calder simply refused to believe in the road. For years, if you drove out that way, you slowed to a crawl because you might find Calder drinking coffee in the middle of the road that wasn't there.

"It wasn't the sawmill or the road that made Calder a ghost, though," says Ashley. "It was water. When they built the Little Turkeyfoot Dam, he didn't believe in that, either."

AROUND Thanksgiving of that fifth grade year, Odie Clark did something which launched him from outcast to cult status in the space of a single afternoon.

Right in the middle of arithmetic class, he screamed a terrible and forbidden word at the top of his lungs.

During the pandemonium that followed, he fell fast asleep.

For a week, Odie's desk was empty.

"Tourette's," announced Jill, conferring with Vonda and Ashley at the library. "He can't help it."

When Odie returned, he still cocked his head around like a chicken. He still smelled. Now, however, he had become the center of a universe of expectation. His classmates developed chicken habits of their own, ears focused in Odie's direction, ready for his next eruption, the next chapter in his legend.

It didn't happen often. When he *did* go off, though, the effect was like a Christmas, Halloween, Birthday and Valentine's Day party rolled into one bright, sixty-second core.

An obscenity would explode from Odie's lips, a war-cry interrupting filmstrips and reading circles, rising in wild glory above the roar of the cafeteria.

The response was always the same. The principal would fetch Odie and walk with him to the farthest reaches of the playground, and stand with him there until he was sure the fit had passed.

After the immediate chorus of joy and the ecstasy of shock, Odie's classmates would watch the playground from the corner of chicken-cocked eyes, observing the figures of Odie and the principal across the intervening distance, through six hundred feet of the mist which seemed at all times to haunt the valleys and low places of Judy, so that the two of them, the old man and the boy with the lazy eye seemed to vanish and reappear, or to hover halfway in-between, like shadows turned inside-out.

ACCORDING to Ashley, Zion Calder was so stubborn he had to die twice before he could become a ghost.

The first time he died was because he had a huge blind spot due to his cotton eye. He wandered into the path of a moving hoist and got knocked into the chipper, a monster of a machine which took in whole trees at one end and spat out chips at the other.

Somehow, Zion Calder went through the chipper and came out the other end without a scratch. No one could believe it, least of all Zion Calder.

"Well," he sighed, "that's it. I'm dead," and marched himself off to the graveyard. He built a little shack out there, and nothing anyone said could convince him to come on home.

Not that anyone said much. There was something patently miraculous about the way the old man had gotten through the chipper in one piece, and a lot of people tended to treat Zion Calder as a sort of accidental holy man after that. They scribbled their most urgent prayers on scraps of paper, then crept out to the cemetery at night to tack them to the door of his shack. Whether Calder read the prayers was unknown, and seemingly immaterial. The door of his shack fluttered with a thousand paper wings.

In 1939, the Tennessee Valley Authority decided to harness the Little Turkeyfoot River with a dam. Much of Judy, Tennessee would be lost underwater, but what remained on higher ground would have electricity.

Zion Calder's graveyard was right in the middle of the proposed reservoir. Calder, naturally, declared there "weren't no such thing as a TVA," and locked his prayer-bedecked door like a fortress.

The dam got built anyway. The waters of the Little Turkeyfoot began to swell and rise, and men from the county engineer's office came to move the cemetery. Calder advised them to go ahead and move whatever they wanted as long as they left his shack alone. This advice was rendered over the barrel of his squirrel rifle, punctuated by the lightning of his cotton eyeball.

They didn't bother him again.

All summer long, graves were opened and coffins pried loose. The diggers wore perfumed handkerchiefs over their faces, and were glad to move on to other work when the cemetery was finally tucked into high ground in the next township. Pilgrims stopped tacking prayers to Calder's door, and by mid-July the old paper scraps had disintegrated in the humidity, leaving only bare wood and a forest of tacks.

SOMETIMES Odie Clark showed up at school with bruises, and everyone knew it was because his mom liked to hit. She wasn't like the people at the school; when Odie screamed awful things at home, the consequences were less than gentle.

Sometimes he had bruises on his arms, sometimes in places you couldn't see them. One time he had a great welt on his neck, and for a whole week he couldn't cock his head sideways and got beaned with the kickball four times. By the end of January, Odie had gone from outcast, to hero, to object of angry pity.

And then, too fast for the minds of his schoolmates to follow, he became a ghost.

One day, his mother grabbed his hair and punched him in the ear for yelling a whole string of evil words while she was on the phone. Odie went out to cry and rub his ear. He went out, like he often did, to put pennies on the railroad tracks, to lower his undamaged ear to the rail and listen for approaching wheels.

He fell asleep with his head on the rail, and vanished into legend.

ZION Calder, Ashley said, sat alone in his shack amidst rows and rows of empty graves. As the water table climbed, the graves slowly filled until they resembled rows of mirrors.

The water table rose, inch by inch, swallowing the basements of abandoned houses, filling the caverns and hollows and valleys, forcing the coal mines to close. At last, one morning in late October, Calder stepped out to find the Little Turkeyfoot River lapping at his toes. He tipped his hat to the water, slipped back inside and waited behind his locked door.

By mid-November, the Little Turkeyfoot River had become Little Turkeyfoot Lake. Its winter-gray surface gave no sign of Calder's shack, the cemetery, or any of the houses it had swallowed. The lake, like Calder, denied everything.

SOMETIMES Vonda wishes her mother were more like Odie Clark's. Even a mother who hits is at least a mother who does *something*. Vonda's mother goes to work and gets tired. She comes home and sits, or disappears into her room at the end of the trailer, straight to sleep. She's a ghost who isn't dead yet.

VONDA goes out alone, sometimes, and puts her ear on the railroad tracks, right where Odie Clark became a ghost. She tells Jill and Ashley that if you go to the tracks at midnight and cover your left eye with your hand and say the F-word three times, a ghost train will come moaning through, a ghost train that's just a headlight and a wind that tosses your hair, followed by the headless ghost of Odie Clark staggering along with his head under his arm, bleeding from the ear where his mom hit him.

Sometimes, too, she tells about her father, pretending to remember him.

"He went by a fake name," she says, "the whole time he lived with my mom. Now he's really famous. If I told you who he was, you'd freak."

"What?" says Ashley, says Jill. *"Who?"*

"You'd freak," repeats Vonda, nothing more.

ASHLEY says the winter the Little Turkeyfoot Lake was born was supernaturally cold, for Tennessee. For the first time in living memory, the temperature dipped below freezing and stayed there for three months. The new lake froze solid from shore to shore. People got in the habit of walking out onto the lake and wondering aloud about old Zion Calder sitting down there in the dark, wondering if he was stubborn enough to breathe underwater.

With the spring thaw, three fishermen decided to give the lake a try. They were floating around out there in the middle when Calder's shack, half-full of air, finally let go of the ground and came rocketing out of the lake near their boat. It hung gracefully in the air for a moment, then landed on its side, more or less whole, floating catawampus in the water. Nearby floated its builder, truly dead at last, and minus his head.

'Eaten by fish,' some speculated.

'Raptured,' said others.

Either way, no one wanted to go out on the lake until Calder's head was accounted for.

The sheriff used dynamite, trying to shock it to the surface.

The head failed to rise.

What did rise, to the displeasure of the valley residents, were parts of old houses and old trees and the mortally wounded steeple of the First Redemption Church.

But that wasn't all.

Something like a wooden submarine splashed to the surface, and bobbed darkly in the water. A second submarine followed, then another, and another.

Coffins.

Apparently the engineers had been less than thorough in their efforts to clear out the cemetery and move on to other, sweeter-smelling tasks.

Like Zion Calder before them, the people of Judy, Tennessee turned their backs.

'Lake? What lake?' they'd say.

"My own grampa," claims Ashley, "will get up and walk out of the room if you so much as mention the lake. He will, I swear to God."

WHEN Vonda gets tired of her mom being tired, sometimes she goes over to Jill's house, which is a real house, not a trailer. Jill has a real dad, too, not a story-dad, even if he's not famous. Jill's dad keeps an electric train in the basement, a huge layout with little towns and hills and lakes and tunnels for the trains to go through.

Sometimes, ever since they were in grade school, he sits at the controls in a high chair like a bar stool, wearing an engineer's cap with dark blue stripes. He lets the girls sit in his lap and open switches, telling the trains where to go.

The summer Vonda and Jill both turned fourteen, the same month Vonda started stealing roaches from her mother's ashtrays, Jill's dad added a new track to the miniature railroad world. The new section had woods, and a perfect model of the haunted underpass.

The girls said the F-word when they first saw the underpass. It seemed kind of sick. Made them feel sick, a little, but they couldn't look away, and Jill's dad stood behind them, watching them.

ASHLEY isn't the only girl in Judy, Tennessee who talks about Zion Calder. His name has been whispered by citizens of all ages, floating stubbornly down the years.

The ghost is not the ghost of Calder's body, just the ghost of his teeth and his long, gray hair, the ghost of his white cotton eye, like lightning or prophecy. He haunts Judy's waters like a fish, like a bad movie which floats in puddles, glares from dishwater, kiddie pools, toilets, and shot glasses, bloated lips curling, speaking silence, cursing the TVA.

JILL says that when they are old, they'll be the old wise women of Judy, Tennessee. People will come to them, mostly little kids, wanting to know about the ghost of Odie Clark, and they'll tell how they knew Odie Clark when he was alive.

Jill says it's important to keep the blood moving in stories like that, so one day when Jill is sitting in her father's lap, opening and closing switches, Vonda grabs a toy whistle off the worktable, a wooden whistle which makes a noise just like an old-fashioned train. She runs upstairs with it and hides it at home in her dresser.

Sometimes she takes the whistle to the real railroad tracks and blows on it, and the idea is that maybe someone will hear it and look and see there's no train, and they'll know, they'll *know* in their souls it's the ghost of the train that nailed Odie Clark, and they'll get the shivers.

She steals a half-smoked cigarette before she goes, and smokes it alone, since Ashley and Jill fear the underpass. Sometimes a train comes, as if summoned by the stolen whistle. A real train, although all trains are ghostly by moonlight. Vonda climbs the right-of-way and stands as close as she dares while the air fills with a wild diesel throb. Rust and steel rocket by, inches away in the dark, shedding mist like a caul. She lifts her eyes, spreads her arms, swimming at the edge of balance, and she wishes. The wish comes from every part of her, rising like fire, like smoke. She doesn't even know what the wish is, but she wishes it real, real hard.

Interview with a Moron

ELIZABETH STUCKEY-FRENCH

SUBJECT: RICHARD MARSHALL LEE, feebleminded man, twenty-five years of age

INTERVIEWER: J.D. LEE, honors student at Purdue University, twenty-one years of age

ON MAY 14, 1892, AT approximately 9:03 a.m., Interviewer boarded the Wabash Special in Lafayette and rode to Logansport in order to conduct this interview. The train stopped at every unincorporated settlement between Lafayette and Logansport and twice ground to a halt in the middle of an empty field, backed up a short way, and then went forward again. The conductor offered no reasonable explanation for these unscheduled stops.

After inhaling coal dust for one hour and fifty-eight minutes on the train, Interviewer disembarked at the station in Logansport. There he hired a hack and endured a wild ride with an inebriated coach driver for another six and a half miles east to St. Bridget's Home for the Feebleminded. The cost of the round-trip train ticket and coach fare equaled exactly half of Interviewer's monthly food and entertainment allowance.

St. Bridget's Home for the Feebleminded is a large, handsome red brick building four stories high, not unlike Cary Quadrangle, the dormitory at Purdue University in which Interviewer currently resides. Interviewer, who had never before set foot in a home for the feebleminded, boldly entered through the front door and was directed into an office barely big enough for a desk and the large Sister sitting behind it. Sister was drinking tea and eating a sugar cookie but did not offer Interviewer any sustenance after his forty-six-mile journey. Sister is missing her left front incisor and has a wattle hanging over her wimple.

Interviewer introduced himself to Sister as Subject's younger brother, J. D. Lee. Sister, who'd been expecting Interviewer, rose from behind the desk to shake Interviewer's hand in a manly fashion. She expressed gratitude that someone from Subject's family had finally come to see him.

Interviewer nodded and did not reveal that he had come in order to satisfy a requirement for Dr. Ernest Grubb's Senior Psychology Seminar, a course that Interviewer was given special permission to take, in spite of the fact that he is only a junior.

Sister explained to Interviewer that Subject, although he had been informed of Interviewer's imminent arrival, had gone outside in order to stand in a hole. Sister reported that Subject often stands alone in this hole, located on the grounds behind the home, for hours on end. Sister smiled as if she found the idea of a grown man standing in a hole amusing.

She was asked why Subject stood in the hole but said she did not know. When asked if he had dug the hole himself, she said she did not know. When asked how long he'd been doing this, her reply was the same.

Sister should know more than she claims to know.

After this unhelpful exchange, Interviewer went outside onto the grounds, which are extensive and well maintained, having the appearance of a pleasant city park. Hardwood trees obscure the iron fence around the property. There are gravel paths that go round in circles and multiple beds of garish tulips.

It was a fine spring day on which there blew a pure breeze untainted by urban coal. Interviewer observed a number of inmates out taking the air—a young man with a thin beard sitting on a bench with his eyes closed and two men in heavy sweaters walking on a path. All three men appeared to be of normal intelligence but must not be, or they would not be in a home for the feebleminded.

Interviewer found Subject on the eastern edge of the grounds, standing in a hole approximately one meter deep and 2.5 meters in diameter. Subject recognized Interviewer and called him by name, offering his hand, which Interviewer shook. Subject and Interviewer had not seen each other in two years; nevertheless, Subject did not feel the need to climb out of his hole. Subject remarked that Interviewer looked like an old man, which is not an accurate observation.

Subject himself looks much younger than his twenty-five years, which might be due to the fact that he has no cares in the world. All his needs are seen to, and he is treated like a child, allowed to stand in a hole for no purpose whenever he so desires and for as long as he so desires. Subject was clean shaven, and despite the dirty hole in which he was standing, his heavy cotton shirt and loose trousers appeared to be neat, clean, and in good repair. Subject asserted that Interviewer was fat and that his cuffs were frayed. Both remarks are clearly inappropriate.

Interviewer asked Subject why he was standing in the hole, and he replied that standing thusly passed the time. When asked what he was looking at, Subject said that he watched whatever was in front of him. There appeared to be nothing in front of him, save some flowering bushes. When asked if he had dug the hole, he said that it had already been there but that he had made it deeper. When asked how long he'd been doing this, Subject said since he was a baby, which is a false statement. Subject has only been residing in this home for two years. Also, babies are unable to dig large holes. When Interviewer pointed this out, Subject began talking about how he had recently invented a machine that shucks corn but said that he could not show it to Interviewer because he was afraid of his idea being stolen and he was, at present, unable to acquire a patent for his shucker.

Interviewer said he had no intention of stealing anything from Subject. Subject brought up a time, many years ago, when both Interviewer and Subject were children, and Interviewer took a pocketknife from Subject's desk drawer. Interviewer reminded Subject that he had simply borrowed the knife, but Subject replied, "Where is it, then?"

Of course Interviewer returned it long ago, has no idea of its present location, and cannot be expected to keep track of Subject's childhood possessions, and said as much to Subject, who did not appear to accept this explanation, as he shook his head and grimaced.

Subject's memory appears to be faulty.

Subject steadfastly refused to show corn-shucking invention to Interviewer but agreed to show him something else he had made instead. He swung himself nimbly out of the hole and walked across the grounds at an unnecessarily brisk pace. Interviewer struggled to keep up. Subject went directly to a telescope of premium quality sitting on a tripod beside the path. Subject claimed that it was his own telescope and that someone had given it to him as a gift.

Have not been able to confirm truth of Subject's claim.

Subject then directed Interviewer to look through the telescope, which was pointed at an object standing on the grass not fifteen meters away. According to Subject, the object under observation was of his own design, a sculpture he'd assembled in the recreation building. The object appeared to be a small heap of rusted metal that could easily be seen by the naked eye. No telescope was needed to view said object.

When asked the purpose of the object, Subject said that if Interviewer looked long enough at the object through the telescope, the purpose would become clear. Interviewer asserted that he didn't have time to stand and gaze through an unnecessary telescope at an uninteresting and nearby object.

Subject countered that the meaning of the object was very profound but could not be put into words and that Interviewer would be sorry if he did not give it a try. To humor Subject, Interviewer gazed through the telescope at the object. Interviewer counted thirteen nails and thirty-nine screws, which were fixed by a length of wire onto a section of iron pipe. As expected, no profound meaning yielded itself to Interviewer. He informed Subject that his experiment was a failure. Subject responded by asking Interviewer if he'd seen a penny on the object.

Interviewer said no.

Interviewer asked Subject if the meaning of the object was related to the penny. Subject said no, and that furthermore, there was in actuality no penny on the object.

Interviewer then asked Subject why Subject had mentioned a penny if there was no penny. Subject said that many things were not on the object and that this was the meaning of the object.

Interviewer reminded Subject that Subject had previously stated that the meaning could not be put into words but that he had just stated the meaning using words. Subject said that Interviewer had misunderstood him. He had said that the deeper meaning could not be put into words.

Against his better judgment, Interviewer gazed again through the telescope at the object while Subject stood at his side. Just then another Sister came along the path and asked Interviewer what he was watching through the telescope.

Interviewer stepped away from the telescope and assured Sister that he wasn't looking at anything. This Sister was a young woman with a pretty face, not unlike the face of one Rosie McCarthy, who used to live in the house next door to Interviewer and Subject.

Sister said to Interviewer, "Oh, I know what you were looking at. Isn't it marvelous? We all find Richard's object very intriguing."

Unlike Rosie McCarthy, this Sister did not appear to have much common sense. Sister and Subject smiled at each other in an unseemly manner. Began to wonder if this home is best placement for Subject. Was relieved when Sister walked off, apparently to attend to an unspecified errand.

Interviewer queried Subject as to whether he'd noticed the similarity between the Sister and Rosie McCarthy. Subject insisted that the Sister actually is Rosie McCarthy, which is a false statement, as Rosie McCarthy is now Mrs. William Weigel of Battleground, Indiana. Subject insisted that the two women are one and the same. Interviewer, though in the right, let the matter drop.

Subject then asked Interviewer when he would be allowed to go back home. Interviewer said that their parents were unable to take care of Subject any longer, because he needed such close supervision. Subject protested, saying that as long as he had a hole and his object that he would never be a burden to anyone. Interviewer was forced to go into the story of how Subject had strained the nerves and the health of his parents by misspending his youth in a variety of ways, including nailing clothing to walls and stealing animals. Reminded Subject of incident with organ-grinder's monkey. Reminded Subject of how their parents had worried and fretted over the Subject's behavior and lavished attention on him, to the detriment of his sibling, whose stellar behavior had gone unnoticed and whose needs had gone unmet.

Subject demanded to know what stellar behavior Interviewer was referring to. Reminded Subject of time when Subject, at twelve years of age, had climbed out the attic window onto the roof, and Interviewer, though only eight years old and terrified of heights, climbed out onto the roof to retrieve Subject, who sat blithely pulling up the edges of the shingles. Interviewer took Subject's hand and led him back across the roof, while Mrs. McCarthy screamed Dear God, Dear God from her yard below. Inside Mother wept and wept, saying she was sorry, she was so sorry she hadn't been watching Subject closely enough, and she would never let him out of her sight again. Mother had no reason to be sorry, in Interviewer's opinion, as she had done nothing wrong, but Interviewer knew better than to state his opinion, because nobody ever listened to anything he said. During and after this event, no one thanked Interviewer or even acknowledged his brave deed, and Subject was never punished.

Subject, who did not appear to be interested in this account of how Interviewer saved his life, again asked when he was going to go home, and whether or not anyone there still loved him, as they never wrote letters to him or came to visit.

Interviewer pointed out that he was there visiting right now.

Subject asked why the rest of the family hadn't come with Interviewer. Interviewer reminded Subject that he now attends Purdue University and no longer lives at home and rarely sees their parents himself. Interviewer admitted that since he left for college he might as well have stepped off the earth, as far as their parents were concerned. He confessed that he had been glad to leave home, because after Subject was taken away Mother had turned into a mouse and Father had increased his drinking. Interviewer then surprised and embarrassed himself by suddenly blurting out that he had been lonely at home without Subject, as he had nobody to look after.

Subject, not seeming to appreciate or comprehend what he had just been told, asked again why Interviewer had not brought Mother and Father with him. Interviewer inquired as to why he alone was not sufficient. Subject said it was because Interviewer was a vile and wicked serpent.

Interviewer reminded Subject that he was the one who had just been crawling around in a filthy hole like a reptile.

Subject reached out and placed his hand on Interviewer's shoulder, stating that even though Interviewer was a silly, stupid, stubborn man, he pitied Interviewer. Interviewer knocked Subject's hand away and said that the only reason he had come to see Subject was because he had been assigned by a professor to interview a moron.

Subject shoved Interviewer.

Interviewer shoved back.

Subject boxed Interviewer's ears, causing extreme pain.

Interviewer leapt on Subject, knocked him down, and sat on him, pinning Subject's arms as a safety precaution.

Subject, using his typical childish maneuver, sank his teeth into Interviewer's wrist and thus managed to wriggle free. Subject ran away laughing and yelling unprintable insults having to do with Rosie McCarthy.

Interviewer pursued Subject but was unable to catch him.

Interviewer was forced to terminate the interview and to take Subject's metal object with him.

On his way out of the home, Interviewer hid his bitten wrist in his pocket. He told the cookie-eating Sister in the office that Subject had hurried off to the recreation building, but before leaving had expressed satisfaction regarding a sudden inspiration for a new invention on which he wanted to start construction directly. Interviewer told Sister that Subject had given the object to him as a gift. Object now sits on Interviewer's desk.

As of this time, no meaning has been derived by Interviewer from the object. Subject would undoubtedly say that it is because Interviewer is not looking at it properly through a telescope. Interviewer would respond to this by declaring that he will never purchase a telescope in order to gaze at the object. The purchase of a telescope in order to gaze at a pile of rubbish close enough to spit on is the act of a moron. Interviewer is certain that the object will never be seen more clearly than he is himself viewing it at the present moment.

However, as a last-ditch effort, and in order to be as fair and unbiased as possible, Interviewer took one of his own pennies, one that might have been spent on well-deserved pastries, and wired it onto the object. Interviewer then sat and studied the object for twelve minutes, to no avail. Subject's object, like Subject himself, remained stubbornly opaque and whimsical. This fact should come as no surprise to Interviewer. Interviewer has never known what to make of Subject, nor has he been able to decipher what makes Subject tick. Furthermore, he has never once been successful in his attempts to clearly communicate his own thoughts and feelings to Subject.

However, Interviewer is not one to give up easily. It is certain that when Interviewer next calls on Subject, Subject will no doubt be engaged in another activity of a pointless and selfish nature and, as no other person seems to want to shoulder the burden of attempting to make Subject face the truth about his actions, Interviewer will once again step into the breach.

On future visits, Interviewer will remain at all times objective. He regrets that he lost his temper and removed an object Subject apparently found to be important, even though it is ugly and useless. If physically attacked, however, Interviewer retains the right to defend himself.

Interviewer is well aware that straightening Subject out will be a difficult feat to accomplish. As Dr. Grubb has said in his lectures, it is nigh on impossible to reason with a moron, and with that statement, Interviewer must heartily concur. His recent interview with Subject has demonstrated as much. In fact, all of Interviewer's experience with Subject has underscored the truth of this assertion. Dr. Grubb has also opined that morons are a corrupting influence on the rest of us, but I must differ with Dr. Grubb on this point.

My brother, Richard, as far as I can see, has never had any influence on anyone, most especially not on me. In fact, neither one of us has ever had any effect on the other.

For example: When Richard was fourteen and I was ten, he tried to enlist my aid in stealing an organ-grinder's monkey, telling me that the organ-grinder was abusing his monkey and that it would be better off living at our house.

I told him that this was a very bad idea, and then I explained why. Stealing was stealing, I told him, and he could be arrested. If he was arrested, Mother and Father would be humiliated. Even if he was not arrested, we could never take care of a monkey in our home. There were too many breakables. Besides, we didn't know anything about the care and keeping of monkeys. Anyhow, I reasoned, the monkey might be perfectly happy capering about in a plaid bathrobe collecting coins in a silver cup. It was not up to us to judge whether or not a monkey was happy, even if we could. The monkey belonged to the organ-grinder. This should have been the end of the matter. But with Richard there is never an end to the matter. Against all my counsel, Richard went downtown, distracted the organ-grinder, snatched the monkey, and ran away. He brought the little monkey, whom we named Willie, back to our house in a shoebox. We attempted to hide Willie in Richard's room, but the creature escaped and Mother caught him pulling the tail feathers out of her stuffed cockatoo. It was an extremely unpleasant day at the Lee house.

However, what I took away from this incident was not that I was right and that morons are incorrigible, and I do not recall that the incident ever created in me a desire to go forth and be wicked also. Nor do I dwell at all upon the upheaval and commotion that resulted from my brother's crime. Instead I remember how Richard, when the police finally arrived, clung desperately to Willie, who only wanted to escape his grasp. I cannot forget how Richard's face looked as he attempted to cuddle the ungrateful monkey to his chest like a ring-tailed baby and how I, forced to stand there and witness this spectacle, would've given anything, anything at all, if the beast would only cease its caterwauling and throw its arms around my brother, just for little while, and love him back.

An Affair Before the Earthquake

SAMRAT UPADHYAY

THE EARTHQUAKE WAS YET TO come.

She promised him before she left for America that she would return in two years and they'd be together.

"Will we marry?" he'd asked.

"That I don't know," she'd said. "What good would that do?"

What good would marriage do! Well, marriage would keep us together, he'd thought. It'd tie us in an official bond, and never would we be apart! Or something like that. But he'd feel foolish uttering these words so he didn't.

When she first told him that she was going away he knew it was coming. They'd been walking in the city center, holding hands, moving from Thamel through Asan, then Indrachowk toward Kathmandu Durbar Square. Soon they'd pass the giant drums to the right, the statue of Hanuman the Monkey God to the left, then, to the right, figures of Shiva-Parvati leaning out of a temple window. On to the square and the nine-stage platform that led to the base of the Maju Deval temple, which was more than three hundred years old, where tourists and locals (now increasingly young lovers) hung out and watched the scenery. In front of the temple she'd say, "Shall we?" and they'd climb the steps, linger for some time as they watched the people below, then they'd come back down. The next stop was the Kasthamandap Temple, where they'd observe the Gorakhnath statue (both of them were not particularly religious), and she'd say, "This temple was made out of a single tree." He was aware of the legend, of course, and he recalled that this structure was nine hundred years old, serving as a resting pavilion, a sanctuary, for merchants who traveled the ancient trade routes. "Our city gets its name from this temple," she said, every time, as though he was unaware of it. And he'd take note of "our city" because that meant that she considered the city to be theirs, theirs together. Our hearth, he thought.

They'd circle the small shrine of Ganesh, still holding hands, and he'd feel that they were consecrating their togetherness.

But she was a free spirit. He knew that. If he'd chosen to ignore it, how was she to blame? Before they became lovers, he'd watched her from afar, and he'd admired her and thought: now there's a free spirit, and I'm not. It was strange, identifying oneself as an un-free spirit. But he'd felt a constriction inside himself ever since he could remember, since childhood. Shy, they used to call him, but he'd always known that it was more than shyness. He was trapped by his own thoughts, which, it became obvious to him by his teen years, went around in circles, or repeated the same patterns—which meant that his life followed the same patterns, over and over. He was free to go wherever he chose, and he traveled quite a bit in the early years of his profession—China, Germany, Australia—yet he was moving within this circle of entrapment.

But she was not restricted to her body, or her mind. Even her laughter (and she laughed often) came from a different, liberated place. She used to work at an INGO, in the same office building as his, one floor below, and her laughter reached up to him from her veranda, where she gathered with her co-workers for breaks. He would be on his own veranda, and he'd lean over so he could see her. He'd see her hair, the top of her head, a part of her face, perhaps the nose and a cheek, and she'd appear beautiful to him in this partial profile. He'd passed by her a few times on the staircase, and she was always with a co-worker, never alone, and she was always smiling or laughing. When their eyes met, he thought she acknowledged him as a person of interest.

For him she was more than a person of interest: she had become, by that time, his lover in his dreams. How could it be, he'd asked himself late at night in his apartment as he lay under his blanket. How could she become his lover so quickly? He didn't know her name, where she lived, whether she was a vegetarian, whether she had family here in the city or elsewhere. He didn't know—he bolted upright in his bed—whether she was married. Why had he assumed that she wasn't? Because she didn't look married, that's why. She didn't wear *sindur* in the parting in her hair, she never wore a *sari* (it was always *kurta suruwal*). Her face looked young: no blemishes, eyes quick and smiling. He reminded himself that there were plenty of married women who looked young, and that sindur and sari no longer signaled married women. In this modern city now many women who had husbands went to work in trousers and shirts and kurta suruwal, often without applying the red powder in their hair. Okay, he thought late at night. I don't know her name, where she lives, who is in her family, whether she has a husband or children, yet she is my lover. Good job.

She would come to him in his dreams. They'd hold hands and walk through the city center, the same path they'd take once they became lovers for real, the same path where she told him she was leaving for America. As dream lovers, they'd make bulging eyes at the fearsome Kal Bhairav statue, watch pigeons coo and flutter next to the Monkey God temple, amble to the main square where they'd climb up the steps of the Maju Deval temple and watch the action below.

She continued to be his dream-lover even after she became his real lover. And becoming her real lover also happened quickly, easily—too easily, he thought. But it all happened in the course of one afternoon and evening, so effortlessly that he wondered if he'd dreamt it. But one afternoon as he stood on his office veranda, leaning to catch sight of her side profile below, she looked up at him and with laughing eyes said, "*Hoina*, what is your name, Sir? I see you all the time but I don't know your name."

He'd shyly given his name, then she asked him whether the Lipton Instant Coffee Machine was working in his office, for the one in her office was broken and she was craving for some coffee. "Am I not?" she asked her two co-workers, whom he couldn't see but who he could hear were tittering. "Oh, yes, broken," her co-workers said, loudly. "Yes, yes, badly broken." He thought one of them said, "Broken like a heart that's broken," but he couldn't be sure.

The next moment she was upstairs and they were drinking coffee and swapping mobile numbers.

AFTER they became lovers, their conversations from his dreams bled into their real conversations. When she sucked on a kulfi ice cream on the steps of Maju Deval, he wasn't sure if it was the dream-she who sucked on a kulfi or the real-she.

"I promise," she said, sometimes in his dreams and sometimes in the real world where the earthquake was yet to come. Sometimes just, "Promise." She loved using the word, as if simply saying it made her feel good about everything.

"Promise?" he asked. "We'll be together?"

"I swear I promise," she said.

SHE liked to sing Nepali songs. She had a soft voice she used to her full advantage. She would start singing without a prompt. "Out of the blue"—that's how he described the abruptness of her singing to a friend to whom he'd confessed how badly he'd fallen in love with her. He'd gone to the friend's house after work, loosened his tie and paced the room, as his friend had watched him as though he were a performer auditioning for a coveted part. It had been an hour of nonstop confession.

"And she starts singing out of the blue," he told his friend. "Out of the blue, I swear. We'll be sitting on the steps of Maju Deval, and I'll be talking to her softly about something, persuading her about something—it seems as though I'm always persuading her, pleading with her—and she'll appear to be listening. I think that I'm beginning to make some headway when suddenly she'll start singing. And it's always a very Nepali song, often the oldies, from the previous generation, like Narayan Gopal, Aruna Lama, Gopal Yonzan, Prem Dhoj, sometimes even the oldy folksy ones like Kumar Basnet.

"Even the ploughing-on-top-of-the-green-hills guy, what's his name? Yes, Dharma Raj Thapa. The surprising thing is that when we talk half of her words are English; she can barely utter one full sentence that's unadulterated Nepali. But when she sings her words are so pure, so Nepali that it's almost as if a different person is singing. What's happening, you think?"

But he wasn't really interested in an answer from his friend, and his friend knew this. The friend also knew what the answer was: she was a different person when she sang. Her singing was a deep, yearning subconscious desire to go back to a time when the Nepali identity wasn't sullied by external forces.

"I'll never meet anyone like her," he continued. He was sweating, so he took off his jacket and went to the window. There was no breeze but he could now look out and talk. The city was crammed with houses. He thought of the phrase "packed like sardines." In that moment, he knew that he wouldn't get to share the city with her, even though she'd said "our city" when she'd talked about the Kasthamandap temple, even though it wasn't until a few days later that she'd tell him she was going away. This is how he knew: when he looked out he saw only himself in the city. He saw himself walking the streets alone, sometimes late at night, perhaps after a rain when the air was fresh. He walked very slowly, pausing every now and then. He watched shopkeepers closing their shops. He moved through the center toward the Durbar Square. A lone woman was bent over the Kal Bhairav statue, praying hard. A couple of drug addicts and drunkards passed him. He looked up at the Maju Deval Temple. In the darkness he saw two figures at the top of the platform—two young lovers. He knew they were looking at him, hoping he'd not come up so they'd remain undisturbed.

After seeing himself alone in the city after the rain, he stopped his monologue. "What happened?" his friend asked. "Go on."

But now the words didn't come. "Is something wrong?"

He shook his head. "It's time for me to leave now," he said.

"But I thought we were going to do some drinking tonight."

"I'm no longer in the mood."

A few days later she told him her plan to go to America, to a large university in the Midwest where there was a lot of greenery.

"When?"

"Next month. I'll return in two years. This degree is a must for me. I need to move up. I need to be the director of my company."

"But what if you change? What if you become like an American?"

She smiled. "How?"

"What if you start talking like an American? Acting like an American?" He talked to her in an exaggerated American accent, or what he thought was an American accent, with wide vowel sounds and hard consonants, all delivered in a nasal twang. She laughed like she was going to drop dead on the street.

He laughed with her, then held her arm and said, in a soft, persuasive voice, "But seriously, what if you change?"

At the top platform of Maju Deval, she began to sing. It was drizzling, enough to make people pick up their pace but not enough to cause panic, and it was nice to watch others hasten as they themselves were protected by the temple's awning that displayed erotic carvings. "Our ancestors were dirty, dirty folks," she'd said a while ago when they'd spotted a scene of bestiality right above their heads.

She sang an old Narayan Gopal song: *yeti chokho, yeti mitho, dulia timlai maya, birsanechan saraley purana premka katha.* Basically: I will give you such a sweet and pure love that people will forget the love stories of yesteryears.

He didn't hear from her once she left for America. He emailed her, called her, Skyped her, Vibered her, contacted another Nepali at her university and had his message delivered to her and received confirmation that his message was indeed delivered to her in person. Nothing. He came upon a photo of her at a university party that someone had posted on Facebook; she was holding a glass of wine, looking happy.

She didn't return in two years. Soon thereafter he too left, for Australia. So, he wasn't there when the earthquake struck and the Maju Deval temple came tumbling down. The Kasthamandap Temple, too, was reduced to a rubble.

Before he left for Australia, he took the route that they used to take, from Thamel to Asan, to Indrachowk, then on to Durbar Square past the ridiculously fearsome Kal Bhairav and the pigeons, the giant drums and the statues of Shiva-Parvati surveying the square from their tiny window. He carried imaginary conversations with her as they walked.

"You think it's going to rain today?" he asked.

"It always drizzles when we come here." She briefly squeezed his hand. "But I like light rains." She twirled in the middle of the square, watched by garland-sellers and ricksaw-pullers. To his surprise, she sang an old Hindi number this time. *Aaj fir jine ki tamanna hai, aaj fir marney ka irada hai.*

Basically: Today I want to live again, and again today I want to die.

Pulsus Paradoxus

DALY WALKER

THE SNOW BEGAN IN THE morning and continued into the afternoon. It was Saturday and I was the surgeon on trauma call. As was my habit when I was tethered to the telephone, I decided to listen to opera. I wanted nothing but a little time to myself so I could lie on the couch and let the music drain me of loneliness and allow me to escape the sadnesses of my life—my estrangement from my troubled daughter, Polly, and the recent and unexpected death of my wife. The opera I chose was a favorite of mine, Mozart's "Magic Flute." The overture began, its heavy chords sounding like knocks on a door. Through the window, I watched the snow fall and let the orchestra's glistening shimmer of sounds flow through me. The music did as I wanted it to. It transported me into a state of reverie where I became the heroic Prince Tamino rescuing my love, Pamina, from the forces of evil. But then phone rang.

"Damn it," I said.

Medicine is a fickle and inconsiderate mistress who holds no regard for her lover's other life, and I knew it would be the emergency room and that the music was over. I muted the sound system and picked up the receiver. The ER nurse's voice was high-pitched with excitation. I was needed stat to attend to a young man who had been shot in the chest. She said he was in shock when he came in, but his blood pressure rose with a rapid infusion on intravenous fluids. I told her to call the OR and to have six units of type specific blood available. I was on my way. I hung up the phone and took a deep breath, thinking of what lay ahead. As I rose from the couch, I felt like Sisyphus must have felt at the bottom of the mountain preparing to roll the stone again.

I pulled on a pair of snow boots and a parka and hurried through the house to the garage. I passed the open door of Polly's room and saw her empty bed. A feeling of abandonment and failure chilled me. I pictured Polly there asleep with her hair loose on the pillow. I thought, *what if it was my daughter on that gurney in the emergency room.* I knew that the young man, however good or bad he was, was someone's child, someone's Polly. Age was beginning to take its toll on my surgical skills. My fingers weren't as nimble as they once were, and operations were harder for me. I wondered if I still had the power to save him. I wished for a magic flute.

I backed my Land Rover out into the falling snow. The radio was playing bad repetitious rock, the kind of music that Polly would listen to. I turned it off and tried to not let myself think of her in the grimy motel apartment where she lived with Wes Mitchell. I tried not to let myself think of the checks she forged or her mother's jewelry she sold to buy their drugs.

I wanted to remember her the way she was in the days before Wes Mitchell, when her mother was alive and Polly was a high-spirited and utterly happy child who filled my heart with gladness. I wanted to remember her as a willowy high school girl with wonderful pale blue eyes and a sense of humor that hit me just right. I wanted to remember the dance of her long brown ponytail as she loped over grassy hills with her cross country team. I wanted to hear the sound of her voice reciting French vocabulary. I wanted to laugh with her and feel together and blameless. It stopped my heart to think how Wes Mitchell had ruined her life, and mine, too. I could never escape the pain and hatred. The thought of him nearly drove me mad.

On the slick street to the hospital, the urgency in the nurse's voice over the phone came back to me, and my thoughts returned to the man who had been shot. I blew my horn and skated the Land Rover through a red light. The fishtailing of my rear wheels heightened my excitation. Big flakes splattered on the windshield. A swirling cloud of white surrounded me with a sense of duty and uncertainty.

Ahead under the ER's canopy, a cone of red light from an ambulance circled in a white gloom. My heart pounded harder. As I had first done thirty years ago as an intern working the Saturday night knife and gun club in the Cook County ER, and later as a battalion surgeon with the infantry in the Mekong Delta, I recited to myself the ABCs of trauma resuscitation. A for airway. B for breathing. Would I have to trach the guy? C for circulation. I told myself to watch for cardiac tamponade or a tension pneumothorax. Bullets bounce off of bones and pinball, boring unpredictable paths through the body. I cautioned myself not to get trapped into assuming that the obvious chest wound was his only significant injury.

I turned on to the plowed obsidian surface of the parking lot, thinking of all the nights I'd spent at the hospital. The stabbings. The shootings. I'd seen pretty much everything and tried not to harden my heart against it. In Nam, it was Pungi sticks, AK 47s, Claymores. Here it was Glocks, switchblades, shotguns, even assault rifles. You thought you lived in a civilized country, but it seemed as if I had spent my life working in a war zone. I knew ballistics, had seen what guns do to people. I detested them and the wounds their bullets created—the lives they destroyed.

I parked in a space next to a police car. Through the windows of the emergency room, I could see a woman pushing an x-ray machine. Nurses flitted about like a covey of white birds in flight. Everyone was moving in fast-forward. I had the feeling that comes from watching disaster from a distance. It was the same way I had felt in Nam hovering above a firefight in a helicopter. I climbed out of the Land Rover and hurried through a dense white snowfall. My breath condensed in little puffs like smoke. From somewhere in the distance came the howl of an anguished dog. Metal doors sprung open, and I burst into the ER. Angie, a tall gangly nurse with ash-blond hair and wearing blue scrubs, raised her hand in greeting.

"Look what the cat drug in," she said feigning cheerfulness.

"What you see is what you get," I said, stomping snow from my boots and casting my parka aside. "Okay. Where's this denizen of our fine city?"

She thrust an x-ray at me and pointed down the corridor.

"Trauma two. He's rocky. Can't keep his pressure up."

For a second, I held the chest film with its smoky images up to the ceiling light. I saw the boot-like shape of his heart and the bullet, a white button superimposed on a gray sternal shadow. My adrenal surged, heating me up.

"What can you tell me about him?" I asked as I hustled behind Angie toward trauma two.

"He's nineteen. Otherwise healthy. Shot with a twenty-two revolver. An accident, of course."

"I'll bet his best friend did it. Just slipped cleaning his gun."

"Doctor, so cynical." She shook her head and sighed. "Actually it's a shame. He's a nice looking kid."

"A real choir-boy I'll bet."

I grabbed the stethoscope that was draped around her neck, and I stepped into the trauma cubical where a burr-headed policeman with a pistol on his belt bent over the stretcher trying to restrain a thrashing, moaning young man. As I approached them, I glanced up at a cardiac monitor that was beeping in a rapid staccato. His QRS complex looked good, and he was in a *sinus tachycardia,* but I didn't like the digital printout that said his blood pressure was only seventy over forty.

I stepped up to the gurney across from the policeman to begin my examination. I lowered my eyes to the patient's ashen gray face. Long lashes. An aquiline nose. A little blond mustache. His features were delicate, almost pretty. In disbelief, I recognized Wes Mitchell, and my heart constricted. I felt as if the blood puddled on the floor was mine, that it had suddenly drained from me.

I gathered myself and made a quick assessment of his wound. His shirt had been ripped open, and over his left nipple there was a tattoo of a little blue and red devil wearing a cape. On the right, there was a small blood-crusted hole in the skin below the clavicle where the bullet had entered. I tried to put his identity out of my mind, but it was impossible to do. I wondered what I had done wrong to cause my daughter to be with someone like him.

Wes jerked his arm away from the policeman and swung it wildly. I grabbed his wrist.

"Lie still, Wes," I said.

"You know him, Doc," the policeman said.

"Yeah. Unfortunately, I do."

Wes flung his head from side to side. He raised up from the gurney and screamed, "Help me! Help me!"

His plea blew through the room like a cold wind. I started to grab him by the hair and jerk his head down, but before I could, the policeman reached up with his big hand and pinned Wes's head to the stretcher.

"Easy, son," he said.

"Let me up." Wes flailed his arms like a drowning man. "Let go. I can't breathe."

"Lie still, goddamn it," I said. "Don't talk."

I wondered who shot him and if Polly was there. I wondered where she was now and if she was safe.

Suddenly Wes quit struggling. His body went limp. I knew if I didn't act he was going to die.

THE last time I saw Polly was a month ago at the Candlelight Motel where she lived with Wes. The run-down motor inn's blue neon sign advertised apartments, efficiencies, rooms—by the day, the week, or the month. Inside unit ten Polly sat at Formica-top table, sipping a can of Mountain Dew and smoking a cigarette. Her eyes were a beautiful cornflower blue and haggard. Her skin was pale as paste. In the corner, the coils of a space heater glowed orange, but the room was cold. The air smelled like singed paper.

For a moment, I scanned the linoleum-floored efficiency. There was a sofa, a television set with rabbit ears, a kitchenette with a sink, a hot plate, and a small fridge. In the corner was Wes' electric bass guitar. Through a door, I could see the metal bed where Polly slept with him. The starkness of the place, the poverty of her life made me want to cry.

"You look thin, honey," I said. "I wish you didn't smoke. Have you been sick?"

I reached across the table and touched her forehead to feel for fever. She pushed my hand away.

"Where's Wes?" I said.

She eyed me suspiciously. "At work," she said. "He works at a music store. Why do you want to know?"

"I just wondered."

"Why are you here?"

"I want you to come home."

I said it gently. My voice seemed thin. I inhaled deeply. I felt as if there wasn't enough air to breathe. I rose from my chair. I moved around the table and laid my hands on her shoulders.

"Don't touch me," she said.

I stepped away from her and looked down through her tangled hair at her slim back. Her shoulders were as narrow as little girl's.

"Come home, Polly," I said. "We can make a new start. You can get off drugs and go to college."

"I'm off drugs," she said. "I'm with Wes." She looked at me with icy blue eyes. "You don't like Wes because he is different from you. Well, I love it that he is different. He's not like you think. He's off of drugs. He has a job. He's playing in a band and writing music. He wants me to go back to school."

"Polly," I said, "please come home."

"Why should I come home? When I was home, you were hardly ever around, and when you were, nothing I did suited you. My grades were never good enough. I wasn't dressed right. My friends weren't good enough." She stuffed her cigarette into the Mountain Dew can. It sizzled and smoke spun out of the hole in the top. "Nothing I do will ever be good enough for you. Why should I come home?"

Suddenly, I was aware of my age and that I might not have long to live. I dreaded nothing more than dying alone. A feeling of desperation came over me. It was as if time were running out.

"I'm sorry," I said, fighting back tears, swallowing to get the words out. "It'll be different now. I've made mistakes. We can learn from our mistakes. We can start over. It's not too late to turn things around."

"I'm not coming home." She lit another cigarette.

"Polly, you can't stay here. This isn't the way to live. You need to come home and get your life together."

"I'm not coming home. Now leave me alone."

She turned from me and walked into the bedroom. I looked through the door at her sitting on the metal bed, back-lit by the neon candlelight of the motel sign winking through a window. We remained lost to each other.

I plugged the stethoscope into my ears and put the bell against Wes Mitchell's chest, over his heart. The lub-dub of its beat was muffled, a distant and sinister sound, as if played softly on a kettledrum.

I glanced up at the monitor with my left hand resting on his chest while I felt his pulse with my right. When his ribs rose under my touch, my fingers on his wrist could feel his blood pressure dampening. It was an ominous sign, something called *pulsus paradoxus,* a rare physiological phenomena that I had learned in medical school. I had seen it in Vietnam with frag wounds to the chest and once when a cardiologist perforated a heart during cardiac catheterization. The paradox of his pulse told me there was blood in the pericardial sack that was tamponading his heart and restricting its beat. He needed to have needle stuck into the pericardium and the blood aspirated. He needed it now or he would die. I looked at his eyes. His pupils were big black tunnels to the brain. They seemed to be staring at me, and I stared back.

"Doctor," Angie said. "His pressure's dropping."

I stood feeling his pulse fade under my fingers. Each beat became weaker. The intervals between the green blips of his heart tracing were a lengthening green line. As if paralyzed, I felt the rise and fall of his chest. His respirations were slowing. Each breath was a labored gasp. Then his chest stopped moving.

When I was a resident, I was part of a surgical team that severed Siamese twins who were joined at the chest. We knew that we were killing one twin to save the other. As I watched Wes with his heart drowning in its own blood, I told myself that if I let him die, I would be sacrificing him to save my daughter. The power of the idea twisted around me like a rope.

A spasm passed through Wes. His body jerked like a condemned man in an electric chair. Through the window over the sink, I could see that it was snowing harder. I sensed that my wife, wherever she was, was watching me through the murky light.

"Oh, God," Angie gasped. "We're going to lose him. He's about to arrest."

"Crash cart." I barked.

Frantically, she rattled a red metal cart on rollers to the bedside. From it I grabbed a long eighteen gauge spinal needle attached to a 50cc syringe. I plunged the needle into Wes's chest just below his sternum and directed its tip toward his left shoulder. I advanced the needle slowly at a 45-degree angle toward the heart while applying suction on the syringe. I kept my eye on a flurry of agonal blips on the heart monitor. My own heart was pounding. Tiny beads of sweat clung to my forehead. Suddenly, I felt the suction pressure give way. I looked down at the syringe. Dark blood flowed into the glass cylinder. As the syringe filled and the pericardial sack was emptied of blood, the ECG waveform returned to normal and Wes's blood pressure rose to eighty millimeters of mercury. It was magical. Sleight of hand. A white dove appearing out of a silk handkerchief. The work of a magic flute. Or maybe it was Biblical. Lazarus rising from the dead.

I stabilized the needle against Wes's chest with my hand. His skin was sticky and moist, like clay. I detached the syringe from the needle and emptied the blood into a metal basin that Angie held in her trembling hands. I repeated the aspiration three times. On the fourth attempt no blood filled the syringe. I felt Wes's heart tapping the tip of the needle. The ECG waveform changed to an injury pattern, telling me I was touching the heart. I quickly withdrew the needle from Wes's chest. I watched the tracing return to normal. I let out a great sigh. *Was it one of relief? Or was it the resignation of defeat?*

"Praise the Lord," Angie said.

With the syringe still in my hand, I stepped back from the gurney and waited to see if his vital signs would hold. When I saw his pulse and blood pressure were stable, I laid the glass syringe on the crash cart. I turned to Angie and told her to notify surgery that we were on the way with the gunshot wound. Then I asked the policeman who shot Wes.

"Some guy who was trying to rob the music store where he works," he said.

"They've got him downtown." He cocked head and looked at me. "How'd you know him?"

I hesitated a moment, and then I answered, "When you've been around as long as I have, you get to know a lot of people."

THE surgery was anticlimactic. A second year surgery resident could have preformed the operation with a little supervision. The bullet had only creased the left ventricle of Wes's heart, sparing his coronary arteries and the electrical conducting system. I quickly repaired the lacerated cardiac muscle with three simple sutures tied over felt plegettes. In my hand, his heart was heavy and rubbery. It rhythmically clenched and unclenched like a determined fist. Its beat felt like forgiveness. Before I closed the chest incision, I cut a small window in the pericardium to prevent tamponade if bleeding reoccurred.

After I changed from my scrubs into street clothes, I stopped by the recovery room and looked at Wes still asleep on the gurney. He was breathing on his own. His slight body was pale as the snow falling outside the window. His eyes were closed and his mouth was set in almost a smile, as if he possessed some secret knowledge. Bathed in fluorescent light, he seemed to glow with a kind innocence. I pictured my daughter held tight in Wes' thin arms. In the dizziness of the moment, I suddenly felt tired. I had a strange urge to lie down beside him.

For a long while, I stood there with my fingers on his pulse and thinking. The green blips of his heart monitor that marched across the screen above him seemed to be spelling out a coded message. It said what brought Wes and I together was more destiny than coincidence. Something told me things would be different now.

WHEN I left the hospital, I stepped out into the silence of a snowy night. It was as if I had entered a large cold white room. A freezing wind made my eyes water. Big flakes were falling. Illuminated by a streetlight, they crisscrossed in the wind like yellow ashes. Everything was blanketed in snow: the winter trees, the roofs of houses where families were eating supper, the police cars in the parking lot, the deserted street. I pictured the snow falling on my wife's lonely and windswept grave. I envisioned it falling, too, on the Candle Light's blue neon sign with its flickering flame. I turned up the fur collar of my parka against the cold and headed to the motel to tell Polly Wes was alive and all was well.

Author Biographies

Kaveh Akbar's poems have appeared in *Poetry, Tin House, Narrative,* and elsewhere. His debut poetry collection, *Calling a Wolf a Wolf,* will be published in 2018. Founder and editor of *Divedapper,* he holds an M.F.A. in poetry from Butler University. Akbar was born in Tehran, Iran, grew up in Warsaw, Indiana, and currently lives and teaches in Tallahassee, Florida. (www.kavehakbar.com)

Phillip Appleman is the author of eight volumes of poetry, including *New and Selected Poems, 1956-1996* and *Darwin's Ark;* three novels, including *Apes and Angels;* and numerous nonfiction books. His awards include an NEA Fellowship, a Pushcart Prize, and both the Castagnola Award and the Morley Award from the Poetry Society of America. Distinguished Professor Emeritus at Indiana University, Appleman was born in Kendallville, Indiana, and currently divides his time between New York, New York and Pompano Beach, Florida.

Francisco Aragón is the author of *Glow of Our Sweat* and *Puerta del Sol* and the editor of the anthology *The Wind Shifts: New Latino Poetry.* His poems and translations have appeared in various publications, including *Chain, Crab Orchard Review, Chelsea, PALABRA, Pilgrimage,* and *Jacket.* He is a faculty member at the University of Notre Dame's Institute for Latino Studies, where he directs their literary initiative, Letras Latinas. He divides his time between Washington, D.C. and South Bend, Indiana.

Marianne Boruch is the author of nine poetry collections, including *Eventually One Dreams the Real Thing* and *The Book of Hours;* a memoir, *Glimpse Traveler;* and three essay collections, including *The Little Death of Self.* A Guggenheim, Fulbright, and NEA Fellow, she is the recipient of the Kingsley Tufts Award, the Eugene and Marilyn Glick National Indiana Authors Award, and numerous Pushcart Prizes. She teaches in Purdue's M.F.A. program and the Low Residency M.F.A. Program at Warren Wilson College. She lives in West Lafayette, Indiana.

Nancy Botkin is the author of two chapbooks and a full-length poetry collection, *Parts That Were Once Whole.* Her poems have appeared in *Poetry East, The Columbia Review, Eclipse, The Laurel Review,* and other journals. She lives in South Bend, where she teaches at IU South Bend. (www.nancybotkinpoet.com)

Maurice Broaddus is the author of the *Knights of Breton Court* urban fantasy trilogy and the co-editor of *Streets of Shadows* and the *Dark Faith* anthology series. His fiction has been published in numerous magazines and anthologies, including *Asimov's*

Science Fiction, Lightspeed Magazine, Cemetery Dance, and *Weird Tales Magazine.* He lives in Indianapolis, Indiana. (www.MauriceBroaddus.com)

Mary Ann Cain is the author of the novel *Down from Moonshine.* Her fiction, essays, and poems have appeared in numerous literary journals. The recipient of degrees in writing studies at IU Bloomington, Colorado State University, and State University of New York at Albany, she lives in Fort Wayne, Indiana, where she teaches writing and rhetoric at Indiana University Purdue University Fort Wayne.

Dan Carpenter is the author of two poetry collections, *More Than I Could See* and *The Art He'd Sell for Love.* A former columnist for *The Indianapolis Star,* he has published selections from his newspaper work in *Hard Pieces* and *Indiana Out Loud.* He is a lifelong resident of Indianapolis, Indiana.

A. Lyn Carol's creative nonfiction has appeared in *The Rumpus, Redivider, Hippocampus,* and *SMITH Magazine.* She was the flash nonfiction winner of the *Redivider* Blurred Genre Contest. Carol holds an M.F.A. from Butler University, where she was fiction editor and nonfiction editor for *Booth: A Journal.* Carol lives in Indianapolis, Indiana, where she designs books and teaches at the Indiana Writers Center.

Jared Carter's sixth book of poems, *Darkened Rooms of Summer,* was published by the University of Nebraska Press. Born in Elwood, Indiana, he currently lives in Indianapolis, Indiana.

Jill Christman is the author of *Darkroom: A Family Exposure* and *Borrowed Babies: Apprenticing for Motherhood.* Her essays have appeared in *Brevity, Fourth Genre, Oprah Magazine,* and other magazines. She received her M.F.A. from the University of Alabama. Christman teaches creative nonfiction at Ball State University and in Ashland University's low-residency M.F.A. program. She lives in Muncie, Indiana. (www.jillchristman.com)

Christopher Coake is the author of the novel *You Came Back* and the story collection *We're in Trouble.* His short fiction has been anthologized in *Best American Mystery Stories 2004* and *The Best American Noir of the Century.* He was the recipient of the PEN/Robert Bingham Fellowship for a first work of fiction and the Eugene and Marilyn Glick Emerging Writers Indiana Authors Award, and was named one of Granta's Best Young American Novelists. He holds an M.F.A. from Ohio State University. Born in Indianapolis, Indiana, Coake now lives in Reno, Nevada, where he directs the University of Nevada, Reno M.F.A. program in creative writing.

Kyle D. Craig is the author of the poetry collection *Invisible Tea*. His poems have been published in *Tar River Poetry, Sou'wester, Blue Earth Review, North Dakota Quarterly* and other magazines. Born and raised in Bloomington, Indiana, he currently lives in Indianapolis, Indiana, where he works as a mental health counselor and teaches writing classes at the Indiana Writers Center. He is a graduate of Indiana University.

Curtis L. Crisler is the author of three poetry collections, four poetry chapbooks, and two books for young adults. His poetry has been adapted for theatrical productions in NY and Chicago. He received his M.F.A. from Southern Illinois University Carbondale. Born and raised in Gary, Indiana, Crisler currently lives in Fort Wayne, where he is an Associate Professor of English at Indiana Purdue University Fort Wayne.

Cathy Day is the author of *The Circus in Winter*, a fictional history of her hometown, Peru, Indiana, and *Comeback Season: How I Learned to Play the Game of Love*, a memoir. Her short fiction and nonfiction have been published in *North American Review, Ninth Letter, Gettysburg Review*, as well as other publications. She earned her M.F.A. at the University of Alabama, and currently teaches at Ball State University. She lives in Muncie, Indiana. (www.cathyday.com)

Mitchell L. H. Douglas is the author of \blak\ \al-fə bet\ and *Cooling Board: A Long-Playing Poem*, which was nominated for an NAACP Image Award and a Hurston/ Wright Legacy Award. His poetry has appeared in *Callaloo, The Ringing Ear: Black Poets Lean South, Crab Orchard Review*, and *Zoland Poetry Volume II* and other magazines. He is the recipient of Lexi Rudnitsky/Editor's Choice Award. A founding member of the Affrilachian Poets, a Cave Canem fellow, and Poetry Editor for *PLUCK! The Journal of Affrilachian Arts & Culture*, Douglas is an Associate Professor of English at Indiana-Purdue University Indianapolis. He lives in Indianapolis, Indiana.

Mari Evans's poetry collections include *Nightstar* and *I Am a Black Woman*. The editor of *Black Women Writers (1950-1980): A Critical Evaluation*, she is also the author of the plays *Eye*, an adaptation of Zora Neale Hurston's *Their Eyes Were Watching God*, and *River of My Song*. Her honors include fellowships from the MacDowell Colony, Yaddo, the National Endowment for the Arts, and the John Hay Whitney Fellowship. She lives in Indianapolis, Indiana.

Mary Fell is the author of *The Persistence of Memory*, a National Poetry Series selection. Her poems and essays have been published in a variety of print and online journals. The recipient of an M.F.A. from the University of Massachusetts, Fell taught at Indiana University East for more than twenty years. She lives in Richmond, Indiana.

Chris Forhan is the author of the memoir *My Father Before Me* as well as three books of poetry, including *Black Leapt In* and *The Actual Moon, The Actual Stars*. His awards include an NEA Fellowship, two Pushcart Prizes, and a "Discover Great New Writers" selection from Barnes and Noble. He earned an M.A. from the University of New Hampshire and an M.F.A. from the University of Virginia. He lives in Indianapolis, Indiana, where he teaches at Butler University. (www.chrisforhan.com)

Karen Joy Fowler is the author of six novels and three short story collections. She's written literary, contemporary, historical, and science fiction. Her most recent novel, *We are all completely beside ourselves,* won the PEN/Faulkner Award, the California Book Award, and was shortlisted for the Man Booker Award. Born and raised in Bloomington, Indiana, she now lives in Santa Cruz, California. (www.karenjoyfowler. com)

Melissa Fraterrigo is the author of the short story collection *The Longest Pregnancy.* Her fiction and nonfiction have appeared in *Shenandoah, storySouth, Notre Dame Review,* and other publications. She received an M.F.A. from Bowling Green State University. A native of Hammond, Indiana, Fraterrigo lives in West Lafayette, Indiana, where she teaches classes on the art and craft of writing at the Lafayette Writers' Studio. (www.melissafraterrigo.com)

Helen Frost is the author of four novels-in-poems: *Keesha's House, Diamond Willow, Hidden,* and *Salt.* Her awards include the New York Historical Society's Children's Book History Book Prize, the William Allen White Award, the Lee Bennett Hopkins Children's Poetry Award, and the Eugene and Marilyn Glick Regional Indiana Authors Award. *Keesha's House* was a Michael L. Printz Honor Book. She lives in Fort Wayne, Indiana. (www.helenfrost.net)

Bryan Furuness is the author of the novel *The Lost Episodes of Revie Bryson* and, with Michael Martone, the co-editor of *Winesburg, Indiana.* His stories have appeared in *New Stories from the Midwest* and *Best American Nonrequired Reading.* Born and raised in Merrillville, Indiana, he currently lives in Indianapolis, Indiana, where he teaches at Butler University.

Eugene Gloria is the author of three poetry collections, including *My Favorite Warlord* and *Hoodlum Birds.* His honors include the Anisfield-Wolf Book Award, a Pushcart Prize, the Asian American Literary Award, and a National Poetry Series selection. Gloria received his M.F.A. from the University of Oregon, and currently teaches English and creative writing at DePauw University. He lives in Greencastle, Indiana. (www.eugenegloria.com)

Matthew Graham is the author of three poetry collections, including *A World Without End.* He received his M.F.A. from the Iowa Writers Workshop and teaches writing and literature at the University of Southern Indiana. He lives in Evansville, Indiana.

John Green is the author of five novels, including *Looking for Alaska, Paper Towns,* and *The Fault in Our Stars.* Recipient of the Michael L. Printz Award, the Edgar Award, and the Eugene and Marilyn Glick National Indiana Authors Award, he has twice been a finalist for the LA Times Book Prize. With his brother, Hank, John is one half of the vlogbrothers (youtube.com/vlogbrothers) and co-created the online educational series CrashCourse (youtube.com/crashcourse). He lives in Indianapolis, Indiana. (@johngreen)

Lucrecia Guerrero is the author of *Chasing Shadows,* a collection of linked short stories, and the novel, *Tree of Sighs.* Her work was anthologized in *Fantasmas* and *Best of the West.* She received her M.F.A. at Spalding University and teaches creative writing part-time at Purdue University Northwest. She lives in Westville Indiana.

Philip Gulley has published twenty books, including the *Harmony* series and the *Porch Talk* series of inspirational and humorous essays. He writes the monthly "Home Again" column for *Indianapolis Monthly* and is a regular contributor to *The Saturday Evening Post.* He was raised in Danville, Indiana, where he lives today. He is a co-pastor at Fairfield Friends Meeting near Indianapolis.

Jean Harper is the author of *Rose City: A Memoir of Work,* recipient of the Mid-List Press First Series Award for Creative Nonfiction. Her writing has appeared in *The Iowa Review, North American Review, Florida Review,* and elsewhere. She has received grants from the National Endowment for the Arts, the Indiana Arts Commission, New Bedford Whaling Museum, and Indiana University. She holds an M.F.A. from Emerson College, and teaches Indiana University East. She lives in the rural northeast part of Indiana. (www.jeanharper.org)

Janine Harrison's work has appeared in *Veils, Halos, & Shackles: International Poetry on the Oppression and Empowerment of Women, A&U, The Wabash Watershed,* and other publications. She received her M.F.A. in creative writing from Chicago State University. The former president of the Indiana Writers Consortium, she teaches creative writing at Purdue Northwest. She lives in Highland, Indiana. (www.janineharrison.live)

Marc Harshman is the author of two poetry collections, including *Local Journeys,* as well as thirteen books for children. His poems have appeared in the *Georgia Review, Emerson Review, Salamander, Poetry Salzburg Review,* and other publications. Poet Laureate of West Virginia, he is the host of "The Poetry Break," a monthly show for West Virginia Public Radio. Harshman was born and raised near Union City, Indiana. He lives in Wheeling, West Virginia.

Joseph Heithaus is the author of the poetry collection *Poison Sonnets* and won the Discovery/The Nation Prize for a group of poems at the core of that book. He co-authored *Rivers, Rails, and Runways* and *Airmail* with the "Airpoets," whose poems are on permanent display at the Indianapolis International Airport. Born in South Bend, Indiana, Heithaus lives in Greencastle, Indiana, where he teaches at DePauw University.

Patricia Henley is the author of two chapbooks of poetry, four short story collections, two novels, a stage play, and numerous essays. Her first book of stories, *Friday Night at the Silver Star,* won the Montana First Book Award; her first novel, *Hummingbird House,* was a finalist for the National Book Award. She attended the Johns Hopkins University. Born in Terre Haute, Indiana, Henley taught at Purdue University for twenty-seven years. Currently, she lives in Frostburg, Maryland.

B.J. Hollars is the author of several books, most recently *From the Mouths of Dogs: What Our Pets Teach Us About Life, Death, and Being Humans,* as well as an essay collection, *This Is Only A Test.* He serves as a mentor for *Creative Nonfiction,* the reviews editor for *Pleiades,* and a contributing blogger for *Brain Child.* Born in Monticello, Indiana and raised in Fort Wayne, Indiana, he lives in Eau Claire, Wisconsin, where he is an Assistant Professor of English at the University of Wisconsin-Eau Claire.

Allyson Horton's poetry has been published in the anthology *Turn the Page and You Don't Stop: Sharing Successful Chapters In Our Lives With Youth* and featured in *The Wabash Watershed.* Her work will appear in the upcoming anthology: *Brilliant Fire!* about the life and legacy of Amiri Baraka. She received her M.F.A. from Butler University. A lifelong resident of Indianapolis, Indiana, she teaches at Park Tudor School.

Marc Hudson is the author of three poetry collections, including *Journal for an Injured Son* and *Afterlight,* which received the Juniper Prize. His poems and essays have appeared in *Poetry, Prairie Schooner, The Sewanee Review,* and other journals. Hudson received an M.F.A. in Creative Writing and a Ph.D. in English from the University of Washington. He taught at Wabash College for twenty-eight years and currently lives in Crawfordsville, Indiana.

Angela Jackson-Brown is the author of the novel *Drinking from a Bitter Cup* and two plays, *Anna's Wings* and *Flossie Baily Takes a Stand.* A graduate of the Spalding low-residency M.F.A. program, she teaches at Ball State University. She lives in Eaton, Indiana. (www.angelajacksonbrown.com)

George Kalamaras is the author of fourteen books of poetry, including *Kingdom of Throat-Stuck Luck,* winner of the Elixir Press Poetry Prize, and *The Theory and Function of Mangoes,* winner of the Four Way Books Intro Series. He served as Poet Laureate of Indiana (2014-2015). Kalamaras grew up in Cedar Lake, Indiana and currently lives in Fort Wayne, Indiana, where he is a Professor of English at Indiana University-Purdue University Fort Wayne.

Karen Kovacik is the author of the poetry collections *Beyond the Velvet Curtain* and *Metropolis Burning,* the editor of *Scattering the Dark: An Anthology of Polish Women Poets,* and translator of Agnieszka Kuciak's *Distant Lands: An Anthology of Poets Who Don't Exist.* Her honors include a Fulbright Research Grant, a Fellowship in Literary Translation from the National Endowment for the Arts, and the Charity Randall Citation from the International Poetry Forum. She served as Indiana's Poet Laureate (2012-2013). Kovacik was born in East Chicago, Indiana, grew up in Highland, Indiana, and currently lives in Indianapolis, Indiana, where she is a Professor of English at Indiana Purdue University Indianapolis. (www.karenkovacik.net)

Norbert Krapf has published twenty-seven books, including *Bloodroot: Indiana Poems, Catholic Boy Blues,* and a prose memoir, *Shrinking the Monster: Healing from the Wounds of Our Abuse.* He released a jazz and poetry CD with pianist-composer Monika Herzig, *Imagine,* and collaborates with bluesman Gordon Bonham to combine poetry and the blues. He served as Indiana's Poet Laureate (2010-2011). A Jasper, Indiana native, Krapf currently lives in Indianapolis, Indiana. (www.krapfpoetry.com)

Sarah Layden is the author of the novel *Trip Through Your Wires.* Her short fiction, poetry, and essays have appeared in the *Boston Review, Booth, PANK, Artful Dodge,* and elsewhere. She earned an M.F.A. in creative writing at Purdue University and lives in Indianapolis, Indiana, where she teaches writing at Indiana University-Purdue University Indianapolis. (www.sarahlayden.com)

Brian Leung is the author of two novels, *Lost Men* and *Take Me Home,* and a short story collection, *World Famous Love Acts.* He is a recipient of the Lambda Literary Outstanding Mid-Career Prize, the Asian-American Literary Award, the Willa Award, and the Mary McCarthy Prize in Short Fiction. Leung received his M.F.A. from Indiana University. He lives in West Lafayette, Indiana, where he is the Director of Creative Writing at Purdue University. (www.readbrianleung.net)

Nancy Chen Long is the author of the chapbook *Clouds as Inkblots for the War Prone.* Her poetry has appeared in *Bat City Review, Pleiades, Superstition Review, Sycamore Review,* and elsewhere. She earned an M.F.A. at Spalding University. Long lives in Brown County and works at Indiana University. (www.nancychenlong.com)

Sean Lovelace is the author of two flash fiction collections, *Fog Gorgeous Stag* and *How Some People Like Their Eggs*, which won the Third Annual Rose Metal Press Short Short Contest. He is also the recipient of the Crazyhorse Prize for Fiction. He received his M.F.A. from the University of Alabama. He lives in Muncie, Indiana, where he teaches in the creative writing program at Ball State University.

Alessandra Lynch is the author of two collections of poetry, *It was a terrible cloud at twilight* and *Sails the Wind Left Behind*. Her poems have appeared in *The American Poetry Review, jubilat, The Massachusetts Review, Ploughshares,* and other magazines. She lives in Indianapolis, Indiana, where she teaches in the creative writing program at Butler University.

Michael Martone is the author of numerous books of fiction and creative nonfiction, including *Winesburg, Indiana, Four for a Quarter,* and *Memoranda,* and the editor of two collections of essays about the Midwest. His honors include the AWP Award for Nonfiction, two NEA Fellowships, a grant from the Ingram Merrill Foundation, and the Eugene and Marilyn Glick National Indiana Authors Award. His stories and essays have appeared and been cited in *The Pushcart Prize, The Best American Short Stories* and *The Best American Essays* anthologies. He holds the M.A. from the Writing Seminars of the Johns Hopkins University, and teaches at the University of Alabama and the M.F.A. Program for Writers at Warren Wilson College. Born and raised in Fort Wayne, Indiana, he currently lives in Tuscaloosa, Alabama.

Bonnie Maurer is the author of five poetry collections, including *Ms. Lily Jane Babbitt Before the Ten O'clock Bus from Memphis Ran Over Her* and *Reconfigured.* Her poems have appeared in the *New York Times, Indiana Review, Nimrod International Journal,* and *Contemporary American Voices 2015,* as well as on IndyGo buses and on the ceiling of St. Vincent Hospital Cancer Wing. She has an M.F.A. in poetry from Indiana University. Born and raised in Indianapolis, Maurer works as a poet-in-the-schools with Arts for Learning, a copy editor for the *Indianapolis Business Journal,* and an Ai Chi instructor. She lives in Indianapolis, Indiana.

Adrian Matejka is the author of the poetry collections *The Devil's Garden, Mixology,* and *The Big Smoke,* which was awarded the Anisfield-Wolf Book Award and was a finalist for the National Book Award and Pulitzer Prize. A graduate of Indiana University, he currently lives in Bloomington, Indiana, where he is the Lilly Professor/ Poet-in-Residence at Indiana University. (www.adrianmatejka.com)

Michael McColly is the author of *The After Death Room,* which won a Lambda Award. His essays and journalism have appeared in *The New York Times, The Chicago Tribune, The Sun, In These Times, NUVO,* and other publications. He earned his

M.F.A. at the University of Washington. McColly was born in Decatur, Indiana, and grew up in Marian, Indiana and in Indianapolis, Indiana where he lives now.

Jim McGarrah is the author of four collections of poetry and three nonfiction books. His memoir, *A Temporary Sort of Peace,* received a national Eric Hoffer Award. He holds an M.F.A. in Writing from Vermont College of Fine Arts. Born and raised in Princeton, Indiana, McGarrah currently lives in Louisville, Kentucky. (www.jimmcgarrah.com)

Kevin McKelvey is the author of *Dream Wilderness,* a collection of poems. His poems, blogs, essays, and stories have appeared in numerous journals, anthologies, and online publications. He received his M.F.A. from Southern Illinois University at Carbondale. Raised near Lebanon, Indiana, he lives in Indianapolis, Indiana, where he is an Associate Professor of English at the University of Indianapolis. (www.kevinmckelvey.org)

Orlando Ricardo Menes is the author of five poetry collections, most recently *Heresies* and *Fetish.* His work has been published in *Ploughshares, Harvard Review, Shenandoah,* and other publications. His awards include an NEA Literature Fellowship and the Prairie Schooner Book Prize in Poetry. Born in Lima, Perú, to Cuban parents, Menes lives in South Bend, Indiana, where he is a Professor of English at the University of Notre Dame. (www.orlandoricardomenes.com)

Norman Minnick is the author of two poetry collections, including *To Taste the Water,* winner of the First Series Award for Poetry from Mid-List Press. He edited *Between Water and Song: New Poets for the Twenty-First Century.* Minnick received his M.F.A. from Florida International University. He taught at Butler University, and has been a featured reader at Poets House, Robert Bly's Great Mother Conference, RopeWalk, Block Island Poetry Project, and other universities and book festivals. He lives in Indianapolis, Indiana. (www.buzzminnick.com)

Mark Neely is the author of the poetry collections *Beasts of the Hill* and *Dirty Bomb.* His awards include an NEA Poetry Fellowship, an Indiana Individual Artist Grant, the FIELD Poetry Prize, and the Concrete Wolf Press chapbook award for *Four of a Kind.* He received his M.F.A. from the University of Alabama. He lives in Muncie, Indiana, where he teaches at Ball State University. (www.markneely.com)

Susan Neville is the author of four collections of creative nonfiction and two collections of short stories, including *The Invention of Flight* and *Indiana Winter.* She is the recipient of the Flannery O'Connor Award for Short Fiction, the Richard Sullivan Prize, and the Eugene and Marilyn Glick Indiana Regional Authors Award. She received her

M.F.A. at Bowling Green State University. Born and raised in Indianapolis, Indiana, she is the Demia Professor of English at Butler University. (www.susan-neville.com)

Roger Pfingston's poems have appeared in *Poet Lore, Rhino, Poetry East, Valparaiso Poetry Review, Spoon River Poetry Review,* and other publications. The recipient of an NEA Creative Writing Fellowship and two PEN Syndicated Fiction Awards, he has held residencies at the MacDowell Colony, Ragdale, and the Virginia Center for the Creative Arts. Born and raised in Evansville, Indiana, Pfingston lives in Bloomington, Indiana.

Richard Pflum is author of three full-length collections of poetry, including *A Dream of Salt.* His work has been published in numerous literary magazines, including *Sparrow, Event, Kayak, The Reaper, The Exquisite Corpse,* and *The New Laurel Review,* and anthologized in *A New Geography of Poets: The Indiana Experience* and *Bear Crossings.* He lives in Indianapolis, Indiana, where he was born and raised.

Donald Platt is the author of six volumes of poetry, including *Man Praying* and *My Father Says Grace.* His poems have appeared in journals, including *The New Republic, Nation, Paris Review, Poetry, Kenyon Review,* and in *The Best American Poetry 2000, 2006,* and *2015.* A recipient of two NEA Fellowships and three Pushcart Prizes, Platt is a professor in Purdue University's English Department and M.F.A. Program. He lives in West Lafayette, Indiana.

Michael Poore is the author of the novel *Up Jumps the Devil.* His short fiction has appeared in *AGNI, Glimmer Train, Fiction, Southern Review, The Pinch,* and *The Best American Non-Required Reading 2012.* Nominated for the Pushcart Prize, the Fountain Award, and the Sturgeon Award, he lives in Highland, Indiana.

Dana Roeser is the author of the poetry collections *The Theme of Tonight's Party Has Been Changed, Beautiful Motion,* and *In the Truth Room.* She is the recipient of the Juniper Prize, the Samuel French Morse Prize, the Great Lakes Colleges Association New Writers Award, and an NEA Fellowship. She holds an M.F.A. from the University of Virginia. Roeser has taught in the M.F.A. Poetry programs at Purdue and Butler Universities. She lives in Lafayette, Indiana. (www.danaroeser.com)

Rachel Sahaidachny's writing has been published in *Southeast Review, Community of Writers Poetry Review, NUVO,* and other publications. She reviews books of poems for *Red Paint Hill.* Awarded first prize in the 2014 *Wabash Watershed Indiana Poetry Awards,* she holds an M.F.A. from Butler University, where she was the poetry editor for *Booth: A Journal.* She is the Programs Manager for the Indiana Writers Center. Born in Peru, Indiana, Sahaidachny was raised in Indianapolis, Indiana, where she lives now.

Scott Russell Sanders is the author of twenty books of fiction and nonfiction, including *Wilderness Plots* and *A Private History of Awe*. His honors include the Lannan Literary Award, the John Burroughs Essay Award, the Mark Twain Award, the Cecil Woods Award for Nonfiction, the Eugene and Marilyn Glick Indiana National Indiana Authors Award, and fellowships from the Guggenheim Foundation and the National Endowment for the Arts. In 2012 he was elected to the American Academy of Arts and Sciences. A Distinguished Professor Emeritus of English at Indiana University, he lives in Bloomington, Indiana.

Sandy Sasso is the author of *Midrash as a Tool for Spiritual Reflection* and co-author of *Jewish Stories of Love and Marriage: Folktales, Legends and Letters*, as well as numerous books for children. Her books have been named to Publishers Weekly's list of "Best Books of the Year," as well as American Library Association's list of "Top Pick, Youth Religion Books." She is the winner of the National Jewish Book Award. Rabbi Emerita of Beth-El Zedeck, she is currently Director of Religion, Spirituality and the Arts Initiative at Butler University and Christian Theological Seminary. She lives in Indianapolis, Indiana. (www.allaboutand.com)

Greg Schwipps is the author of the novel *What This River Keeps*. He is the recipient of the Eugene and Marilyn Glick Emerging Indiana Authors Award. Schwipps received an M.F.A. from Southern Illinois University at Carbondale. Born and raised on a working farm in Milan, Indiana, he currently lives in Greencastle, Indiana, where he is a Professor of English at DePauw University.

Barbara Shoup is the author of eight novels, including *An American Tune* and *Looking for Jack Kerouac*, and co-author of *Novel Ideas: Contemporary Authors Share the Creative Process*. She was the recipient of the PEN Phyllis Reynolds Naylor Working Writer Fellowship and the Eugene and Marilyn Glick Regional Indiana Author Award. Two of her novels were selected as American Library Association Best Books for Young Adults. Born and raised in Hammond, Indiana, Shoup lives in Indianapolis, Indiana, where she is the Executive Director of the Indiana Writers Center. (www.barbarashoup. com)

David Shumate is the author of three books of prose poems, including *Kimonos in the Closet, The Floating Bridge*, and *High Water Mark*, winner of the 2003 Agnes Lynch Starrett Poetry Prize. His poetry has appeared widely in literary journals and has been anthologized in *Good Poems for Hard Times, The Best American Poetry, The Writer's Almanac*, as well as other anthologies and university texts. He was the recipient of an NEA Fellowship and an Arts Council of Indianapolis Creative Renewal Fellowship. Shumate is Poet-in-Residence Emeritus at Marian University and a lecturer in Butler University's M.F.A. program. He lives in Zionsville, Indiana

Kevin Stein has published eleven poetry collections, including *Sufficiency of the Actual,* and three books of literary criticism. His honors include the Vernon Louis Parrington Medal for Distinguished Writing, the Devins Award for Poetry, the Society of Midland Authors Poetry Award, an NEA fellowship, and the Frederick Bock Prize for Poetry. In 2003 he was named the fourth Poet Laureate of Illinois. Born and raised in Anderson, Indiana, he received his M.A. from Indiana University. He lives in Peoria, Illinois, where he directs the creative writing program at Bradley University.

Elizabeth Stuckey-French is the author of three novels, including *The Revenge of the Radioactive Lady* and *Mermaids on the Moon,* and the short story collection, *The First Paper Girl in Red Oak, Iowa.* She is a co-author of *Writing Fiction: A Guide to the Narrative Craft.* She was awarded a James Michener Fellowship and a Florida Book Award and has won grants from the Howard Foundation, the Indiana Arts Commission, and the Florida Arts Foundation. Born and raised in Lafayette, Indiana, she currently lives in Tallahassee, Florida, where she teaches fiction writing at Florida State University. (www.elizabethstuckeyfrench.com)

Jessica D. Thompson is the author of the poetry chapbook *Bullets and Blank Bibles.* Her poetry has appeared in numerous journals, including *Atlanta Review, Sow's Ear Poetry Review,* and *Tiferet Journal,* and was anthologized in *Circe's Lament: Anthology of Wild Women Poetry* and *New Poetry from the Midwest.* She was the recipient of the James Baker Hall Memorial Prize in Poetry and the Kudzu Poetry Prize. She lives in New Harmony, Indiana where she works as a Human Resource Professional.

Kelsey Timmerman is the author of *Where Am I Wearing: A Global Tour to the Countries, Factories, and People That Make Our Clothes* and *Where I Am I Eating: An Adventure Through the Global Food Economy.* He is the recipient of the Eugene and Marilyn Glick Emerging Writers Indiana Authors Award. He is the cofounder of the Facing Project, a national community storytelling project. Born in Union City, Indiana, he currently lives in Muncie, Indiana. (www.kelseytimmerman.com)

Samrat Upadhyay is the author of five novels, including *Arresting God in Kathmandu* and *Buddha's Orphans,* and a story collection, *The Royal Ghosts.* The recipient of a Whiting Writers' Award, the Asian American Literary Award, and the Society of Midland Authors Book Award, he has appeared on BBC Radio and National Public Radio. He lives in Bloomington, Indiana, where he teaches creative writing at Indiana University. (www.samratupadhyay.com)

Shari Wagner is the author of *The Harmonist at Nightfall: Poems of Indiana* and *Evening Chore,* and coauthor, with her father, of *A Hundred Camels: A Mission Doctor's Sojourn* and *Murder Trial in Somalia* and *Making the Rounds: Memoir of* *a Small-Town Doctor.* Her poems and nonfiction have appeared in *North American Review, The Writer's Almanac, American Life in Poetry,* and *Shenandoah.* Wagner has an M.F.A. from Indiana University. She is the current Indiana Poet Laureate, and teaches at the Indiana Writers Center. Born in Goshen, Indiana, she now lives in Westfield, Indiana. (www.shariwagnerpoet.com)

Dan Wakefield is the author of five novels and eleven books of nonfiction, including *Going All the Way, Starting Over,* and *New York in the Fifties.* He received a Neiman Fellowship in Journalism, a Rockefeller Grant for Creative Writing, and a fellowship from the National Endowment for the Arts. His novel, *Going All the Way,* was nominated for the National Book Award. He currently lives in Indianapolis, Indiana, where he was born and raised. (www.danwakefield.com)

Daly Walker is the author of *Surgeon Stories,* a collection of short stories, and *Little Creek: Finding Elemental Life in Brown County,* a collection of essays. His fiction has appeared in *The Atlantic Monthly, The Sewanee Review, The Southampton Review, The Catamaran Literary Reader, The Sycamore Review,* and other publications. Born and raised in Winchester, Indiana, he now divides his time between Quechee, Vermont and Boca Grande, Florida. (www.dalywalker.com)

Elizabeth Weber is the author of three poetry books, including *Small Mercies* and *The Burning House.* Her poems and essays have appeared in *Calyx, Verse, Kalliope, Puerto del Sol, Prairie Schooner,* and other publications. Her poem "City Generations" is part of the Indianapolis Cultural Trail. She lives in Indianapolis, Indiana, where she teaches at University of Indianapolis.

Marcus Wicker is the author of *Maybe the Saddest Thing,* a National Poetry Series winner. His work has appeared in *The Nation, Poetry, American Poetry Review, Boston Review,* and other magazines. His honors include a Ruth Lilly Fellowship, a Pushcart Prize, and fellowships from Cave Canem and The Fine Arts Work Center. He holds an M.F.A. from Indiana University. Wicker lives in Evansville, Indiana, where he is an Assistant Professor of English at the University of Southern Indiana and the editor of Southern Indiana Review. (www.marcuswicker.com)

Lili Wright is author of the novel *Dancing with the Tiger* and the travel memoir *Learning to Float.* Her essays and journalism have appeared in *The New York Times, Newsweek, The Chicago Tribune, Down East,* and other publications. She holds an M.F.A. from Columbia University. Wright teaches at DePauw University and in Butler University's M.F.A. program. She lives in Greencastle, Indiana. (www.liliwright.com)

Publishing Credits

Kaveh Akbar. "Being in this World Makes Me Feel Like a Time Traveler" was originally published in *American Poetry Review*.

Marianne Boruch. "Big Little" was originally published in *The Massachusetts Review*.

Nancy Botkin. "Love is Blue" was originally published in *Cimarron Review*.

Mary Ann Cain. "Tomato Soup" was originally published in *From the Edge of the Prairie*.

Dan Carpenter. "Returning to Rilke" was originally published in *The Flying Island*.

Jared Carter. "The Measuring" was originally published in *Sou'wester*.

Jill Christman. "What You Remember: An Essay in Third Person" was originally published as "Family Portrait: An Essay in Third Person" in *Superstition Review*.

Kyle D. Craig. "My Buddhist Lessons" was originally published in *Haibun Today*.

Cathy Day. "Not Like the Rest of Us: A Hoosier Named Cole Porter" was originally published in *Literary Hub*.

Chris Forhan. "Solo Act" was originally published in *The Georgia Review*.

Melissa Fraterrigo. "Ruin" was originally published in *Sou'wester*.

Helen Frost. "Valentine's Day, Sixth Grade" was originally published in *A Chant a Mile Long*.

Eugene Gloria. "Alfonso Street" was originally published in *Drunken Boat*.

Matthew Graham. "The Sadness of Youth" was originally published in *Inertia*.

Lucrecia Guererro. "Rings" was originally published in the *Antioch Review*.

Janine Harrison. "Restavek" was originally published in *Weight of Silence*.

Marc Harshman. "Grandmother at the Dressmakers'" was originally published in *Still: The Journal.*

Patricia Henley. "The Invention of Cartwheels" was originally published in the *Atlantic Monthly* and *Best American Short Stories.*

B.J. Hollars. "Ft. Wayne is Still 7th on Hitler's List" was originally published in the *North American Review.*

Marc Hudson. "Final Bath" was originally published in *Poet Lore.*

Angela Jackson-Brown. "Vacation" was originally published in *A Narrow Fellow: Journal of Poetry.*

Karen Kovacik. "Assemblage: Lake County" originally appeared in somewhat different form on www.indianahumanities.org.

Norbert Krapf. "Bach in the Morning" was originally published in *Bittersweet Along the Expressway: Poems of Long Island.*

Sarah Layden. "House" was originally published in *Artful Dodge;* "Skin" was originally published on Pindlelbodyboz.com.

Brian Leung. "Shuhua's Suite" was originally published in *Blythe House Quarterly.*

Nancy Chen Long. "On Seeing *The Embroiderer, Or Mette Gauguin*" was originally published in *Alaska Quarterly Review.*

Michael Martone. "Contributor's Note" was originally published in the *Columbia Review.*

Bonnie Maurer. "Himmler's Lunch in Minsk, 15 August 1941" was originally published in *Wabash Watershed.*

Adrian Matejka. "Map to the Stars" was originally published in *Poetry.*

Jim McGarrah. "When the Stars Go Dark" was originally published in *Open 24 Hours.*

Mark Neely. "Extremist Sonnet" was originally published in *Black Warrior Review.*

Susan Neville. "Jubilee" was originally published in *Arts Indiana.*

Roger Pfingston. "1948" was originally published in *I-70 Review*.

Donald Platt. "Chartres in the Dark" was originally published in *Shenandoah*.

Michael Poore. "The Story of the Ghosts of Judy, TN" was originally published in *Story Quarterly*.

Dana Roeser. "The Fire Academy" was originally published in *Sou'wester*.

Rachel Sahaidachny. "The Sky Turned Orange on the Eastern Side at Twilight" was published in a somewhat different form in *Community of Writers Poetry Review*.

Scott Russell Sanders. "Neighbors" was originally published in *Notre Dame Magazine*.

Barbara Shoup. "Working a Jigsaw" was originally published in *Other Voices*.

David Shumate. "Bringing Things Back from the Woods" was published in the collection *Kimonos in the Closet* and used with permission from the University of Pittsburgh Press.

Kevin Stein. "The Tragedies" was originally published in *Poet Lore*.

Elizabeth Stuckey-French. "Interview with a Moron" was originally published in *Narrative Magazine*.

Jessica D. Thompson. "This God of My Waking" was a finalist in the Janet B. McCabe Poetry Prize and originally published in *Ruminate Magazine*.

Kelsey Timmerman. "The Labors of Our Fathers" was originally published in *Wabash Magazine*.

Shari Wagner. "The Lerner Theatre, 1953" was originally published in *The Harmonist at Nightfall*.

Marcus Wicker. "Taking Aim at a Macy's Changing Room Mirror, I Blame Television" was originally published in *Poetry*.

Lili Wright. "How I Spent My Summer Vacation" was originally published in *The Normal School*.

Index

CPSIA information can be obtained
at www.ICGtesting.com
Printed in the USA
FSOW01n1702031216
27927FS

9 780996 743839